Challenges of Democracy in the European Union and its Neighbors

Aylin Ünver Noi and Sasha Toperich
Editors

Center for Transatlantic Relations
Paul H. Nitze School of Advanced International Studies
Johns Hopkins University

Aylin Ünver Noi and Sasha Toperich, eds. *Challenges of Democracy in the European Union and its Neighbors*

Washington, DC: Center for Transatlantic Relations, 2016.

Center for Transatlantic Relations
The Paul H. Nitze School of Advanced International Studies
The Johns Hopkins University
1717 Massachusetts Ave., NW, Suite 525
Washington, DC 20036
Tel: (202) 663-5880
Fax: (202) 663-5879
Email: transatlantic@jhu.edu
http://transatlantic.sais-jhu.edu

ISBN 13: 978-0-9907720-6

Cover image: Shutterstock.com

Contents

Part I
Challenges of Democracy in the European Union

Part II
Challenges of Democracy in the Aspirant Countries

Preface

This timely volume explores challenges of democracy in the EU and challenges of democracy in EU aspirant countries and their neighbors. Authors take a close look at the effect of EU democracy-promotion efforts on the EU's international role and normative power.

A quarter century ago, the Soviet Union dissolved and the Cold War ended. Since then, and particularly after the Balkan wars of the 1990s, a generalized sense took hold in Western capitals that the natural state of the post-Cold War era would be European peace, stability and inexorable expansion of Europe's democratic space. Central and southeast European countries joined the EU and NATO to extend the spaces of Europe where democracy and market economies prevailed and war simply did not happen. The EU created a variety of means to associate neighboring countries not yet willing or able to join its structures.

In the West, consensus grew that the post-Cold War security order in Europe was stable; that the magnetic qualities of life within the European Union would eventually lead eastern and southeastern European neighbors to align themselves to its standards; and that Russia, while still distant, could, with Western support, modernize and eventually arrange itself within Europe's evolving order.

History, it turns out, did not end with the Cold War. Walls came down, but throughout the unsettled spaces of wider Europe, that vast area beyond the EU, other walls remained—historical animosities, ethnic hatreds, unresolved borders, and struggles for power and control.

Meanwhile, a dizzying array of domestic and foreign challenges has exposed fault lines among EU member states themselves in a generation. Such divisions are nothing new, but they have taken on a new quality as a surge of refugees, terrorist fears, high youth unemployment, and uneven growth give life to popular anxieties and illiberal responses that are challenging some of the EU's most fundamental premises and structures.

The vision of a Europe, whole and free, is being tested today by the realities of a Europe that is fractured and anxious, which leaves Europe's west with less confidence and readiness to reach out in any significant way to Europe's east.

Our authors tackle these challenges and propose ways forward. We are grateful to them, and to our editors, Aylin Ünver Noi and Sasha Toperich.

Daniel S. Hamilton
Austrian Marshall Plan Foundation Professor
Executive Director
Center for Transatlantic Relations

Acknowledgements

This book is based on the proceedings of a conference held on March 30, 2015, at the Johns Hopkins University SAIS Center for Transatlantic relations. Some of the contributors to this book participated in the conference, and their conference papers were updated and revised according to changes that have since occurred in the region. Other authors also joined us in an effort to analyze and present additional perspectives on the challenges of democracy in the European Union and its Neighbors. We would like to express our gratitude to all our SAIS colleagues for their valuable support in organizing the conference and to the authors for their hard work on this project.

We wish to express special thanks to our editor for the careful attention given to the manuscript. Our special thanks go to Andy Mullins and Heidi Obermeyer for their dedication to timely and incisive edits in the last phase of production.

We are grateful to Peggy Irvine for working out the publishing details of this and many other CTR publications.

The opinions expressed in the following essays are the authors' alone, and do not necessarily represent the views of any government or institutions, or those of their fellow contributors.

Aylin Ünver Noi
Non-Resident Fellow, Center for Transatlantic Relations SAIS

Sasha Toperich
Senior Fellow; Center for Transatlantic Relations SAIS

Abbreviations

AA	Association Agreement
AKP	Justice and Development Party (Adalet ve Kalkınma Partisi)
ANAP	Motherland Party (Anavatan Partisi)
APT	Azerbaijan Partnership for Transparency
ASEAN	Association of Southeast Asian Nations
BiH	Bosnia and Herzegovina
BMENA	Broader Middle East and North Africa Initiative
CCE	Center for Civic Engagement
CEECs	Central and Eastern European Countries
CeSID	Center for Free Elections and Democracy
CoE	Council of Europe
DAD	Democracy Assistance Dialogue
DCFTA	Deep and Comprehensive Free Trade Agreement
DSP	Democratic Left Part (Demokrat Sol Parti)
EaP	Eastern Partnership
EC	European Community
ECB	European Central Bank
ECHR	European Convention of Human Rights
EDL	English Defence League
EEAS	European External Action Service
EED	European Endowment for Democracy
EFP	European Foreign Policy
EFPR	European Foreign Policy Research
EIDHR	The European Instrument for Democracy and Human Rights
ENAR	European Network Against Racism
ENP	European Neighborhood Policy
EP	European Parliament
EU	European Union
FPÖ	Austrian Freedom Party
GDP	Gross Domestic Product
GIZ	Deutsche Gesellschaft für Internationale Zusammenarbeit GmbH
GYLA	Georgian Young Lawyers Association
IC	International Community
ICTY	International Criminal Tribunal for the former Yugoslavia
IEE/ULB	Institut d'Etudes Europeennes

IOM	International Organization of Migration
ISFED	International Society for Fair Elections and Democracy
IMF	International Monetary Fund
IREX	International Research & Exchanges Board
MENA	Middle East and North Africa
MEP	Member of the European Parliament
MERCOSUR	Common Market of the South (Latin America)
MHP	Nationalist Action Party (Milliyetçi Hareket Partisi)
NATO	North Atlantic Treaty Organization
NDI	National Democratic Institute
NGNI	New Generation New Initiative
NGO	Non Governmental Organization
NPE	Normative Power Europe
OHR	Office of High Representative
OECD	Organization for Economic Cooperation and Development
OGP	Open Government Partnership
OSCE	Organization for Security and Cooperation in Europe
PEGIDA	Patriotic Europeans against the Islamisation of the Occident
PIC	Peace Implementation Council
PMMG	Public Movement for Multinational Georgia
RCI	Rational Choice Institutionalism
SDC	Swiss Agency for Development and Cooperation
SFRJ	Socialist Republic of Yugoslavia
SEDA	Social Economic Development Agency
SI	Sociological Institutionalism
SIGMA	Support for Improvement in Governance and Management
SVP	Swiss People's Party
TESEV	Turkish Economic and Social Studies Foundation
TEU	Treaty on European Union
TFEU	Treaty on the Functioning of the European Union
TI	Transparency International
UDHR	Universal Declaration of Human Rights
UK	United Kingdom
UN	United Nations
UNAG	United Nations Association of Georgia
UNM	United National Movement
US	United States
USAID	United States Agency for International Development
USSR	The Union of Soviet Socialist Republics
WB	The World Bank Group
WW2	Second World War

Figures and Tables

Introduction

Aylin Ünver Noi and Sasha Toperich

The classical theory of democracy defines democracy as "the will of the people" and "the common good."[1] Accordingly, "the democratic method is that institutional arrangement for arriving at political decisions which realizes the common good by making the people itself decide issues through the election of individuals who are to assemble in order to carry out its will."[2] Joseph Schumpeter made a modern formulation of the concept of democracy in 1942, claiming that the "democratic method is that institutional arrangement for arriving at political decisions in which individuals acquire the power to decide by means of a competitive struggle for the people's vote."[3]

The definition of democracy when referring to elections takes a minimalist form, reducing to the term "ballot box". Yet elections—open, free and fair—are the essence of democracy. The true democracy incorporates also features of a liberal democracy, that is, liberty, equality, effective public control over policy, a separation of powers, rule of law, responsible government, transparency and accountability in politics, equal participation and various other civic virtues.[4]

Democracy, along with human rights and peace, are the core values of the EU and are embedded in European integration. They have also become concrete goals guiding the actions and tools of EU foreign policy. The promotion of democracy was determined as the primary aim of both the European Security Strategy (2003) and the U.S. National Security Strategy (2002), and this has been supported by both the European Union and the United States in several different initiatives. In this regard, the EU's unique and *sui generis* international identity has been described by various sources as "civilian power", "magnetic force", "gentle power", "normative power", "ethical power", a "Kantian paradise or

---

1. Joseph A. Schumpeter , *Capitalism, Socialism and Democracy*, (UK: Taylor & Francis e-Library, 2010), pp. 225.

2. Ibid., p. 225.

3. Ibid., p. 241.

4. Samuel P. Huntington, *The Third Wave: Democratization in the Late Twentieth Century*, (Norman and London: University of Oklahoma Press, 1991), p. 9.

Venus" and a "European superpower"; while the United States has been described using the terms "military power", "smart power" and "Hobbesian or Mars" as a result of the means they have used to reach this end.[5]

Huntington, in his famous book *The Third Wave: Democratization in the Late Twentieth Century*, described the process of democratization in the modern world in three democratization waves, which were followed by reverse waves.[6] The latest part of third wave of democratization flourished with the victory of economic and political liberalism over communism, and facilitated the membership of the Central and Eastern European Countries to the EU. Once the wave of democratization had swept through Central and Eastern Europe, there was no longer an alternative competing regime.

There was a prevalent view, in Dankwart Rustow's words, that "almost all wealthy countries are democratic and almost all democracies are wealthy",[7] and this correlation was echoed by Ronald Inglehart in his reference to economic development and democracy. Economic development provided the basis for democracy, and crises produced by either rapid growth or economic recession weakened authoritarianism in the 1970s and 1980s.[8] The EU has become a model to be aspired to due to the stability, prosperity and peace enjoyed by its citizens, along with its success as both a powerful international economic actor and a regional community. The EU's economic, social, environmental and political norms, which are part of the European experience of modernity, and the construction of more open, tolerant and just societies[9] have

---

5. Françoise Duchene, "Europe's Role in World Peace," in Richard Mayne, *Europe Tomorrow: Sixteen Europeans Look Ahead*, (London: Fontana, 1972). Ian Manners, "Normative Power Europe: A Contradiction in Terms," *Journal of Common Market Studies*, vol. 40, no. 2, 2002, pp. 235-258. Joseph S. Nye, *Soft Power: The Means to Success in World Politics*, (New York: Public Affairs 2004). Tommaso Padoa-Schioppa, *Gentle power, Europa, Forza Gentile* (Bologna: Il Mulino, 2001), p. 29. Lisbeth Aggestam, "Introduction: Ethical Power Europe?" *International Affairs (Royal Institute of Inetrnational Affairs)* vol 84, no. 1, 2008, pp. 1-11. Richard N. Rosecrance, "The European Union: A New Type of International Actor" 1998. Robert Kagan, *Of Paradise and Power: America and Europe in the New World Order*, (New York: Alfred, 2003). A. Knopf. John McCormick, *The European Superpower*, (Hampshire and New York: Palgrave Macmillan, 2007). Jan Zielonka, *Paradoxes of European Foreign Policy*. (Great Britain: Kluwer Law International).

6. Huntington, *op. cit.* p, 15.

7. Ibid., p. 34.

8. Ibid, p. 59.

9. Ian Manners, "The European Union as a Minervian Actor in Global Institution Building" in Yves Tiberghien, ed., *Leadership in Global Institution Building: Minerva's Rule*, Hampshire and New York Palgrave Macmillan, 2013), pp. 33-49.

combined to make the EU a force of attraction for its periphery. The enlargement was the EU's most successful foreign policy tool due to its transformative power over third countries.

This view, however, has today lost its validity due to the rise of emerging powers that are economically developed but politically less democratic. The value-based identity and its normative actions as a norm and value promoter led to the EU's power and its role in international politics being called into question. Yet recent events—which have prevented Armenia and Ukraine, from signing association agreements – indicated that the EU's monopoly on transformative power, which had been largely unrivalled, has come to an end.[10] The negative consequences of the Eurozone Crisis, the inward looking trend, the image of a declining power and the re-nationalization of external policies are complicating both domestic and foreign policy in the EU.[11] Borrowing from Fareed Zakaria, "illiberal democracies"[12] pose a grave threat to freedom, even in some EU member states like Hungary and Poland within the new reverse wave being seen today.

This reverse wave would appear to be more prevalent in the EU neighbors that are in transition to democracy, and even in some of the more democratic ones. In recent years, the increasing illiberal tendencies in existing democracies, in the newly established democratic regimes or in the transition countries have brought discussions on the sustainability of democracy. Some scholars, like Robert Kaplan, have even argued that democratic elections in many countries may hinder efforts to maintain ethnic peace, social stability and economic development.[13] This may also validate Zakaria's argument, which was based on American diplomat Richard Holbrooke's words related to a problem on the eve of the September 1996 elections in Bosnia: "Democratically elected regimes, often ones that have been reelected or reaffirmed through referenda, are routinely ignoring constitutional limits on their power and depriving their citizens of basic rights and freedoms."[14]

---

10. Heather Grabbe, "Six Lessons of Enlargement Ten Years On: The EU's Transformative Power in Retrospect and Prospect," *Journal of Common Market Studies*, vol. 52, 2014, pp. 40-56, p. 40.

11. Mario Telò, "Introduction" in Mario Telò and Frederik Ponjaert, eds., *The EU's Foreign Policy: What Kind of Power and Diplomatic Action?* (UK: Ashgate, 2013), pp. 1-15.

12. Fareed Zakaria, The Rise of Illiberal Democracy. *Foreign Affairs*, 1997.

13. Robert D. Kaplan, "Was Democracy Just a Moment?" *Atlantic Monthly*, (December 1997), pp. 55-80.

14. Zakaria, *op. cit.*.

This edited book, which is an outcome of the March 30 2015 conference held at the Johns Hopkins University SAIS Center for Transatlantic Relations in Washington, DC, chaired by **Aylin Ünver Noi**, explores the challenges to democracy in the European Union member states and in its neighboring countries by focusing on the factors that facilitated reverse waves in democratization processes, as well as the roles of the transatlantic partners and their foreign policy approaches. The book discusses in several chapters the types of challenges these countries have faced, and continue to face, during their democratization process.

In Part I, we examine the challenges of democracy in the EU and the EU member states. Conceptual challenges to transnational democracy in the EU and the racism that represents severe challenge to the liberal democracies in the EU are topics discussed in this chapter.

In "The Challenge of a Democracy beyond the State in the European Union," **Mario Telò** argues that "building a democracy beyond the State is a difficult challenge, as the first European attempts in the history of human being well show." He defines Europe as the most sophisticated laboratory of transnational democracy beyond the state, focusing in his chapter on the impact of the Eurozone crisis on the transnational democratic process and the risks of degradation of the EU's internal multilateralism. Related to this subject, he draws attention to the link between the current socio-economic crisis and the possible dissipation of previous achievements in democracy, as well as internal multilateralism. Telò argues further that the current social crisis and the long-lasting austerity policies are affecting European transnational democracy in many ways.

Telò also argues that in its social dimension, transnational democracy requires a long-term idea of solidarity, as well as a historical and social background. He discusses two classical challenges that are faced by constitutional states: internal democracy and external policy, suggesting that it is increasingly impossible to consolidate domestic participatory democracy without developing transnational democracy beyond the State; and that it is impossible to develop transnational democracy without an enhanced shared collective security framework. He assesses the internal/external dimension of democratic legitimacy in the face of the increasing relevance of external opportunities and threats.

In "Racism in Europe: A Challenge for Democracy," **Leila Hadj-Abdou** analyzes two interrelated manifestations of racism in the current

European context: the rise of *Islamophobia*, and the growth of populist right-wing parties and social movements. Her analysis looks at current debates in Europe including the current 'refugee crisis', and discusses parties such as the Austrian Freedom Party, the Hungarian Jobbik party, as well as the PEGIDA movement in Germany.

Hadj-Abdou argues that today the terms "migrant" and "Muslim" serve increasingly as surrogates for the term "race." She demonstrates, that instead of using overt forms of biological racism and anti-Semitism, right wing parties and movements in Europe emphasize the incompatibilities of different cultures in order to legitimize its opposition to international immigration and ethno-cultural diversity. She, moreover, points out that rather than being an anomaly of liberal democracy, racisms are an expression of the paradoxes inherent in democracy.

Part II examines the challenges of democracy in the aspirant countries to the EU, candidate, and potential candidate countries. This part includes chapters evaluating the EU's transformative power over third countries through enlargement—the EU foreign policy approach that is considered the most successful—focusing primarily on reform processes and the factors facilitating these processes in the respective countries.

In "Challenges of Democracy in Turkey: Europeanization, Modernization and Securitization Revisited," **Aylin Ünver Noi** claims that credible conditionality, along with the demands of society and government related to democracy, make Europeanization more likely. This was witnessed particularly during the reform process in Turkey that reached a peak with the 2001–2004 constitutional amendments and harmonization packages that led to the launch of accession negotiations in 2005. The period after 2005, however, was marked by a less credible EU membership perspective following a decrease in enthusiasm at both a public and governmental level towards the EU based on a loss of mutual trust between the two parties. Furthermore, the electoral support gained by the Justice and Development Party (AKP) in the post-2005 period led the Turkish government to take a more "Europeanization *a la carte*", approach, picking and choosing from the EU policies to both satisfy their constituencies and consolidate their political power.[15]

---

15. Tanja A. Börzel and Didem Soyaltin "Europeanization in Turkey: Stretching a Concept to Its Limits?" *Working Paper Freie Universitat Berlin-KFG The Transformative Power of Europe*, No. 36, (February 2012), p. 14.

Ünver Noi's examination of the democratization process in Turkey for the 2001–2015 period focuses not only on Europeanization, but also on modernization and securitization, all of which are interlinked in the Turkish case. In this context, she assesses the expected positive role of the Islamic middle class in Turkey's modernization and democratization by analyzing the argument that identifies a correlation between economic development and democracy based on modernization theory. She evaluates also the internal and external developments by drawing upon the securitization theory of the Copenhagen School, and the impacts of securitization on the democratization process in Turkey.

Daniel Serwer analyzes Serbia and its gradual journey towards democracy, taking the 1990s disintegration of the Federal Republic of Yugoslavia as the starting point. He argues that in Serbia, there is a popular desire to join the European Union, which encourages the elite to make reforms to this end. He claims that Serbia has made significant progress in many respects since the Milosevic era, and can now claim to be on the road to democracy and to a European future.

Despite the improvements and the correct functioning of Serbia's electoral mechanisms, Serwer argues that there are number of areas that need further improvement in Serbia, such as minority rights, freedom of the press, rule of law and reconciliation with its neighbors. He goes further to analyze the external factors in which the democratization process is changing society slowly in Serbia. In this context, he evaluates the government of Serbia's endeavors towards EU accession, despite the presence of a well-financed and well-organized vocal opposition that is closer to Russia, and the anti-NATO sentiments among Serbians that make the anti-Western agenda easier to advance for the opponents of Western integration and their ideas. He concludes with a discussion of the EU's capacity for the absorption of new member states, arguing that Serbia's membership process seems to be taking longer than that of Croatia.

In "Challenges of Democracy in Bosnia and Herzegovina," **Sasha Toperich** and **Mak Kamenica** claims that Bosnia-Herzegovina can be considered a "defective democracy" or a hybrid regime. He suggests that there is a lack of effort to transform values, standards and that political culture, particularly among the elites, who are very comfortable with the dysfunctional political environment. Most Bosnian-Herzegovinian citizens believe corruption is increasing, that most politicians are involved in it and that the government is ineffective in fighting it, while the extremely complex and multi-layer legal system in Bosnia-Herzegovina contributes to a weak rule of law. The public must be willing to hold politicians accountable, and a recently launched robust program of socio-economic reforms may finally be a breakthrough in this regard. Political and institutional reforms must follow if the country is to be more functional and able to provide good quality of life for its citizens.

Part III examines the challenges of democracy in neighboring countries, focusing on the European Neighborhood Policy and the Eastern Partnership. In addition, an evaluation is made of one of the major challenges to democracy, being corruption both in the EU and in its neighbors.

In "Rethinking the European Union's Neighborhood Policy," **Michael Leigh** asks fundamental questions about whether the policy should be maintained at all, and, if so, what adjustments should be made. He evaluates the main policy instruments of the ENP that were first developed under the "Eastern Partnership", and then extended in principle to North Africa and the Levant, being the new generation of Association Agreements (AAs), incorporating Deep and Comprehensive Free Trade Agreements (DCFTA), as well as action plans, progress reports, assistance, overlapping policies, the EU's efforts to promote religious freedom, the EU's core values and their effectiveness regarding Europe's neighbors.

He notes that the aim of the European Neighborhood Policy was to incentivize reform in neighboring countries so as to create a ring of well-governed states around the EU. However, the "ring of friends" now finds itself surrounded by a "ring of fire", and this has caused difficulties in identifying a clear and single approach to issues by EU institutions on one side and the member states on the other. The Eastern Partnership countries face a number of challenges and external pressures, most notably from Russia, and so in order to maintain credibility, EU institutions and member states must speak increasingly with one voice. While the EU institutions put forward strict political conditionality, the EU member states' engagement on the basis of traditional considerations encapsulates in the EU a "dual approach" that harms its credibility in terms of the promotion of democracy. Leigh emphasizes the need for the EU and its member states to act quickly and pragmatically in a variety of fields beyond the ENP if Europe is to endure the threats to security and stability emanating from the east and south.

Alexander Sokolowski assesses the challenges and potential paths for democracy building in the Southern Caucasus in his chapter "Challenges of Democracy in the Caucasus." He argues that in the Caucasus, the key common challenges to democracy include a lack of democratic experience; disputes over boundaries that raise questions about membership in the political community; wars and perceived threats from neighbors that lead to the perception of democracy as a deferrable luxury; relatively small middle classes, which are needed for democratic transformation; economic disparities between the center and the periphery within the country; low levels of political trust among the ruling elite and toward politicians and political institutions; and most notably the centralization of power in executive branch authorities.

He points to three additional conditions that complicate the adoption of democracy in Georgia, Armenia and Azerbaijan. Where the adoption of democratic norms are perceived a deviation from traditional values, the reform process to bring the country in line with EU standards can be seen as an abandonment of local culture, and inculcate the belief that democracy is being externally imposed. The uncertainty surrounding if and when Caucasian states will be welcomed to the Euro-Atlantic community and a more assertive posture from their northern neighbor are other challenges to democracy in the region that are discussed in this chapter.

Shaazka Beyerle, in her chapter entitled "Challenges of Democracy: Corruption," examines the linkages between corruption, authoritarianism and violent conflict, their legacy in Europe and neighboring countries, and the implications for European democracy and security. She discusses how corruption erodes public trust in government and undermines democracies and state-building, identifying it as a problem in both the EU and its neighbors. The EU member states have in place most of the necessary legal instruments and institutions to prevent and fight corruption, but the results in many places have been unsatisfactory. There are frequent failures to enforce the law to its fullest extent, systemic problems are not dealt with and the responsible institutions lack the capacity to enforce the law. She argues that these issues make the EU's efforts to urge neighborhood countries to fight corruption more difficult.

In the EU's neighbor countries, the legacy of authoritarianism—impunity and a lack of accountability among the elites- ensures the continuance of corruption after transition. As states were structured to aid self-enrichment prior to democratization, the process does not guarantee reforms will be automatic. After a transition from a dictatorship to a democracy, corruption does not evaporate. When the citizens are faced with obstructive politicians, corrupt parties and weak institutions, representative democracy alone cannot deliver accountability and justice. Any belief that the establishment of anti-corruption structures will automatically ensure corruption is dealt with is false. Beyerle demonstrates the role of citizen-led campaigns, their synergies with top-down efforts, and she offers five takeaways for curbing corruption and reinforcing democracy.

Part IV examines the success of the EU's efforts to promote democracy, focusing on its international role and its normative power. In "*Constructing the EU as a Global Actor: A Critical Analysis of European Democracy Promotion*", **Münevver Cebeci** discusses the debate over the EU's actorness, especially at a global level, underlining the EU's *difference* as an actor in the world as a post-modern and post-sovereign bloc that can be considered a model in terms of successful regional integration and the promotion of democracy, human rights and the rule of law, and which acts as a normative power. She attempts to look into how the EU's identity in global politics is constructed in a specific way—both as a global actor and as an "ideal power"; how such construction legitimizes its democracy-promotion activities through various tools, such as enlargement and trade conditionality, political dialogue, etc.; and how the latter feed into such constructions in return.

She analyzes European foreign policy in a discussion based on the "'ideal power Europe' meta-narrative" argument, which is a concept used by the author to underline the power-knowledge relations behind the construction of the EU's identity as an ideal. She states that the EU's efforts to promote democracy do not go beyond the portrayal of the EU as an ideal entity that promotes universal values and norms, and of its others (the target societies) as imperfect—as societies which need the EU's help in order to become democratic, etc. She argues that the image of an "ideal power" is maintained (produced and reproduced) even when the EU is facing hardship, if not failing outright.

Geoffrey Harris discusses human rights and the promotion of democracy under the intriguing title "Human Rights and Democracy Promotion: EU Blows on an Uncertain Trumpet," taking us from the European Community's first enlargement in 1973 to the present day, and then explaining the challenges ahead. Keeping up the courage of their convictions that has carried the European countries for last forty years but also to determine EU aims on what they will bring to life as the "European consensus on democracy" are vital elements in looking forward, as engagement with unpleasant regimes is unavoidable.

He assesses the issue in three terms, beginning with the 1973–1989 period under the title "Steady Progress based on Common Values". He continues with a look at the 1990–2008 period under the title "From Hubris to Uncertainty", before concluding with a section entitled "New Challenges, Economic Crisis and Upheaval in the Neighborhood". He also evaluates the resurgence of Russia, the mass influx of refugees into the EU, as well as transatlantic partners' responses and cooperative engagement of the EU and the United States to provide the reader with an understanding of the factors that have had an effect on efforts to promote democracy in the EU.

Together, we have attempted to offer our readers ongoing challenges of democracy in the EU and its neighbors that led to several arguments. Guy Hermet words on the decline of political democracy in the EU member states as a result of the limited available resources for the financing of the welfare state is one of the interesting ones: "democracy is spreading at the peripheries of the world, but is exhausted at the center."[16] Developments in the EU neighborhood test this argument, since the negative trends in the periphery also pose a clear challenge to one of the main and shared values around which the EU and the US transatlantic partners formulated their foreign policy approaches—the promotion of democracy—through coercion, conditioning and attraction.

All of the contributors to this publication have tried to evaluate the state of democracies, as well as the normativized image of Western democracy, as a universal model to which non-Western societies aspire. We have attempted to come up with an answer to the question of whether illiberal tendencies in democracies and/or the de-democratization trend in the EU neighborhood that challenges its positive image would evolve into a different model of "quasi-democracy", or whether Western-style democracy would recover as a model and continue to transform its neighbors in line with its own ideal model.

---

16. Parliamentary Assembly, Doc. 11623, June 6, 2008, *The State of Democracy in Europe: Specific Challenges Facing European Democracies: The Case Diversity and Migration*.

Part I

Challenges of Democracy
in the European Union

Chapter One

The Challenge of a Democracy Beyond the State in the European Union

Mario Telò

Building a democracy beyond the state is a difficult challenge, as the first European attempts in the history of the human being well show. It is an inevitable step for true democrats, because the traditional national democracies are increasingly unable to cope with the transnational and supranational challenges of our time: addressing financial unbalances, building an international order and facing new security threats, limiting climate change and environmental degradation, regulating migration flows, combating infectious diseases, fighting against transnational criminality, drug traffic and terrorism.[1] It would not be serious denying the open and increasing contradiction between the supranational nature of the most important challenges of our time and the national limits of the democratic State.

However, even defining "democracy beyond the State" is not an easy task. Theoretically, we are exploring a research field that is epistemologically off-limits for the mainstream U.S. neorealist school of International relations[2] because according to them democracy has nothing to do with the international realm. It is also out of reach for the French "republican" tradition, which still asserts that democracy can be implemented only at the national level.[3] For this innovating endeavor we need to take stock of critical approaches to International relations while combining them with comparative politics and European studies.

On the basis of the current academic debate, we could define *democracy beyond the State:*

---

1. David Held, *Models of Democracy,* (Cambridge: Cambridge University Press, 1996); Jürgen Habermas, Toward a Cosmopolitan Europe, *Journal of Democracy,* Vol. 14, no. 4, 2003, pp.86–100.

2. Kenneth Waltz, *Theory of International Politics,* (Reading Massachusset: Addison Wesley Publishing, 1979).

3. Gauchet M. *L'avènement de la démocratie. I: La révolution moderne,* (Paris: Folio Essays, 2013).

(a) As an institutional settlement of *democracy among the States*—conceptually opposed to democracy within the State.[4] Of course, in the EC/EU understanding, transnational institutions and transnational citizenship do interact with domestic democracy and citizenship in multiple ways: on the one hand, every member of the EU supranational democratic polity in the making must be ("Copenhagen criteria," 1993), and remain (Article 7,TEU) a democratic State, since transnational democracy is impossible with unreliable pre-constitutional States. Austria was the target of intergovernmental political sanctions in 2000 due to a national government considered as xenophobic by the other 14 EU members. The problem is that, compared with the decade of the "liberal peace" following 1989, façade democracies are increasing in number and arrogance[5] not only outside the EU, like Russia, but also within, like Hungary.

On the other hand, once established, intergovernmental and supranational institutions develop a complex interplay with national democracies[6]—defined as a multiple and multifaceted "Europeanization" process,[7] acting both bottom-up and top-down. The first theoretical question to cope with is the dynamic and changing relationship between democracy within the State and democracy beyond the State in the troubled context of the early 21st century.

(b) We need also a further conceptual distinction. While the *confederal* concept of democracy is focusing on the democratic nature of member States represented in the multilateral bodies like the Council of Ministers and the European Council, a democracy beyond the State in Europe looks as closer to—even if not coincident with—*federal* democracy. Contrary to a democratic polity constructed by sovereign but interdependent States (e.g., the United Nations assembly), the European supranational democracy building process has been compared with the democratic path constructed according to the Hamilton's model of U.S. federalism.[8] Both share the need to cope with the theoretical chal-

---

4. Kalypso Nikolaidis and Paul Magnette, "The European Union's Democratic Agenda," in Mario Telo, ed., *EU and Global Governance*, (London & New York: Routledge, 2009), pp 43-63.

5. Larry Diamond, *In Search of Democracy*, (Abingdon: Routledge, 2015).

6. Philip C. Schmitter and al, *Governance in the European Union*, (London: SAGE 1995).

7. Claudio Radaelli and Susana Borras, "The Transformation of EU Governance, the Open Method of Coordination and the Economic Crisis," in Maria Joao Rodrigues and Eleni Xiarchogiannopoulou, eds., *The Eurozone Crisis and the Transformation of European Governance*, (Farnham: Ashgate, 2014), pp 41-57.

lenge firstly addressed by Montesquieu: how to combine democratic citizens' representation with the need to protect the *demos* from external threats? A small State is close to the citizens but weak within the international arena, whereas the big State is strong against external threats but far from domestic audience. The union of multiple States within a federal State is the best possible compromise according to Montesquieu and the American federalists.

The European federalist thought is one of the main sources of inspiration for transnational democracy indeed (from Spinelli to De Rougemont). However, if not disentangled from the federal State tradition[9] it would be associated with the teleological perspective of building in Europe a kind of second United States. Nobody speaks about *democracy beyond the State* in the U.S., while for Europe, given the deep historical roots of various nations and member States, the distinction between the federal State model and democracy beyond the State is of crucial relevance. What firstly matters is the conceptual independence of these two concepts from one other.

(c) A second source of inspiration for a democracy beyond the State is the tradition of *cosmopolitan democracy*. Differently from the tradition of federal democracy, the *cosmopolitan* concept of democracy is clearly far from a State model, as Immanuel Kant already stated more than two centuries ago.[10] Yet both concepts focus on cross-border relations among individuals and social groups, independently from—or parallel to—inter-State relations. Both traditions draw the attention on social ties, on mobility and relations at level of civil societies, on the plurality of social and institutional actors networking across national borders. The political philosophical background of both innovating approaches has to be found in the work of Immanuel Kant rather (as recently revived by Habermas and others) than in Montesquieu.

However, the experience of the European Union shows the differences between cosmopolitan democracy and democracy beyond the State. While the first one is focusing on the universal dimension, which

---

8. Larry Siedentop, *Democracy in Europe*, (London: Allen Lane, 2002); Sergio Fabbrini, *Which European Union? Europe After the Euro Crisis*, (Cambridge: Cambridge University Press, 2015).

9. See Olivier Beaud ,*Théorie de la Fédération*, (Paris: PUF, 2007); Nicolas Levrat éd. in cooperation with Frédéric Esposito, *Europe: de l'integration a la Fédération*, (Louvain-la-Neuve, Academic –Bruylant, 2010).

10. Immanuel Kant, *Treaty for Perpetual Peace*, 1795.

entails universal values, notably human rights protection (Held, Archibugi 2000), the second one is a political concept and a more consciously limited concept. *When we discuss a transnational democracy beyond the State in Europe we address the question of the construction of a democratic system limited to a certain territory, developed not at the global but the regional level, in the sense of a territorial region of the world, including borders and frontiers.* Even the most open concept of borders entails a distinction between insiders and outsiders, and also the intermediate status is legally fixed (status of "candidate country"). On the one hand, transnational and territorially based democracy could be conceived as a step towards the cosmopolitan utopia; on the other, it could also be developed as an independent and political project.

In this second version, it entails a complex relationship between democracy and a political decision making process based on a particular region, a distinct territory and grouping of States. Even if Europe is not a State and probably will never become one, it is already a regional polity, a political project as proved by the two political pillars of CFSP and JHA as well as by the Euro, which is a political project. The project of building up a democracy beyond the State means in Europe a limited transnational democratic polity, with borders. The EU is, however, a particular polity, compared with the universal dimension of the cosmopolitan vision.[11] The distinction between Europe and the World is much more evident in the 20th and 21st century than at the times of Kant.[12] Neglecting this crucial difference would with right provoke multiple and serious criticism by non-European scholars, even beyond the post-colonial school of thought.[13] Even within the European continent, some States (Turkey, Russia or other States) could decide, by free decision, to stay out (or exit from, like the UK) of the EU transnational democracy project and establish friendly neighborhood relations.

Cosmopolitan thought is challenged. The Habermas approach[14] is characterized by an internal tension: on the one hand, he and his school revived the cosmopolitan tradition in relation to Europe, focusing on

---

11. Kalypso Nikolaidis and Robert Howse, eds., *The Federal Vision: Legitimacy and Levels of Governance in the United States the European Union*, (Oxford: Oxford University Press, 2001).

12. Anthony Pagden, ed. *The Idea of Europe: From Antiquity to the European Union*, (Cambridge: Cambridge University Press, 2002).

13. Amitav Acharya, *The End of American World Order*, (Cambridge: Polity Press, 2014).

14. Jürgen Habermas, "Toward a cosmopolitan Europe'. *Journal of Democracy*, vol. 14, no. 4, 2003, pp. 86–100.

transnational networks and bottom-up citizen's participation, the need of combining parliamentary democracy with a public sphere, all elements which are essential to transnational democracy. On the other hand, when talking not only about a European "public sphere" but also including elements of European "republicanism" ("constitutional patriotism" according to the Habermas language; see his recent ARENA paper on European democracy 2014, as well as Fossum and others) he emphasizes the political dimension of a European transnational democracy, its clear distinction from cosmopolitanism and from the global or continental (in its broadest understanding) dimension.

What are We Learning from the EU's experience?

Europe is, by general assessment, the most sophisticated laboratory of transnational democracy beyond the State. According to the EU/EC Treaties, since Maastricht (1992), the citizen is twice sovereign, as member of his/her nation and as member of the European Union (Articles 9 and 10, TEU). A "common citizenship" is announced in the Lisbon Treaty Preamble: it entails the recognition of the rights, freedoms and principles listed in the "EU Charter for Fundamental Rights" and makes explicit reference, in Article 6 of the TEU, to both the European Convention for Human Rights and the member States constitutional traditions. The European citizenship includes several rights: free mobility not only as a worker, as it was since the early Rome treaty (now Articles 45-48, TEU), but as an ordinary citizen, which breaks with the traditional identification of national citizenship and residence. Furthermore, it includes the right to vote (at local and European level), petition, and diplomatic representation. The provisions related to the European space of freedom, security and justice further deepen several aspects of transnational democracy and citizenship.

Moreover, the gradually enhanced power of the EP, from 1979 to the Lisbon treaty, was the flag of several generations of European democrats because it was expected to compensate the citizens for the diminished national parliament sovereignty provoked by the centralization of the EU decision making process, with the national sovereignties sharing and pooling process (within the Council and the European Council), strengthening supranational regulations and empowering the Council of Minister (and the national governments) against the respective national parliaments. Well, what we have learned since the early nineties (notably after the Maastricht Treaty ratification referenda, "no" in Denmark and short "yes" in France in 1993) is a kind of paradox: *despite tremendous progresses of the European parliament as its co-decision power with the Council is concerned, the Eurosceptical feeling of a European democratic deficit is stronger then ever.*

Further strengthening the EP powers as strongly called upon by federalist movement (F. Herman, G. Verhofstadt, Cohn Bendit, and others, according to the Altiero Spinelli tradition) on the one hand, was necessary given the evidence of the declining EC/EU's early "substantive legitimacy"[15] provided by the high economic efficiency during the thirty Golden years; but, on the other end, it looks as insufficient to cope with the social consequences of the hardest economist crisis since the 1930s provoking the explosion of populist movements.

Already ten years ago, before the financial crisis imported from the U.S., the Constitutional Treaty rejection in 2005 and the Lisbon Treaty difficult ratifications in 2007-8, were totally unexpected. The new evidence is that, combining relevant steps towards "federal" centralization at supranational level (treaties of Amsterdam 1997, Nice 2000, Rome 2004, and Lisbon Treaty, 2007) with enhanced parliamentary power is absolutely not enough to cope with the largely diffused popular feeling of a too far decision making process combining technocratic governance and intergovernmental hidden negotiations. The strengthening of the EP continued until the top reached with the full co-decision power with the Council, provided by the Lisbon Treaty. However, never the Euroscepticism was so strong and diffused as in the last decade. This paradox was already addressed by the scholars in the 90s[16] when the emergence of the limits of the idea of importing from USA the Hamiltonian tradition paved the way to a more complex and mature understanding of democracy beyond the State. Actually, European referenda are becoming nightmares for Europhiles and no government (with the single and paradoxical exception of the UK) asks for new Treaty revision because of the fear of serious complications during the national ratification process.

---

15. Joseph H. Weiler, *The Constitution of Europe: 'Do the New Clothes have an Emperor?' and Other Essays on European Integration*, (Cambridge: Cambrige University Press, 1999).

16. Mario Telò, ed., *Démocratie et Construction Européenne*, (Bruxelles: Editions de l'Université de Bruxelles, 1995) Eric Remacle and Paul Magnette, eds., *Le Nouveau Modèle Européen*, (Bruxelles: Editions de l" Université de Bruxelles, 2000).

Which remedy? It is well known that, in order to understand and address this theoretical challenge, F. W. Scharpf proposed to distinguish between *output legitimacy* (based on the efficiency of EU policies and real benefits for citizens) from input legitimacy (based on proactive citizens' participation). On that basis, a various political stream supported by academics suggest to make of the EU democracy something more similar to national democracies, and of the European Parliament something more similar to national Parliaments, notably the Westminster Parliament, ignoring that the EP was—and still is—a "strange" Parliament.[17]

Should and could the increasing democratic deficit of the EU democratic system be addressed by a process of *political polarization* of the European electorate according to the left-right cleavage and could the European Parliament consequently change according to the Westminster model? In other world, should transnational democracy beyond the State become more politicized, similarly to the cleavages of domestic politics of larger States?

The comparative political science school led by Simon Hix[18] focusing on elections, parliaments and parties, is supporting this perspective, by underlining the actual and potential similarities with national politics. Consequently this school is fostering the transformation of the EP into a true political Parliament electing the Commission *on a political basis (according to the left-right cleavage).* This change is expected also to counteract the declining turnout and mobilize the citizens' participation. Well, the provision of the Lisbon Treaty related to the election of the Commission President by the Parliament (TEU, art 17.7) looked to many as paving the way to this perspective. Actually, this politicization process made some progress in 2014, with the *Spitzenkandidaten* indicated by the 5 main EU parties and the eventual election of the winner, the leader of the winning party—the EPP- notably Jean-Claude Junker, as the new President of the European Commission. However, there is some relevant *caveat*: the campaign in many countries was not at all inspired by this political innovation (the *Spitzenkandidaten* were not even invited to put their foot on the UK soil for example).

Secondly, the more political and "politicized" new Commission, chaired by Jean- Claude Junker, is not a politically homogeneous gov-

---

17. Pascal Delwit, Jean-Michel De Waele, Paul Magnette, eds., *A Quoi Sert le Parlement Européen?*, (Bruxelles: Complexe, 1999)

18. Simon Hix, *The Political System of the European Union*, (Basingstocke: Palgrave, 1999).

ernment of the EU: it is a matter of facts, that both the Commission internal political composition and the large supporting parliamentary majority correspond to a "consensual"[19] democratic model, including a multiplicity of actors and interconnected levels of governance and, politically, both center-left and center-right parties, rather than to a Westminster democratic majority democratic model. The EU transnational democracy beyond the State is definitely much more comparable with consensual democratic national systems, like Austria, Belgium, and Switzerland than to the UK; and some of its forms are consistent with the particular ways of deliberative democracy by addressing internal conflicts/disagreements and justifying binding decisions.[20]

All in all, notwithstanding the innovations, the European transnational democracy experiment beyond the State confirms its distinctive features and cannot be confused with classical national majority system democracy. Politicization according to the classical right-left cleavage, only to a limited extent fosters citizens mobilization and is not the panacea: the turnout remains relatively low (less than 50%) and 17% was won by Eurosceptical parties, which made it necessary to build a "great coalition" (3 parties, EPP, Social Democrats and Liberals) electing and supporting the Junker Commission. All in all, in Europe, transnational democracy beyond the State will hardly follow the national democratic model, notably the model of great powers like UK or France or US. The special circumstances of the existence of many European *demoi* instead of a single European *demos*,[21] the internal discrepancies and divergences increased with the Eastern enlargement, the extremely sensitive issue of the fair balance between smaller and larger member States,[22] the relevant unbalances of the constituencies electing EP parliament members in various countries, all make it impossible to apply the Westminster model of majority democracy. Not only but the consensual and centripetal EU experience has inspired similar consensual and/or " technical" governments in several Member States.

---

19. Arendt Leijpart, *Patterns of Democracy: Government Forms and Performance in Thirty-Six Countries,* (New Haven: Yale University Press, 1999).

20. Amy Guttmann and Dennis Thomson, *Why Deliberative Democracy?* (Princeton: Princeton University Press, 2004).

21. Jürgen Habermas, Toward a Cosmopolitan Europe. *Journal of Democracy,* vol. 14, no. 4, 2003, pp. 86–100.

22. Kalypso Nikolaidis and Paul Magnette, "The European Union's Democratic Agenda," in Mario Telo, ed., *EU and Global Governance,* (London and New York: Routledge, 2009), pp 43-63.

For similar reason (obstacles to trivial transplantation into the EU system of national models), the multiple proposals of recovering the legitimacy deficit by the direct election of the President of the EU, combining the two functions of Commission president and European Council president, is typical of intellectuals who are underestimating the consequences of the complexity of the EU system and the impossibility of over simplification following the example of strong national democracies. In conclusion, it is very doubtful that a political European transnational democracy beyond the State should replicate the domestic politics of the larger States like France, UK or the USA.

The EU laboratory shows that transnational democracy beyond the State is not only a multilevel but also a mixed an multiform polity. While following—as experts- the works of the European Convention (2002/2003), we tried to conceptualize the four forms of EU transnational democracy included in the new draft-Treaty and transferred four years later in the text of the Lisbon treaty (TEU, art 9-12):

1. A central body of representative democracy as the legislative power is concerned (EU Parliament, or EP) completing the second legislative body (the Council of Minister) and balancing the executive power shared by Council and Commission and the juridical power (the Court of Justice); the relevant status acquired by the EP fosters an increasing role of European political parties.[23]

2. An incipient multilevel parliamentary system, including not only the EP but also the participation of national Parliaments (TEU, Article 12, and Protocol n.1, attached to the Lisbon Treaty with the "early warning" procedure);

3. A structured social transnational democracy, strengthening the socio-economic side of democratic participation, by underpinning the role of *social partners dialogue*, both between them and with the Commission and the rotating Presidency (Spring social forum), which includes the social dimension of democracy within the European decision making process (TFEU, Article 154, 155). The Socio/Economic Committee is also a form of representative social democracy (TFEU, Part 6, Title 1, chapter 3,1 consultation bodies), combined with the territorial representation of sub-national entities, like the European Regions (TFEU, Part 6, Title 1, Chap-

23. Robert Ladrech, *Europeanization and Political Parties: Towards a Framework for Analysis*, Keele University paper , 2001

ter 3,2). Decisions regarding employment and social policies are taken after interplay with social partners and consultative bodies.[24]

4. A fledging European *public sphere*, legally framed by treaty provisions for enhanced transparency, consultations, and also the first steps towards a *participatory democracy* (according to Article 11.4, one million citizens could "invite the Commission to make a proposal" to Council and Parliament (however, a disappointing record of implementation has to be mentioned). Public sphere is also matter of civil society participation, multilingual media like Euronews, dialogue between the EU institutions and churches, local powers, experts, transnational networks and lobbies, etc.

This institutional complexity of the democracy beyond the State has an obvious implication. Each provision for a European transnational democracy entails distinct legitimacy procedures: direct (EP) or indirect (European Council and Council of Ministers) election; technocratic and substantive efficiency; openness and dialogue with civil society.

A large debate is open regarding the link between democratization and *constitutionalization*. On the one hand, the need for a coherent framework and for a general consistency of the transnational democratic system would call, according to relevant scholars, for a written constitution, a constitution not only beyond the national State but also without a federal supranational State; and without a single *demos*.[25] On the other hand, according to an alternative approach,[26] a *constitutional process*, without a written Constitution, better fits with the specific and complex nature of the European polity. The history of European construction and notably three failed attempts to approve a constitutional treaty suggest the second option as the most appropriate.[27]

---

24. M. Joo Rodrigues and Eleni Xiarchogiannopoulou, eds., *The Eurozone Crisis and the Transformation of European Governance*, (Farnham: Ashgate, 2014).

25. Jürgen Habermas ,Toward a Cosmopolitan Europe. *Journal of Democracy*, vol. 14, no. 4, 2003, pp.86–100

26. Joseph H. Weiler, *The Constitution of Europe: 'Do the New Clothes have an Emperor?'and Other Essays on European Integration*, (Cambridge: Cambrige University Press, 1999).

27. Sonia Lucarelli, Furio Cerutti and Viven A. Schmidt, *Debating Political Identity and Legitimacy in the European Union*, (Abingdon: Routledge 2010).

Democracy beyond the State as a Work in Progress: New Challenges for Research

Multiple relevant research agendas are emerging in the current times of uncertainty, and deepening the distinctive political perspective of European transnational democracy we presented in this chapter, notably: A) theoretically, a third way between the federal and the cosmopolitan concepts of democracy beyond the State; B) empirically, exploring a complex political way to transnational democracy in Europe which cannot be identified to trivial and oversimplified copies of national democracy and is confronted with a globalized and disordered world. We limit our review to some ongoing research projects:

The Impact of the Eurozone Crisis on the Transnational Democratic Process and the Risks of Degradation of the EU Internal Multilateralism

The Nobel Prize winner Amartya Sen did recently draw the attention on the increasingly dramatic link between the current socio-economic crisis and the possible dissipation of previous achievements in democracy, internal multilateralism and social ethics.[28] At a recent conference Sen addressed the question of the negative interplay between the quality of the European democracy and the contents of the economic policy. In his words, a policy of austerity would undermine the social basis of democracy, while an alternative "Social-democratic economic policy" would not. In principle, this argument is not easy to accept: how a particular economic policy and a distinctive ideology should be more coherent with democracy, whereas others—like the Liberal or Christian or Green—would not? However, there is no doubt that the current social crisis and the long lasting austerity policy-adopted by every national government—was affecting the European transnational democracy in many ways.

We are witnessing a paradox: the EU is expanding democracy beyond the limits of nation State, while the EU integration risks empowering executives and lobbies which are more able to quickly adjust to the supranational dimension. Secondly, the Commission and ECB popular perception as bodies "governing by numbers" within the

---

28. Amartya Sen, in *Actes Du Colloque La Démocratie, Enrayée?* F.De Smet, ed., (Bruxelles: Académie, 2014).

context of a "multilayered regional governance," is *de facto* increasing populism while limiting the national government's policy agenda.[29]

Moreover, even accomplished progresses in crisis management and in anti-crisis policy efficiency often result in enhanced democratic deficit both at the national and EU level. For example, there is a little doubt that the key moment of the Euro-crisis solution was the famous sentence of July 2012 by Mario Draghi, the President of the ECB, saying that "the ECB was ready to do whatever in its power to save the Euro." Did the ECB, by these very effective declarations, become the political government of the EU? This was the perception by a large swath of public opinion. Trivial and populist oppositions of national democracy to supranational technocracy were addressed. Even if the ECB President Mario Draghi acted only after the 21 June 2012 European Council green light, there is no doubt that the perception of the President of the ECB as "the EU's most powerful political leader" was and is problematic from the democratic theory point of view.

Efficiency by crisis management, if framed by austerity policy, looks to many as contradictory with the democratic legitimacy of the EU's decision making. Research is critically analyzing stereotypes as the Greek criticism to "EU and German diktats" are concerned. It is a matter of facts that both Southern crisis-States (like Greece) and Northern creditor States are democracies. Not only Tsipras is a legitimate winner of democratic election but all EU member States leaders; for instance, A. Merkel has to look for the internal legitimation by the German *Bundestag*, *Bundesrat* and *Bundesverfassungsgericht* (supreme court). Secondly, the bodies of the European democracy beyond the State were not truly marginalized: democratic procedures matter more than the usual oversimplification by Eurosceptic criticism. For example, the European Parliament role, notably its "negative" role, its critical function is resilient, as a consequence of the Lisbon Treaty reform and the procedures of codecision. Thirdly, the concept of "best practices" draws the attention on the relevant role of some national democracies, notably Scandinavian parliaments and parliamentary committees, by developing democratic accountability of the EU council of Ministers and the need of diffusing these examples within the EU member States.

---

29. Philip C. Schmitter and Zoe Lefkofridi, "A Good Crisis or a Bad Crisis for the EU?' in Maria Joao Rodrigues and Eleni Xiarchogiannopoulou, eds., *The Eurozone Crisis and the Transformation of European Governance*, (Farnham: Ashgate, 2014), pp 11-28.

What is more pertinent in the Sen critique? The EU's transnational democracy is framed by a dynamic multilateral polity represented by the Council of Ministers, the Euro-group (18 members of euro), and the European Council. Contrary to domestic democracy, this intergovernmental multilateral framework is crucial and only an idealistic picture of Europe may ignore that this is a pillar of the EU "beyond the State democratic polity" since the EU's legitimacy cannot be built against the States but in cooperation with them. Well, as a consequence of the hard intergovernmental negotiations, the EU's internal multilateralism looks to critical observers as gradually transformed into a increasingly hierarchical decision making process: the intergovernmental cooperation is increasingly influenced either by power relations, or affected by populist domestic pressures, which is inevitably undermining to some extent the mutual trust, and making the room for transnational democracy narrower. We know from experience and scientific literature that multilateralism is normatively based on two principles: the first is the "generalized principle of conduct" which is opposed – by definition—to hegemonic or imperial relations, which entail a hierarchical dimension;[30] and the second is "diffuse reciprocity."

The first principle is no longer respected when uneven application of the common rules and procedures occurs. This is relevant for the EU case, since derogations to the "Stability Pact" rules have been welcomed for Germany and France in 2003, while not for Portugal at the end of the decade. On the other hand, this is relevant also by analyzing opposite cases: for example, the same austerity rules risked of not being of application for Greece after the 2015 elections, while Spain, Ireland, Portugal and other countries had to implement them is a strict way in 2012-15. Also rejecting the general principle of conduct by exploiting its own national weakness as more than an argument, a weapon, is inconsistent with transnational democracy beyond the State while consistent with a populist downgrading of national democracy.

A promising research field is precisely the dynamic interplay between transnational democracy and the changing EU's internal multilateral set, on the one hand, and the troubles of national democracies, on the other.

---

30. James A. Caporaso, International Relations Theory and Multilateralism: The Search for Foundations, in *Multilateralism Matters: The Theory and Praxis of an Institutional Form*, edited by John Gerard Ruggie, (New York: Columbia University Press, 1993), pp. 51-89.

The Social Dimensions of Transnational Democracy beyond the State: Deepening Diffuse Reciprocity and Bridging with Neighbors

The second principle of multilateral cooperation affected by the crisis—"*diffuse reciprocity*" has been opposed to "specific reciprocity" by Robert Keohane in 2003[31] and by myself in 2013. This principle means that the exchange among States may evolve from mere cost-benefit calculations (*do ut des*, as in specific reciprocity), towards two deeper dimensions: firstly, expanding the time dimension of the exchange between partners, which implies an enhanced trust between them. Giving and receiving back do not need to be simultaneous exchanges as in specific reciprocity. Secondly, a diffuse reciprocity means making issue-linkage possible: the fields of the multilateral exchange may be quite diverse and interplaying with one another, from trade to economic cooperation, from political dialogue to financial cooperation, from commitment to human rights protection to fight against the climate change. *Diffuse reciprocity* is the way for transnational democracy expansion in the experience of the EU democracy beyond the State and between the States.

On the basis of a large literature on social exchange, political scientists (for example Anna Caffarena 2008)[32] analyze the role of mutual trust as a "social capital" composed of diffused reciprocity, networks of social relations and social norms, and its current decline in bilateral/multilateral interstate relations as a major problem.[33] According to this point of view, what is needed is reviving and further institutionalizing the social capital of mutual trust by fostering rich relationships of dialogue, communication, shared long-term aims and cooperation, which should be underpinned by transnational democratic networks. The simple fact that even the Westphalian Treaty of 1648 revived the principle of "friendship" as a necessary context for a successful peace treaty (The Christianity during the Middle Ages underesti-

---

31. Robert O. Keohane, Reciprocity in International Relations. *International Organization*, vol. 40, no. 1, pp. 1–27. 1986

32. Anna Caffarena, "Couples and Trust Building in International Society. A Social Capital Perspective," paper presented at ISA Annual convention, San Francisco 2008

33. Russel Hardin, *Trust*, (Cambridge: Cambridge University Press, 2006) (quoted by Anna Caffarena, ivi) James S. Coleman, Social Capital and the Creation of Human Capital. *The American Journal of Sociology*, n. 94, 1989, pp. 95-120 (quoted by Anna Cafferana, Ivi); Robert D. Putnam, *Democracy in Flux: The Evolution of Social Capital in Contemporary Society*, (Oxford: Oxford University Press, 2002).

mated the concept of friendship), we do understand that this social capital is really essential for the EU democracy to survive the crisis.

However, let's imagine that the internal trust and friendship is truly revived, strengthening the internal solidarity within the Euro-group of 18 countries. Would a successful process of "bonding" of peoples of similar sort discourage "bridging" and openness to neighbors? In other words, it is possible that developing diffuse reciprocity, friendship and solidarity within a limited regional polity (as a domestic democracy, or even the Euro-group) make more difficult openness to other external actors, people of a different sort, to candidate States, or to the universal dimension? Which balance is wise between bonding and bridging in the current world characterized by connectivity and conflicts? Under which conditions are trade-offs possible?

Along a similar research strategy, the social scientist Maurizio Ferrera underlines in a forthcoming book chapter the internal "fault lines" aggravated by the economic and social crisis notably between South and North as shown by the conflict between Greece and Germany.[34] Well, in the current critical juncture, transnational democracy needs, on the one hand, a long-term idea of solidarity where what looks as a cost in the short term may be seen as a gain for every country including the creditor ones in the long term. On the other hand, the crisis-States should never forget two things: firstly, that a multilevel transnational democracy needs to *fairly* respect also the national democracies of creditor countries; and secondly, that the post-1945 process of reconciliation between aggressors and victims of WW2 is a "common good," a precious achievement without which transnational democracy would be impossible. German leaders have been universally and many times recognized as sincere in apologizing for Nazi war crimes. Ignoring how hard this *catharsis* has been, and undermining it for instrumental purposes would be irresponsible. Jacques Delors quoted in 2012 Hannah Arendt and her plea in favor of the couple "pardon and promise," as a precondition to create a Weberian-style *Vergemeinschaftung*, or *"neighborhood communities"* based on spatial proximity. This double principle is a founding value, a regional "common good," for the peaceful and democratic relations between Germany and all the victims of the Nazi

---

34. Ferrera, M . "Governing the European Union after the 'Phase Change:' New Ideas, New Values," in Van Middelaer L /Van Parijs Ph., eds., *What is the Future of Democracy in Europe and Can the Union be Part of it?*, (Brussels: Lanoo, 2015).

regime within the common European home.[35] A democracy beyond the State needs this historical and social background.

The Internal/External Dimension of Democracy.

We are approaching a third big issue for democracy beyond the State within the EU limits. The question how to combine two classical challenges for constitutional States: internal democracy and external policy. In comparative terms, the Swiss case is an interesting laboratory. On the one hand, if an even exemplary national democracy only focuses on the first, it risks several traps (for example, isolation, or referenda raising international problems, with the consequence of forcing the government to look for compromises with neighbors (as is happening after the referendum of 2014, about the free cross-border movement of people). On the other, one has to keep in mind how the need of avoiding the risk of weakening the citizens' representation side and provoking massive internal contest. It is increasingly impossible to consolidate domestic participatory democracy without developing transnational democracy beyond the State and is impossible to develop transnational democracy without an enhanced shared collective security framework.

This issue is relevant also for other EU Member States who may develop the practice of participatory democracy and national referenda to address relevant dilemmas, including both enlargement of the EU and exit from the EU. How to combine national traditions of participatory democracy and free public opinion with openness and notably the recognized need of an enhanced cooperation between the hard core of the Eurozone and the surrounding circles, including the neighbors and in particular candidate countries? The current de facto evolution towards a "multi-speed Europe," by concentric circles architecture, may be the best available solution. The strengthening of the Eurozone economic governance (and internal legitimacy) may be compatible with a larger transnational European polity and democratic framework, respecting national cultural diversities and including all the multiple trans-democratic dimensions, from social solidarity to the convergence on a humanitarian and mainly civilian common foreign policy.

---

35. Ibid.

The Internal/External Dimension of Democratic Legitimacy Facing the Increasing Relevance of External Opportunities and Threats. The European Transnational Democracy and the Global Level

Europe is not an island and European states are not the only ones who are facing what Norberto Bobbio defined in 1989 as "the external limits to democracy" (power of external actors, States, multinational companies, violent networks and other international threats).[36] International autonomy is the precondition for the quality of democracy: how does European transnational democracy interact with the surrounding disordered world? This research field is at the crossroad between comparative regionalism, EU studies and international relations/globalization studies: are international relations and globalization limiting the efficiency of a democratic polity by protecting citizens' sovereignty? How to cope with these external limits in Europe and at macro regional and global level? Is the enhanced a diffused call for global governance (regarding the financial imbalances, poverty reduction, coping with challenges such as climate change, terrorism, criminality, infectious diseases, etc.) contradictory with democracy at the national, global and regional levels?

a) At the regional level. Proximity and neighborhood matter and transnational democracy may affect domestic democracies. For example, the EU may play a more proactive role by expanding democracy to both candidate countries and partners of the EU's Neighborhood Policy. The development of transnational democracy (parties, various kind of networks, inter-parliamentary dialogue, and so on) may be more relevant on the one hand to prevent steps back in the democratization process of weak regimes that have met minimum standards of democracy, and on the other hand, to press authoritarian regimes to democratic pluralism, both in Eastern Europe and in the Mediterranean sub-region. Often, democratic transitions need social, economic and cultural linkages to established Western national and transnational democracies. After the end of the optimism of the 1990s about a global third wave of democratization (Huntington 1991), regionalism and geographic proximity are more concrete and efficient resources for democratization than the global agenda. The EU as a favorable neighbor may press for democratic consolidation in a way that is an alternative to the "U.S. way".[37]

---

36. Norberto Bobbio, *I limiti della democrazia*, (Torino: Einaudi, 1989).

37. See U.S. New Security Strategy 2002.

provided a correct trade-off between *bonding and bridging*, EU and candidate or neighboring countries may develop transnational linkages at level of civil society in a broader understanding. Against the enhanced assertiveness of alternative authoritarian regimes and their growing attractiveness in the name of economic efficiency in the current globalized economy, strengthening linkages become more important than in the 1990s. For example, open immigration and asylum policies, networks at the level of municipalities, companies, universities, advocacy groups, parallel to trade negotiations, may not only spotlight violations of democratic rules, but also enhance the resources of local democratic forces.[38]

b) We focused this chapter on the process of building a democracy beyond the State at regional level, notably in Europe, including members and surrounding countries. However, even at the global level, transnational democracy may be developed, in the context of a multi-level model of cosmopolitan democracy (which is quite far from the classic Kelsen model). Robert Keohane, the leader of neo-institutionalist International relations studies, addressed what he defined as this growing "governance dilemma": the more we need supranational governance to cope with the limits of national democracy, the more we need democratic governance at a transnational level. Every level of governance, whether national, regional or global, is to some extent increasingly challenged by a democratic deficit that is enhancing the efficacy deficit as well. Secondly, this kind of governance dilemma should be addressed by "less contingent forms of democratic legitimacy" compared with the golden times of the Bretton Woods multilateral system.[39] His former pupil, A. Moravcsik, pretends that democratic deficit is not relevant for the EU, composed by democratic States and democratic governments, which meet in the Council and European Council.[40] What is more and more evident is that we need to be exploring a third way between the realistic approach of Moravcsik and the utopian view of Held. What Andrew Moravcsik argues is true but insufficient given the increasing relevance of transnational governance for the citizens'

---

38. Stephan Haggard, Democratization during the Third Wave. *Annual Review of Political Science*, in press.

39. Robert O. Keohane, *After Hegemony. Cooperation and Discord in the World Political Economy*, (Princeton: Princeton University Press, 2004). Garnet Paper, 2004.

40. Andrew Moravcsik, In Defence of the "Democratic Deficit:" Reassessing Legitimacy in the European Union. *Journal of Common Market Studies*, vol. 40, no. 4, 2002, pp. 603-624.

life: a distinctive and specific development of democracy beyond the State is needed. Moreover, contrary to the cosmopolitan view, the European concept of democracy beyond the State is a political project at the regional level (similarly with the process occurring, by alternative ways, in ASEAN, MERCOSUR and other regional entities), including a territorial political dimension and multiple circles of membership. Which are the main components of a less contingent legitimacy of transnational democracy? On the following points the EU experiment of a democracy beyond the State may be seen as a forerunner of a multi-faceted global tendency:

- *Output legitimacy* means that democratic governance beyond the State should provide true benefits for the ordinary citizens. Transnational democracy cannot be legitimate in a context of economic failure and missed security provisions. A positive trade-off between efficiency of transnational governance and democracy is essential.

- *Knowledge and democracy*: epistemic community legitimacy, education are the soul of democratic life at transnational level, balancing the shift towards technocracy and contingent legitimacy.

- *Accountability*: the fight against corruption of non-national institutions should be more reliable (at every level of transnational organization including staff and budget), and mainly organized at the national level.[41]

- *Representation*: no transnational democracy at the global level without a profound reform of the shares within the organizations.[42] The Western States' inevitable withdraw from dominating positions in the legacy of WW2 and Bretton Woods could be balanced by a enhanced joint action of regional entities, among them the cohesion of the hard cores, notably in the EU.

- *The role of shared values*. Non-contingent democratic legitimacy should increasingly be also based on shared *values*. But against Eurocentric approaches, balancing universalism and relativism will be crucial: every region shares distinctive "cognitive priors,"[43] among them various understandings of universal values, different

---

41. Charlotte Ku and Harold Jakobson H.(eds) *Democratic Accountability and the Use of Force in International Law*, (New York: Cambridge university Press, 2003)

42. Amandina Orsini, ed., *EU in International Organizations*, (Farnham: Ashgate, 2014).

43. Amitav Acharya, *The End of American World Order*, (Cambridge: Polity, 2014).

combinations between procedural and substantial democracy, individual and social rights. A third level of norm setting between the national and the global is emerging in many continents. The agenda of normative transnational democracy will be increasingly affected by macroregional features.

- *Input legitimacy at regional level should be more able to address external governance, and if possible global governance*: multiple forms of distinctive democratic participation (even if they cannot trivially replicate national democracy features: regional parliaments, regional social dialogue, regional citizens' direct participation, involvement of national parliaments, involvement of sub-national bodies, from sub-national regions to municipalities...).

Europe remains a unique laboratory for combining multilevel democracy and diffuse reciprocity among States. Contrary to the idea of a "post-modern Europe as an island within a modern world," the need of a transnational democracy beyond the State is rising up within other regional contexts: for example, the ASEAN Charter (2007), the Parlasur within Mercosur, the African Union parliament... Comparative research between regional entities is strongly fostered addressing the question of the various regional forms of transnational democracy beyond the State. And transnational democracy is also relevant as the multiple *interregional partnerships* between regional democratic bodies are concerned, like TTIP, ACP, the Mediterranean dialogue, Rio Process: the role of NGOs, transparency, balance between democracy and institutionalized dispute-settling mechanisms. The emergent interregional ties are not only structural features of multilevel global governance (in the context of the decline of global multilateralism) but also potential components of global democratization[44] inter-parliamentary dialogue, transnational advocacy and knowledge networks among national/regional institutions, political parties, universities, cities, unions, interest groups...

It is an innovative, fresh, bottom-up approach to the democratic agenda beyond the State avoiding one of the most negative scenarios: a process of internal *bonding that makes bridging impossible*. That would mean avoiding the risk of "a Swiss paradox" at a large scale (deepening

---

44. Olivier Costa and Clarissa Dri, "How Does the European Parliament Contribute to the Construction of the EU's Interregional Dialogue?" in F. Baert, T. Scaramagli and F. Söderbaum, eds., *Intersecting Interregionalism: Regions, Global Governance, and the EU*, (Heidelberg: Springer Dordrecht, 2014), pp. 129–50.

regional social and diffuse transnational democracy at the expenses of openness and bridging with surrounding countries) and place the EU experiment of a republican democracy beyond the state as a driving force of a larger multilevel process of democratization.

Chapter Two

Racism in Europe: A Challenge for Democracy?

Leila Hadj-Abdou

> *Democracy is a form of government, not a steambath of popular feelings.*
> —Ralf Dahrendorf[1]

The Anti-Racist Founding Myth of Europe and the Perseverance of Racism

In recent decades the Shoah has become a central reference point for a common European identity. Especially in the 1990s, after the end of the Cold War, the heritage of the Nazi past and the involvement of many European countries in the exploitation and extermination of Jews gained a special role in the public discourse of the newly unified Europe.[2] The commemoration of the Shoah is not only a source of symbolic legitimacy, but it also suggests a commitment to political values such as the rejection of racism, antisemitism, and xenophobia[3]. In 2007, denial of the Shoah became a punishable crime across the European Union.[4] However, despite the relevance of this founding myth it would be misleading to believe that it implies a clear cut rupture with Europe's racist past, and the end of exclusionary practices.

On the contrary, several factors indicate that racism continues to be a feature of contemporary Europe. For instance, in a publication released by the civil society organization European Network Against Racism (ENAR) in 2015, it was revealed that in 2013 alone there were 47,210 racist crimes reported across the European Union. The organization stressed that this is only the tip of the iceberg as many crimes go unre-

---

1. Margaret Canovan, "Trust the People! Populism and the Two Faces of Democracy," *Political Studies*, vol. XLVII, (1999), pp. 2-16.

2. Lothar Probst, "Founding Myths in Europe and the Role of the Holocaust," *New German Critique* Vol. 90, 2003, pp. 45-58.

3. Ibid., 53.

4. Claus Leggewie, "A Tour of the Battleground: The Seven Circles of Pan-European Memory," *Social Research*, Vol. 75, No. 1, (Spring 2008), pp. 217-234.

ported.[5] Because of the ongoing economic recession in Europe, the report assumes that these figures will continue to rise in subsequent years.

Given these alarming developments, this chapter will take a closer look at two interrelated manifestations of racism in the current European context: the rise of Islamophobia, and the growth of populist right wing parties and right wing social movements across Europe.

It demonstrates that new cultural forms of racism are omnipresent in Europe, and that we witness nowadays an "entitlement racism,"[6] in which racism has been newly established as a legitimate way in which to express negative sentiments about Europe's "others." The chapter eventually concludes that rather than being an anomaly of liberal democracy, racism is an expression of the paradoxes inherent in democracy.

Before we discuss these two interrelated expressions of contemporary racism in Europe in more depth, it is useful to provide a definition of racism and to explain why the existence of racism is usually perceived as incompatible with liberal democracy.

Racism—a Tool of Social Inequality and Exclusion

Racism has been often understood as an ideology that ascribes inferiority to persons with distinct biological features such as skin color. However, it is important to acknowledge that there are different variants of racism. One major feature of racist ideology is its flexibility and adaptability, i.e. its ability to reinvent itself.[7] This inherent feature makes it more accurate to speak of racisms plural rather than racism. Phenotypical biological features such as skin color are only one type of marker used in racist ideology. Further markers, which operate in a very similar way to skin color, are employed in processes of racialization. Hence, many scholars have tended to include in theories of racism cate-

---

5. Felicity Capon, New report exposes huge increase in racist crimes in Europe, 2015, http://europe.newsweek.com/new-report-exposes-huge-rise-racist-crime-europe-326929 (accessed 25/8/2015)

6. Philomena Essed, "Entitlement Racism. License to Humiliate," 2013, http://www.antigone.gr/files/en/library/selected-publications-on-migration-and-asylum/eu/ SymposiumReport_LR%20final.pdf#page=44 (accessed 25/8/2015).

7. Etienne Balibar, "Is there a neo-racism," in Immanuel Wallerstein and Etienne Balibar, *Race, Nation and Class* (New York and London: Ambiguous identities Verso,1991), pp. 37-67.

gories such as culture, ethnicity and religion in addition to biological features. As Reisigl and Wodak[8] have pointed out, even the classical pseudoscientific racisms of the 19th and 20th centuries included a reference to cultural or national character. The Nazi anti-Semitic racist ideology is a case in point. Most prominently Adolf Hitler emphasized that the true danger posed by the Jew is rooted in his spirit/culture rather than any biological "racial" trait:

> We speak of the Jewish race only as a linguistic convenience, for in the true sense of the word, and from a genetic standpoint, there is no Jewish race.... The Jewish race is above all a community of the spirit.... A spiritual race is tougher and more enduring than a natural race. The Jew wherever he goes remains a Jew ... and to us he must appear as a sad evidence for the superiority of spirit over flesh. [9]

The increasing use of culture as a surrogate for race has led scholars of racism to the conclusion that we are witnessing the emergence of a new racism, or neo-racism. The use of the term neo-racism is based on the misleading idea that there is actually something new about this mode of racism. Yet despite the fact that there is relatively little new about the "new racism," the increasing reference to culture in contemporary racist discourses poses a considerable challenge to anti-racist struggles, namely the denial of racism. By avoiding the word race and related signifiers such as color, forms of racism that refer to culture claim to be non-racist. Therefore, as Grofoguel[10] poignantly point out, if racialized subjects "experience higher unemployment rates, higher poverty rates, higher dropout rates, lower quality of education in public schools, lower salaries for the same jobs [...] or are placed in the "dirty jobs of the labor market" it is because they are "unassimilated" and have an "un-adapted/inadequate culture," and not because they are racially oppressed and marginalized.

---

8. Ruth Wodak and Martin Reisigl, "Discourse and Racism: European Perspectives," *Annual Review of Anthtropology*, Vol. 28 (1999), pp. 175-199.

9. Gunnar Heinsohn, "Hitler's motive for the Holocaust," in Wolfgang Bialas and Lothar Fritze, eds., *Nazi Ideology and Ethics*, (Newcastle: Cambridge Scholars Publishing, 2014), pp. 103-126, p. 113

10. Ramon Grosfoguel and Laura Oso and Anastasia Christou, "Racism, Intersectionality and Migration Studies: Framing Some Theoretical Reflections," *Identities: Global Studies in Culture and Power*. Online September 2015.

It is vital therefore to acknowledge the omission or the plain denial of racism in many contemporary debates as a particular challenge for anti-racist struggles. On the other hand, it is useful to look at the inherent continuities of racism across time and space, such as the process of naturalization.

Naturalization is the process that renders categories such as ethnicity and culture into effective instruments of racism. It is the depiction of differences as natural and fixed[11], as exemplified by the above-cited statement by Hitler ("the Jew always remains the Jew"), or by contemporary discourses that portray immigrants as unable to integrate into Western societies because of their cultural differences. These allegedly natural, static features are then assumed to determine the behavior of those people to whom these differences are ascribed; and these differences are evaluated negatively.

A related immanent feature of racism is its group-constructing mechanism. Racism is always exercised by groups, or by individuals that conceive of themselves as a member of a group, and is targeted at other groups or individuals as members of groups. The seminal work on "the established and the outsiders" by the sociologists Elias and Scotson, and their concept of "pars pro toto" distortion, have provided an important insight into these group dynamics that play out during processes of racialization.[12] As they have observed, a more powerful, established group (in the case of racism, the racializing group) tends to attribute to the entire outsider group (the racialized group) the "bad" characteristics of that group's worst section, the "anomic minority." In contrast, the self-image of the established group is modelled on its exemplary, most nomic, or norm-setting section, i.e. the minority of its best members. The figure of the "illiberal Muslim terrorist" versus the "liberal non-Muslim law-abiding citizen" is an illustrative example of such a pars pro toto distortion. In sum, racist ideology de-individualizes people. The individual only exists as a member of a group, and alleged deficiencies don't have to be identified individually but are instead automatically attributed to the individual qua being identified as a member of the particular group. The underlying function of these processes is to exclude

---

11. Robert Miles, *Racism*, (London: Routledge, 1989).

12. Norbert Elias and John Scotson, *The Established and the Outsiders: A Sociological Enquiry into Community Problems* (London: SAGE, 1994).

the racialized other from material and immaterial resources and/or to legitimize their exclusion.[13]

In order to fully grasp the phenomenon of racism, however, we must recognize that it includes several dimensions, of which ideology is only one. As Essed[14] has noted, racism is an ideology, a structure and a practice (or process as she calls it). It is an ideology that hierarchizes groups and puts them in opposition to each other. At the same time it is also a structure of rule, law and regulations that establishes unequal access to rights, entitlements and resources. Essed, moreover, highlights that racism is also a practice, since "structures and ideologies do not exist outside the everyday practices through which they are created and confirmed."[15] Racism hence classifies and performs acts of boundary-making through its ideological component; it excludes through structures, and it (re-)activates these excluding structures and ideas (ideologies) through everyday practices. In the interplay of these three components, racism becomes a powerful system of creating, maintaining, and legitimizing social inequality.

Racism and Liberal Democracy

The issue of racism has been largely under-theorized in academic scholarship on democratic theory. This fact seems surprising at first; however, this scholarly omission is embedded in democratic ideas. Democratic theorists are guided by a disregard for difference and the liberal conviction that democracy is primarily a matter of assuring an equal right to vote and to majority rule, as Gould[16] has rightly emphasized. In dominant democratic theoretical accounts the promotion of justice and equality consequently requires non-discrimination, i.e., the employment of the same principles to all persons regardless of their particular social position or backgrounds.[17] The equality principle

---

13. Philomena Essed, *Understanding Everyday Racism: An Interdisciplinary Theory*. (London: Sage, 1991). Stuart Hall, Rassismus als ideologischer Diskurn," in *Das Argument 178*, (Hamburg: Argument Verlag. 1989), pp. 913-921

14. Essed, *op.cit.*, p.

15. Essed, *op.cit.*, p. 43.

16. Carol Gould, "Racism and Democracy Reconsidered," *Social identities* Vol. 6, No. 4, (2000) pp. 425-439.

17. Iris Marion Young, "Structural Injustice and the Politics of Difference," Paper for the AHRC Centre for Law Gender and Sexuality. *Intersectionality Workshop* 21/22 May 2005, Keele University, UK.

enshrined in liberalism has thus demanded that gender, racial, sexual and other differences are disregarded rather than taken as a starting point for discussion and deliberation in democratic societies. Even more striking is the fact that not only has most democratic theory little to say about racism, but many democracies have actually coexisted in practice with racism for centuries.[18]

Only relatively recently have activists and scholars of democracy developed approaches that take into account the need to address the inequalities, including racial inequalities, that are preserved in many liberal democracies. They have pointed out that the difference-blind equality principle enshrined in liberal democratic ideas is actually part of the reason why inequalities continue to exist. Defining equality as equal treatment, they have emphasized, blends out differences in "social position, division of labor, socialized capacities, normalized standards and ways of living" to the detriment of members of historically excluded groups.[19] Scholars such as Iris Marion Young have consequently proposed a "politics of difference," which endorses the idea that substantial equality will be produced not necessarily by treating everyone in the same way, but instead by implementing measures such as compensation.

Without going into more detail regarding this immensely rich and important strand of scholarship, it is important to note that this approach has challenged the underlying biased equality paradigm of liberal democracies, and in relation to racism has stressed that where racialized structural inequality influences so many institutions and potentially stigmatizes and impoverishes so many people, a society that aims to redress such injustice must notice the processes of racial differentiation before it can correct them.[20]

These accounts have made it clear that racism is a challenge to democracy because it hampers participation, which in turn is a basic condition of democracy. Participation however, is not understood here as mere voting rights or formal institutional equal access to the democratic process. The crucial point is that, in order to be able to fully participate, one has to be free from any form of domination. Finally, it is also important to note that different axes of inequality, such as race, class and gender, intersect with each other, and hamper full participa-

---

18. Gould, *op. cit.*, p. 426.

19. Young, *op. cit.*

20. Young, *op. cit.*

tion in the democratic processes in complex ways. Hence, it is rarely racism as an isolated phenomenon and form of exclusion that comes into play, but the interaction of different forms of domination, that jointly construct a system of social inequality. In sum, racism indeed poses a severe challenge to liberal democracies, but in much more complex ways than classical liberal democratic theories would suggest.

Europe and its Different Internal Others

In the following sections two manifestations of racism in Europe are discussed: the success of the "New Right" and the interrelated emergence of Islamophobia. It has to be emphasized though that racism in Europe is certainly not directed solely towards Muslim communities. Roma communities in particular are continuously racialized and consequently marginalized in Europe.[21] Another highly relevant manifestation of racism is targeted at international immigrants and refugees in general. Thousands of refugees have died in the Mediterranean in recent years; the figure for 2015 alone (as of mid-September 2015) was 2900 people.[22] The influx of refugees and migrants is often accompanied by dehumanizing discourses about them from political elites, as well as from the public in general. In spring 2015, for example, the British newspaper "The Sun" published a piece by the columnist Kathie Hopkins, who compared immigrants to cockroaches:

> No, I don't care. Show me pictures of coffins, show me bodies floating in water, play violins and show me skinny people looking sad. I still don't care [...] Make no mistake, these migrants are like cockroaches. They might look a bit 'Bob Geldof's Ethiopia circa 1984,' but they are built to survive a nuclear bomb. They are survivors.[23]

---

21. Liz Fekete, "Europe against the Roma," *Race & Class*, Vol. 55, No. 3, (January/ March 2014), pp. 60-70.

22. IOM (2015): Missing migrants project. http://missingmigrants.iom.int/ (number retrieved 9/25/2015)

23. UN human rights chief denounces Sun over Katie Hopkins "cockroach" column. http://www.theguardian.com/global-development/2015/apr/24/katie-hopkins-cockroach-migrants-denounced-united-nations-human-rights-commissioner, April 25 2015

The column was published just hours before a fishing boat packed with migrants capsized off the coast of Libya, with the loss of 800 lives.[24]

Meanwhile, as this chapter is being written, pictures of the maltreatment and mass detention of refugees at the EU's eastern border circulate in Europe on a daily basis. This maltreatment, particularly by the Hungarian government, is considered so severe that it has evoked analogies to Nazi deportations during the Holocaust in public debates.[25] The statements of government leaders such as Hungary's Viktor Orbán have made explicit the link between the dehumanization of these people and their racialization:

> Those arriving have been raised in another religion, and represent a radically different culture. [...] There is no alternative, and we have no option but to defend our borders.[26]

These incidents represent only the most visible of the dehumanizing discourses and practices against Europe's "others." Many other processes of "othering" are more subtle, and require a careful, case-by-case analysis to determine whether processes of racialization are at stake or not. However, while contextual analyses are undoubtedly necessary, it is important to acknowledge that racism certainly plays a role in contemporary European migration politics. As the scholars Wieworka[27] and Balibar[28] remind us, the increasing use of culture in racist ideology is directly linked to the transformation of Europe from a colonizing continent to an immigrant-receiving continent. Whereas more classical forms of biological racism during colonial times were designed to subordinate the "other," in times of increasing migration (partly a direct consequence of decolonization) to Europe, cultural forms of racism increasingly function to deny people access and belonging in the first place.[29]

---

24. Ibid.

25. Austria's Faymann likens Orban's refugee policies to Nazi deportations. http://www.reuters.com/article/2015/09/13/us-europe-migrants-idUSKCN0RC0GL20150913

26. Migration crisis: Hungary PM says Europe in grip of madness. http://www.theguardian.com/world/2015/sep/03/migration-crisis-hungary-pm-victor-orban-europe-response-madness, September 3 2015.

27. Michel Wieworka, Racism in Europe Today. *European Sociologist (Newsletter for the European Sociological Association)* Vol. 35, (2013), pp. 3-5.

28. Balibar, *op. cit.*, p.

29. Ibid., p.

Right Wing Extremism in the New Europe

As we have indicated above, immigration and immigrants have become one of the most politicized issues in Europe today. The question of immigration has moved in most liberal democracies "from the dark corridors of parliament committees to the often populist and emotionally charged public sphere."[30] As a consequence, the politicization of immigration has led to significant electoral gains for populist right-wing forces (or even right-wing extremist parties) in many European states. The Austrian Freedom Party (FPÖ) and the Swiss People's Party (SVP) are paradigmatic instances of this evolution, but these cases are no exception. For example, only a few years ago academic articles were published on the puzzling question: "Why is there no extreme right party in Greece?"[31] In 2015, the extreme right-wing party Golden Dawn holds 17 seats (seven percent) in the Hellenic parliament. Minkenberg[32] reminds us though that the analysis of right-wing extremism should not focus exclusively on those groups represented in parliaments. He distinguishes three types of groups. The first is office-seeking groups, which organize themselves in political parties. Second are groups that mobilize within social movements. The third type comprises groups that are best described as sub-cultures, which operate relatively independently from political parties and larger social movements, do not exhibit formal organizational structures, and may have a particular propensity for violence. All three types are an increasingly relevant phenomenon in contemporary Europe.

What is alarming about these developments is not the mere existence of these parties and movements, but their (electoral) popularity and their simultaneous integration into the political establishment. Much of this shift from "pariah" to mainstream and the accompanying electoral success is a consequence of the radical transformation of right-wing parties and movements in Europe. The "new modernized right" is often characterized by a toned down anti-democratic rhetoric, including a sig-

---

30. Andrej Zaslove, "The Politics of Immigration: a new electoral dilemma for the right and the left?" *Review of European and Russian Affairs* vol. 2, no. 3, 2006, p. 15.

31. Vassilis Lambropoulos, "Why is There no Extreme Right in Greece?" *The Journal of the International Institute* vol. 10, no. 1, (Fall 2002). http://quod.lib.umich.edu/cgi/t/text/text-idx?c=jii;view=text;rgn=main;idno=4750978.0010.106. , p. 15.

32. Michael Minkenberg, "The European Radical Right and Xenophobia in West and East: Trends Patterns and Challenges," in Ralf Melzer and Sebastian Serafin, eds., *Right Wing Extremism in Europe: Country Analyses, Counter-Strategies, and Labor-Market Oriented Exit Strategies* (Berlin: Friedrich Ebert Stiftung, 2013).

nificant reduction of its previous anti-Semitic shibboleths, and a generic willingness to behave in a way compliant with basic principles of liberal democracy. Instead of using overt forms of biological racism and anti-Semitism, the new right emphasizes the incompatibilities of different cultures in order to legitimize its opposition to international immigration and ethno-cultural diversity.

A paradigmatic example is the Austrian Freedom Party. In the 2013 general election, the FPÖ gained 20.5 per cent of the votes, making it one of the most successful right-wing parties in the European Union. In recent decades it has transformed itself, from a fringe party, which relied heavily on references to the national-socialist past and was based upon a German nationalist ideology, into a successful right populist party. The party even entered national government at the beginning of the 2000s. During its time in office in the 2000s it was significantly weakened, but has revived under its new leader Heinz Christian Strache. While the move from fringe to mainstream was often faltering under the previous leadership of Jörg Haider, who still used blatantly anti-Semitic rhetoric and regularly deployed codes such as "East Coast" (referring to the American Jewish population) to criticize his political competitors, the party's current discourse is much changed. This does not imply that anti-Semitic attitudes and ideology no longer exist within the party, but they are clearly less relevant to the party's electoral strategy.

Instead, from the mid-2000s Islam became one of the most salient issues in the political mobilization of the party. Strache used the issues of Islam and Muslim immigration as a means of sharpening the profile of the FPÖ against its political competitors on the right.[33] The FPÖ's strengthened anti-Islamic agenda also matched the increasingly Islamophobic tendencies within the Austrian population. In the European Value Survey of 1999, 15 per cent of correspondents said that they did not want to live next to a Muslim. In the 2000s, this number more than doubled: in 2008, 31 per cent of respondents stated that they did not want to have a Muslim neighbors.[34]

---

33. The party split in 2005 into The Alliance for the Future of Austria led (until his death) by Haider, and the Freedom Party led by Strache. Leila Hadj-Abdou and Sieglinde Rosenberger, "Islam at Issue: Anti-Islamic Mobilization of the Extreme Right in Austria," in Brian Jenkins, Emmanuel Godin, and Andrea Mammone, eds., *Varieties of Right-Wing Extremism in Contemporary Europe*, (Routledge: London, 2013), pp. 149-163.
34. Christian Friesl, Regina Polak, and Ursula Hamachers-Zuba, *Die Österreicherinnen. Wertewandel 1990-2008*, (Vienna: Czernin, 2009), p. 265.

The anti-Islamic agenda of the Strache-FPÖ is based on two main arguments. The first is that fundamentalist Islam poses a threat to national security. The second argument is that Islam is an inherently alien culture, which threatens the cultural identity of the Austrian nation state. The concept of cultural identity as used in the party's discourse remains rather vague. However, it is evident that in the rhetoric of the FPÖ, Islam is constructed as a monolithic entity that promotes a culture that is irreconcilable with that of Western societies. In line with this position, in the mid-2000s the party even launched an association named SOS-Occident ('SOS-Abendland') to save "Western cultures and customs."

The party's solution to these supposed cultural and security threats is to restrict immigration. Islam is used in the party's rhetoric as a simple synonym for unwanted immigration and immigrants. Hence, from the mid-2000s onwards, the term "Muslim" has to some extent replaced the term "immigrant" in the party's rhetoric. It serves as a means to divide those who are supposedly Europeans, and hence can be part of the Austrian nation, from those who are not and cannot.

Similar developments are at play in other Western European right-wing populist parties. The result has been increased transnational cooperation of the populist right, and the use by these parties of very similar concepts and ideas. As Wodak[35] have highlighted, Islamophobia is at the core of a transnational project to unite the European populist right under one common banner: the defense of Europe's heritage and its Western and liberal democratic values against the "third invasion of Islam in Europe," as the party leader of the Belgian Vlaams Belang has tellingly paraphrased it.

New forms of mobilization that rely strongly on an anti-Islamic rhetoric have also been at the core of new right social movements, such as the PEGIDA ('Patriotic Europeans against the Islamisation of the Occident') in Germany, or the English Defence League. Goodwin[36] has pointed out that it would be wrong to assume that their supporters are giving up on mainstream democracy; such movements are nevertheless an important symbol of the overall decline of public trust in politics.

---

35. Ruth Wodad, Majid Koshravinik, and Brigitte Mral, *Right Wing Populism in Europe. Politics and Discourse*, (New York and London: Bloomsbury Academic, 2013), p. 74.

36. Matthew Goodwin, The Roots of Extremism: The English Defence League and the Counter-Jihad Challenge. *Chatham House Briefing Paper*, March 2013.

People who affiliate with these movements are "more dissatisfied with politics, more distrustful of institutions and more likely to think that the political system has serious faults that need addressing."[37] PEGIDA's slogan, "The system is finished—we are the change," is emblematic. Right-wing street protesters don't simply understand themselves as victims of a wrong politics, but of a failed system.[38] However, as noted above, this is a general development: it is merely more pronounced among members of these movements. In the broader population, large majorities are similarly distrustful of politicians and institutions.[39]

What is particular and new about these movements, though, is their denial of racism or the refraining from using overt forms of racism. Instead they make strong references to liberal democracy and liberal values, a feature which they share with right-wing populist parties in Western Europe. A paradigmatic example is the mission statement of the English Defence League published in 2011, which explicitly refers to the organization as non-violent and non-racist, and underlines:

> The EDL promotes the understanding of Islam and the implications for non-Muslims forced to live alongside it. Islam [...] runs counter to all that we hold dear within our British liberal democracy. [...] The EDL is [...] keen to draw its support from all races, all faiths, all political persuasions, and all lifestyle choices. Under its umbrella all people in England, whatever their background or origin, can stand united in a desire to stop the imposition of the rules of Islam on non-believers. In order to ensure the continuity of our culture and its institutions the EDL stands opposed to the creeping Islamisation of our country, because that presents itself as an undemocratic alternative to our cherished way of life.[40]

One of the strategies deployed by the New Right is, thus, "illiberal liberalism," or what Triadafilopoulos[41] has called "Schmitterian liberalism," i.e., the idea that some (immigrant) cultures contradict liberal uni-

---

37. Ibid. p. 8.
38. *The Pegida Brand: A Right-wing Populist Success Product.* http://www.socialeurope.eu/2015/03/pegida-brand/
39. Goodwin, *op. cit.*, p. 8.
40. English Defence League (2011), *Mission statement.* http://www.englishdefenceleague.org/
41. Triadafilos Triadafilopoulos, "Illiberal Means to Liberal Ends? Understanding Recent Immigrant Integration Policies in Europe," *Journal of Ethnic and Migration Studies*, vol. 37, no. 6, (July 2011), pp. 861-880.

versal values and thus have to be excluded. Here the new right uses universal, liberal values in an instrumental way. By alleging that the collective "other" does not share universal, liberal values, the boundaries of who belongs and who does not are effectively redefined.

The fact that the prominent reference to liberal values by the New Right is a political strategy rather than a conviction is suggested by several contradictions in the actions of these movements. EDL protests, for instance, have often exhibited racist chanting, and Nazi salutes[42] and thus conform in many ways to traditional far right movements. New populist right wing parties show similar incoherencies when it comes to the endorsement of liberal values. The idea of gender equality, for instance, is a major reference point in right wing populist discourses, including the above-mentioned Austrian Freedom Party, as a means of demarcating Muslim immigrants. However, if we look more closely this commitment to gender equality and women's rights proves largely inconsistent with the parties' views on family values and policies, which tend to reflect a nationalist concept of the family as the central organizing unit of society.[43]

Finally, it has to be noted that the radical right in Eastern Europe, as well as in Greece, differs considerably from the New Right in Western Europe. Right-wing parties such as the Hungarian Jobbik (Movement for a better Hungary) or the Golden Dawn in Greece are ideologically extreme parties. Despite being extremist they are far from being politically marginalized: both are the third largest party in their respective countries, and have acted as agenda setters for parties further to the center. They can be defined as extremist because they reject democracy; the Jobbik, for example, has a clearly anti-democratic paramilitary wing: the "Hungarian Guards" sport black uniforms identical to the ones worn by the Nazis in World War II, organize anti-Roma rallies and marches, are involved in violent attacks, and incite hatred.[44] They were

---

42. English Defence League: Chaotic Alliance Stirs up Trouble on Sreets. The Guardian, 12 September 2009, http://www.theguardian.com/world/2009/sep/11/english-defence-league-chaotic-alliance

43. Susi Meret and Birte Siim, "Gender, Populism and Politics of Belonging: Disourses of Right Wing Populist Parties in Denmark, Norway and Austria," in Monika Mokre and Birte Siim, eds., *Negotiating Gender and Diversity in an Emergent European Public Sphere*, (Basingstoke: Palgrave Macmillan, 2013), pp.78-95.

44. Margareta Matache, "The Deficit of EU Democracies: A New Cycle of Violence Against Roma Population," *Human Rights Quarterly*, vol. 36, no. 2, (May 2014), pp. 325-348.

banned in 2009, but quickly re-emerged under a new name: "For a Better Future Civic Guards Association."

Golden Dawn exhibits a similarly anti-democratic attitude. It has called Greek democracy the "dictatorship of parliamentarism."[45] The party has been regularly involved in violent attacks against immigrants, Roma, sexual minorities as well as political opponents. These types of parties and movements use an unequivocally racist rhetoric including anti-Semitism,[46] whereas anti-Muslim racism, i.e. Islamophobia, is employed relatively rarely. The statements of Golden Dawn's political candidate Alexandros Plomaritis, who argued that immigrants must be dealt with by reopening "ovens" and turning them into "soap,"[47] are indicative of this overt rhetoric. The explicit racism of these parties mirrors the attitudes of their electorate. For instance, in Hungary, a survey conducted in 2015[48] by the Hungarian polling company Median showed that 54 percent of Jobbik voters hold strongly anti-Semitic views.

It is clear, then, that several types of right-wing movements co-exist in Europe today. On the one hand, traditional right wing, neo-fascist parties and movements have re-emerged; these mobilize in an overtly racist manner and target minoritized groups such as Jews and Roma. At the same time we also see the emergence of a "New Right," which primarily focuses on immigrants, and in particular Muslim(s) (immigrants) as Europe's "others."

In order to understand the emergence of the New Right and to fully grasp its "newness," we turn now to the emergence of Islamophobia in Europe.

The Emergence of Islamophobia in Europe

The term Islamophobia was introduced in contemporary discourses by the English Runnymede Trust in 1997, who described it as "unfounded hostility towards Islam."[49] The term has since become

45. Antonis A. Ellinas, "The Rise of Golden Dawn: The New Face of the Far Right in Greece," *South European Society and Politics*, vol. 18, no. 4, (2013), pp. 543-565.

46. Minkenberg, *op. cit.*, p. 27.

47. Fekete, *op.cit.*, p. 62.

48. Mellbevago felmeres a budapestiek fele antiszemita. http://vs.hu/kozelet/osszes/mellbe-vago-felmeres-a-budapestiek-fele-antiszemita-0331#!s0

49. Raymond Taras, "Islamophobia never stands still: Race, religion and culture," *Ethnic and Racial Studies*, Vol. 36, No. 3, (March 2013), pp. 417-433.

widespread, demonstrating the increasing prevalence and social accept-ance of hostility against Muslims; or as the then UN General Secretary Kofi Annan, put in at the beginning of the 2000s:

> When the world is compelled to coin a new term, to take account of increasingly widespread bigotry, that is a sad and troubling de-velopment. Such is the case with Islamophobia.[50]

At the same time the use of the term is also misleading to some extent, since it conceals the racial component of the phenomenon. It might be more accurate to speak of anti-Muslim racism. In this chapter, the term Islamophobia is very much understood as a form of racism that is targeted against Muslims. Islamophobia draws from a "historical anti-Muslimism and anti-Islamism and fuses them with racist ideologies of the twentieth century to construct a modern concept."[51] The 9/11 bombings are often cited as a triggering event for the spread of Islamo-phobia. However, its emergence in its current form in Europe predates 2001. It is closely linked to the end of the Cold War in 1989, when political attention started to shift from materialist concerns, questions of class and distribution of resources, to questions of immaterial values, such as culture. It is no accident that the first debates to fundamentally question Muslim practices, and the belonging of (visibly identifiable) Muslim(s) (immigrants) to Europe, emerged precisely in 1989. These debates pertained to the wearing of the hijab (headscarf) in French pub-lic schools.

Islamophobia, like other forms of racism, involves processes of natu-ralization and group-essentializing. As Bleich[52] rightly argues, "ques-tioning or even criticizing aspects of Islamic doctrine or practices of specific subgroups of Muslims is not automatically Islamophobia." However, if from these examples it is concluded that Islam or Muslims "as a whole are worthy of condemnation, it becomes an indiscriminate attitude that constitutes Islamophobia."[53] Moreover, it is crucial to see that Islamophobia is based on the concepts of civilization and culture. It holds the view that Islam, and ergo Muslims, are fundamentally "incom-

---

50. Erik Bleich, "What Is Islamophobia and How Much Is There? Theorizing and Measuring an Emerging Comparative Concept," *American Behavioral Scientist*, vol. 55, no. 12, (December 2011), pp. 1581-1600.

51. Taras, *op.cit.*, p. 419.

52. Bleich, *op. cit.*, p. 1585.

53. Ibid., p. 1585.

patible with and inferior to" Western culture.[54] Hence, as noted above, illiberal liberalism—that is, the reference to liberal values that are defined as innately Western/European—is widely employed to exclude and racialize the Muslim "other."

The fact that Islamophobia rests on the assumption that Islam is incompatible with the West also reveals its close relationship with the process of European integration and the accompanying formation of a European identity. As Bunzl highlights, modern anti-Semitism as a product of the 19th century was closely related to nationalism and the emergence of the nation state, whereby the Jewish "other" served primarily as a marker of who did or did not belong to the national community. Islamophobia, on the other hand, determines who belongs or does not belong to Europe. As Bunzl remarks, Islamophobes are not worried whether Muslims can be good Germans, Italians or Danes; rather they question whether Muslims can be good Europeans.[55] Islamophobia hence functions less in the interest of national, ethnic purification than as an instrument to fortify Europe in face of international (to a great extent Muslim) migration.[56] "Culturally unassimilated, ideologically unassimilable and transnationally implicated in disloyalty,"[57] the racialization of Muslims has produced "intolerable subjects." The emergence and spread of Islamophobia thus provides proof anew of racism's ability to adapt to new historical circumstances, and to create allegedly immutable differences between groups.

Racism and Right Wing Mobilization: An Expression of the Contradictions of Liberal Democracy

In the previous sections I have suggested that racism is not a paradoxical anomaly within liberal democracy; instead it is better understood as an expression of contradictions inherent in liberal democracy. I want to reiterate this point in the following.

---

54. Matti Bunzl, "Between anti-Semitism and Islamophobia," *American Ethnologist*, vol. 32, no. 4, (November 2005), pp. 499-508.

55. Ibid., P. 502.

56. Ibid., p. 502.

57. Alana Lentin and Gavin Titley, "The Crisis of Multiculturalism in Europe: Mediated Minarets, Intolerable Subjects," *European Journal of Cultural Studies*, Vol. 15, No. 2, (April 2012). p. 124.

We saw in the section on Liberal Democracy and Racism that the liberal democratic principle of equality is actually one of the reasons why inequalities, including racial inequalities, continue to exist. Focusing on formal equality as a matter of equal treatment falls short of ensuring substantial equality, which relies on taking into account the different positions of groups in society.

In the section on Right Wing Extremism in the New Europe, I have, moreover, highlighted that the success of the "New Right" is a consequence of the increasing erosion of political trust among European citizens. To put it differently, fewer and fewer people believe that democratic governments can actually achieve anything. This erosion of trust is not solely a consequence of the decreasing power of national governments in the face of globalization. Again it is the result of contradictions inherent in liberal democracy.

Democracy, as Margaret Canovan[58] has argued, comprises two visions: the redemptive and the pragmatic. These visions rely on each other as much as they contradict each other. The redemptive vision promotes the idea of democracy as a form of government by the people for the people. Pragmatically, democracy means institutions. Institutions do not simply limit power; they also constitute it and make it effective.[59] Redemptive democracy, however, is characterized by a strong impulse against institutions, and the urge to instead act directly, and spontaneously, and to overcome alienation.[60] However, in the words of Ralf Dahrendorf: "democracy is a form of government, not a steambath of popular feelings."[61] In particular, the liberal principles enshrined in liberal democracies put constraints on the power of the people and their popular feelings (i.e. the redemptive side of democracy). Liberal principles restrain a crude majoritarianism that neglects or overrides the rights of minorities.[62] It is these contradictions that the New Right in Europe effectively instrumentalizes for its political goals.

Lastly, this chapter has also highlighted that new forms of racism, such as Islamophobia, are (ab)using liberal values in order to racialize and exclude the "other." Through accusing the "Muslim other" collec-

---

58. Canovan, *op. cit.*, p. 12.
59. Ibid., p. 10.
60. Ibid., p. 10.
61. Canovan, *op. cit.*, p. 12.
62. Ibid., p. 7.

tively of not sharing universal, liberal values, the boundaries of who does and who does not belong to Europe are (re)defined.

The Duty Not Only to Remember but to Think

At the beginning of this chapter I referred to the Shoah as a founding myth for the "New Europe." Observing the emergence of this myth at the time, Claude Lefort pointed out that:

> For the last few years, we have been taught that it is our duty to re-member. That is certainly a positive development. Yet the doctrine that urges us not to forget the crimes against mankind is accompa-nied by the hope that this memory will prevent us from repeating the atrocities of the past. But without the duty to think, the duty to remember will be meaningless.[63]

More than ever since WWII, Europe today needs to think, and to understand that the "migrant" or the "Muslim" serve increasingly as a surrogate for race, and that these groups are subjected or are extremely vulnerable to racism. Liberal democracy as an institution alone will not save us from racism, nor do the current political leaders in Europe seem likely to come to our rescue. In Europe the electoral dynamics still work largely against ethnicized and racialized minorities. And as we have emphasized, while liberal democracy is challenged by racism it is its own blind spots and inherent paradoxes that partly provide the basis for that challenge and enable new strategies for racist discourse to exclude the "other." What is needed, therefore, is vocal and dynamic popular opposition to current discourses about immigrants, Muslims and other European "others." We need a Europe that thinks and speaks out.

At the time of writing this chapter (autumn 2015) the emergence of such an opposition is in full bloom. In many Western European coun-tries, such as Austria and Germany, a significant number of people are heading daily to the streets to support refugees, to provide those that are usually portrayed as Europe's "others" with a helping hand and a warm welcome. It remains to be seen, however, whether European citi-zens will also counter racism and processes of racialization at the ballot box. As things stand, it seems plausible that right-wing populist parties will continue to grow.

---

63. Probst, *op.cit.*, p. 58.

Part II

Challenges of Democracy in the Aspirant Countries

Chapter Three

Challenges of Democracy in Turkey:
Europeanization, Modernization, and Securitization Revisited

Aylin Ünver Noi

Turkey's experience with democracy is longer than most of the neighboring countries of the European Union (EU), longer even than some EU member states. Turkey, which introduced a multiparty system and democracy in 1946, is also a founding member state of the Council of Europe (CoE) (1951), an organization that serves as the guardian of democracy and human rights; the OECD (1961), a forum for countries describing themselves as committed to democracy and the market economy; and the OSCE (1975), an organization of countries declaring their commitment to democracy based on human rights and fundamental freedoms.

Although democracy in Turkey was in the past interrupted by military intervention (1960), the "half coup" (1971), the military takeover (1980), and the "postmodern coup d'état" (1997), it has achieved significant progress, particularly in the early 2000s, in areas such as the abolition of the death penalty, the fight against torture, the reform of prisons and detention centers, freedom of thought and expression, freedom of association and reunion, freedom of religion, the functioning of the judiciary, civil-military relations, economic, cultural and social rights, and the fight against corruption. The credible EU membership perspective attained at the 1999 Helsinki Summit served to accelerate the reform processes that were already underway in Turkey.

Since the beginning of the 2000s, Turkey has been presented as a role model due to the freedoms enjoyed by its population in comparison to the majority of the Muslim world, its economic growth (seventeenth largest economy of the world), and its ability to combine Islam and democracy. Moreover, in 2004, Turkey joined the West as a pioneering country in the promotion of democracy in the Broader Middle East and North Africa region (BMENA). Turkey as one of the Democracy Assistance Dialogue (DAD) countries along with Italy and Yemen, hosted several events to promote democracy, focusing on empowering women and increasing women's role in social, economic and political life in the region. During the Arab Spring, Turkey was one of the countries supporting the democratic transformation of the MENA region.

Yet, in recent years, the democratization process in Turkey—like in some EU member states and neighboring countries—has become part of a reverse wave. This chapter examines democratization process in Turkey for the 2001–2015 period, with particular focus on three concepts—Europeanization, modernization and securitization—that are interlinked in the Turkish case.

This study first attempts to identify the role of the EU in Turkey's transformation, with particular focus on the country's Europeanization—that is, the influence of the EU or the domestic impact of the EU on Turkey's policies, and political and administrative structures—as a candidate state. A further discussion of this Europeanization is opened with reference to securitization, with the intention being to explain how the de-securitization of the issues facilitated through the Europeanization process led to further democratization. The paper then evaluates the directions of democratic change in the country, with particular focus on the new Islamic middle class that has emerged over the last twenty years under the modernization part. Within this context, it draws upon modernization theory to assess the argument that establishes a correlation between economic development and democracy. Finally, it evaluates developments both internal and external according to the securitization theory of the Copenhagen School, as well as the impact of securitization on the democratization process in Turkey.

Europeanization

Europeanization has gained popularity in European studies since the 1990s, gaining widespread currency among scholars as a term that refers to a variety of changes within European politics and international relations. Featherstone describes Europeanization "as a process of structural change affecting actors and institutions, ideas and interests";[1] while Radaelli defines Europeanization in general terms "as processes of a

---

1. Kevin Featherstone and Claudio M. Radaelli, *The Politics of Europeanization*, (Oxford: Oxford University Press, 2003).

construction, diffusion, and institutionalization of formal and informal rules, procedures, policy paradigms, styles, 'ways of doing things', and shared beliefs and norms which are first defined and consolidated in the making of EU public policy and politics and then incorporated in the logic of domestic discourses, identities, political structures, and public policies."[2] In this chapter, Europeanization refers to the European Union's domestic impact on its member states, candidate countries and associated countries,[3] but before analyzing the impacts of Europeanization on Turkey's democratization process, the effects of Europeanization on the EU candidate states is analyzed in this section.

In the case of the candidate states, certain policies and institutions of the EU can lead to policy or institutional misfits, where the EU requirements for accession clash with domestic policies. This leads to Europeanization only if it is acted upon by the domestic actors and if the process is mediated by domestic institutions. Mediating conditions can be categorized as those identified by rational choice institutionalism (RCI) and those identified by sociological institutionalism (SI).[4]

RCI assumes it to be rational that actors who seek to maximize their power and welfare behave according to the logic of consequences.[5] Accordingly, European integration and the misfit outcome changes the domestic opportunity structure for domestic actors, which in turn leads to a differential empowerment of domestic actors if the favored actors are able to exploit the new resources that are made available to them.[6] In RCI, the three active mechanisms in accession Europeanization are conditionality, domestic empowerment and lesson-drawing. The main variables in the conditionality model are external rewards and sanctions, as well as a cost-benefit analysis of rule adoption by the applicant government. The model expects logic of consequences to operate in the adoption of rules in the non-member state under the conditions of external incentives offered by the EU as a reward for membership. From the perspective of the external incentive model developed by

2. Claudio M. Radaelli, "Whither Europeanization? Concept Stretching and Substantive Change," *European Integration Online Papers*, vol. 4, no. 8, 2000, http://eiop.or.at/eiop/texte/2000-008a.htm.

3. Yonca Özer and Çigdem Nas, "Introduction," in Yonca Özer and Çigdem Nas, eds., *Turkey and the European Union: Process of Europeanisation*, (Aldershot: Ashgate, 2013), p. 1.

4. Ali Tekin and Aylin Güney, "Introduction," in Ali Tekin and Aylin Güney, eds., *The Europeanization of Turkey: Polity and Politics*, (Oxon and New York: Routledge, 2015), p. 5

5. Tekin and Güney, *op. cit.*, p. 5.

6. Ibid., p. 5.

Schimelfennig and Sedelmeier, the reward for EU membership may exert strong pressure for change, altering the cost-benefit calculations of domestic actors.[7] The second mechanism of accession of Europeanization is domestic empowerment, in which the EU can alter domestic opportunity structures by providing incentives to societal actors, which can in turn lead to a change in the cost-benefit calculations of the government of the candidate state. The final mechanism in accession Europeanization is lesson-drawing, with both the government and societal actors able to draw lessons from the EU to better tackle any problems they may face.[8]

SI assumes that actors behave in accordance with logic of appropriateness[9]—a perspective that sees human activity as being driven by rules of appropriate or exemplary behavior, organized into institutions.[10] Accordingly, rules are followed because they are seen as natural, expected, rightful and legitimate. Actors are guided by a collective understanding of what constitutes proper, that is, socially acceptable behavior within a given rule structure. These collective understandings and inter-subjective meanings influence the ways in which actors define their goals and what they perceive as rational actions. Actors that are motivated by internalized identities, norms and values seek conformity with social norms, and rationality is socially constructed.[11] In this framework, Europeanization is considered to be a provision of new norms defining legitimate and rational behavior domestic actors strive to comply.[12]

From a SI perspective, Europeanization entails a process of social learning as another way of stimulating rule-adoption behavior in non-member states. According to this variant, domestic actors are socialized into European norms and logic of appropriateness through a process of persuasion and social learning. The EU may either convince the government of the appropriateness of its rules, or may persuade societal groups

---

7. Frank Schimmelfennig and Ulrich Sedelmeier, "Introduction: Conceptualizing the Europeanization of Central and Eastern Europe," in Frank Schimmelfennig and Ulrich Sedelmeier, eds., *the Europeanization of Central and Eastern Europe*, (Ithaca & London: Cornell University Press, 2005), p. 18.

8. Ibid., pp. 5-6.

9. Tekin and Güney, *op. cit*, p. 6.

10. James G. March and Johan P. Olsen, The Logic of Appropriateness, *Arena Working Papers*, WP 04/09, Arena Centre for European Studies, (University of Oslo, 2009), p. 2.

11. Ibid., p. 493.

12. Tekin and Güney, *op. cit.*, p. 6.

and organizations to lobby their government for rule adoption. In such a situation, domestic actors redefine their interests and identities accordingly.[13] In other words, political elites learn from the EU, internalize its norms and develop new identities. In this regard, successful Europeanization depends on the existence of an important mediating factor: the existence of norm entrepreneurs, that is, actors from the candidate country and/or the EU.[14] These agents of change, or *norm entrepreneurs*, mobilize at the domestic level to pressure policy-makers to initiate change by increasing the costs of certain strategic options, while using moral arguments and strategic constructions in order to persuade actors to redefine their interests and identities, engaging them in processes of social learning. The mechanisms by which these norm entrepreneurs try to induce change are persuasion and argument,[15] but rather than aiming to maximize their subjective desires, their intention is to fulfill social expectations. From this perspective, Europeanization can be understood to be the emergence of new rules, norms and practices to which the member states are exposed, and which they have to incorporate into their own domestic practices and structures.[16] A government will adopt EU rules if it can be convinced of their appropriateness.[17]

In brief, Europeanization, in the case of candidate countries, brings adaptation pressure for change under the EU anchor in almost all policy areas. The credibility of the EU perspective, the clarity of the EU model and the clear delineation of the timing of EU rewards in response to the candidate country's fulfillment of EU criteria facilitate a successful adoption of EU norms, legislation and policies. The EU acts as a legitimization device empowering those groups able to internalize and act on line with EU norms and values.[18]

The outcomes of Europeanization distinguished by Börzel and Risse as "three degrees of domestic change" are absorption, accommodation and transformation. The degree of domestic change is low in absorption, in that the member states incorporate European policies into their

---

13. March and Olsen, *op.cit.*, p. 493.

14. Tekin and Güney, *op.cit.*, p. 6.

15. Tanja A. Börzel and Thomas Risse, "Conceptualizing the Domestic Impact of Europe," in Kevin Featherstone and Claudio Radaelli, eds., *The Politics of Europeanization*, (Oxford: Oxford University Press, 2003), pp. 57-82, 67.

16. Ibid., p. 66.

17. Schimmelfennig and Sedelmeier, *op. Cit.*, p. 18.

18. Özer and Nas, *op. cit.*, pp. 1, 2.

domestic structures without substantially modifying existing policies and institutions. The degree of domestic change is modest in accommodation, since member states accommodate Europeanization pressure by adapting existing processes, policies and institutions without changing their essential features and the underlying collective understandings attached to them. Finally, the degree of domestic change is high in transformation, since member states replace existing policies, processes and institutions with new, substantially different ones, or alter existing ones to the extent that their essential features and/or underlying collective understandings are fundamentally changed.[19]

Europeanization from a RCI perspective is largely conceived as a political opportunity, offering some actors additional resources to exert influence while severely constraining the ability of others to pursue their goals.[20] In this approach, actors engage in strategic interactions using available resources to maximize their utilities on the basis of given, fixed and ordered preferences. They follow an instrumental rationality by weighing up the costs and benefits of different strategy options, while taking into account the (anticipated) behavior of other actors. According to RCI logic, we can conceptualize the adaptation pressures or the degrees of misfit emanating from Europeanization as providing new opportunities for some actors and severely constraining the freedom of movement of other actors.[21] In the following section, the impact of Europeanization on Turkey's democratization process is analyzed.

Impact of Europeanization on Democratization in Turkey (1999–2015)

Turkey's relationship with the European Community (EC) dates back to 1959 when it applied for association with the EEC. This relationship continued with an association agreement—the Ankara Agreement—signed in 1963,[22] and an Additional Protocol signed in 1970. Yet, the

---

19. Börzel and Risse, *op. cit.*, pp. 69, 71.

20. Tanja A. Börzel, "Non-State Actors and the Provision of Common Goods: Compliance with International Institutions," in Adrienne Windholt-Heritier, ed., *Common Goods: Reinventing European and International Governance*, (Maryland: Rowman and Littlefield, 2002).

21. Börzel and Risse, *op. cit.*, p. 9.

22. Aylin Ünver Noi, "Should Turkey Coordinate its Foreign Policy with the European Union?" *Mediterranean Quarterly*, vol. 23, no. 3, (Summer 2012), pp. 63-82.

complicated relationship between Turkey and the EC was interrupted during the 1970s when Turkey froze unilaterally the Ankara Treaty in 1978, invoking the self-protection clause. Following the Turkish military coup d'état in 1980, European Parliament suspended the Association Agreement in 1982.[23]

In the second half of the 1980s democracy was restored in Turkey, and the country re-applied for EC membership in 1987. Following the 1985 Southern European countries enlargement, in 1989 the EC suggested Turkey operationalize the Association Agreement rather than taking the track of a direct application for membership, citing economic, social and political reasons. As foreseen in the 1963 Ankara Agreement, the Customs Union decision was taken by the Turkey-EU Association Council in 1995.[24]

Turkey's bid for EC membership was further complicated by the application for membership of a number of Central and Eastern European countries. The 1993 Copenhagen Summit acknowledging the membership of these states, but not Turkey, was an important watershed in the evolution of the EU's approach to enlargement. At this summit, the EU set out economic and political criteria that raised the bar for membership[25] that required candidate states to meet a number of political criteria, including the stability of institutions guaranteeing democracy, the rule of law, human rights and respect for and protection of minorities; as well as some economic criteria, including the maintenance of a functioning market economy, and the capacity to cope with competitive pressure and market forces within the Union.[26]

The Luxembourg European Council of December 1997 declared the candidacies of the CEECs, Malta and the Greek Administration of Southern Cyprus, but not Turkey, merely confirming at the highest level "Turkey's eligibility for accession to the European Union" and its intention to draw up a strategy "to prepare Turkey for accession by bringing it closer to the European Union in every field." Turkey reacted negatively to the results of the European Council, considering that it had been subjected to discriminatory treatment when compared to the

---

23. Meltem Müftüler Baç, "Turkey's Political Reforms and the Impact of the European Union," *South European Society & Politics*, vol. 10, no.1, (March 2005), pp. 16-30.

24. Ibid. p. 19.

25. Ibid., p. 17.

26. European Council in Copenhagen, Conclusion of the Presidency (21-22 June 1993), p. 13.

other applicant countries. This led Ankara to state that it would not participate in the European Conference, and that it was suspending political dialogue with the Union and therefore no longer wished to discuss with it such issues as the relations between Greece and Turkey, the Cyprus issue or human rights. According to Ankara, EU-Turkey relations would henceforth be based on existing texts (the Association Agreement, Additional Protocol and Customs Union).[27] At the Cardiff Summit in 1998 it was announced that a progress report would be prepared annually for Turkey, and the enlargement process was revised during the Vienna Summit in December 1998, when the decision was taken to strengthen relations between Turkey and the EU.[28]

The EU declared Turkey as a candidate country at the Helsinki Summit of December 1999. This made the membership ideal an attainable objective for Turkey, marking a turning point in Turkey-EU relations in general and Turkey's democratization process in particular, since it stimulated Turkish political and legal reforms. Accordingly, the Europeanization of Turkey intensified after the Helsinki Summit. The Turkish government had already adopted a major package of constitutional changes in order to satisfy the European Parliament's demands for democratic development in Turkey prior to its vote on the Customs Union in December 1995;[29] and while the EU had already bolstered Turkey's Europeanization process within the premise of the Association Agreement, it had not been as effective as the candidate Europeanization that emerged following the Helsinki Summit.

Between 1999 and 2005, with credible conditionality, Turkey accelerated its efforts to join the EU, and adopted various democratization packages to meet the Copenhagen criteria based on the hope that the EU would open accession negotiations.[30] This democratic transformation reached a peak with constitutional amendments and harmonization packages, with the EU's influence on constitutional changes in Turkey being felt most strongly between 2001 and 2004. The table below shows the constitutional amendments and major changes taken first by the tripartite coalition Democratic Left Party (DSP), Motherland Party

---

27. Regular Report from the Commission on Turkey's Progress towards Accession 1998 http://ec.europa.eu/enlargement/archives/pdf/key_documents/1998/turkey_en.pdf
28. IKV (2013) A Chronology on the Accession Process
http://oldweb.ikv.org.tr/icerik_en.asp?konu=adayliksureci&baslik=Candidacy%20Process
29. Müftüler Baç, *op. cit.*, p. 19.
30. Müftüler Baç, *op. cit.*, p. 20.

Table 1. Reform Packages 2001–2004

Date	Type	Major Changes
3 October 2001	1st Constitutional Package	34 amendments to the 1982 Constitution
November 2001	New Civil Code	Gender equality in marriage
February/ March 2002	2nd Constitutional Package	Constitutional amendments
2 August 2002	3rd Constitutional Package	Abolition of the death penalty/revised anti-terror law, permission to broadcast in languages other than Turkish
3 December 2002	4th Constitutional Package	Operationalize previous reforms/revise penal code for torture
4 December 2002	5th Constitutional package	Retrial of all cases decided in State Security Courts
May 2003	6th Constitutional package	Adoption of Protocol 6 of the ECHR, convert all death sentences to life imprisonment/ repeal Article 8 of Anti-Terror Law
July 2003	7th Constitutional Package	Revision of the National Security Council
7 May 2004	8th Constitutional package	Ten amendments to the Constitution, freedom of press, and priority given to supranational treaties over domestic law, abolition of State Security Courts.
24 June 2004	9th Constitutional Package	Changes to Article 48 of the Penal Code, revision of Higher Education Board and the Censure Board
25-26 September 2004	New Turkish Penal Code	Revision of laws on violence against women and children/changes to penalties for various offences and redefinition of offences.

Source: Müftüler Baç, Meltem (March 2005), "Turkey's Political Reforms and the Impacts of the European Union," *South European Society & Politics*, Vol.10, No.1, pp. 16-30, 22.

(ANAP) and Nationalist Movement Party (MHP) government, and then by the Justice and Development Party (AKP).

Turkey's Europeanization was greatly motivated by the EU, as the prospects of EU membership provided powerful stimulus for constitutional reforms, as well as the harmonization packages. The prospect of full membership provided much-needed external stimulus for the legitimization of the reform process, and the credible EU accession perspective empowered pro-reformist domestic actors—*norm entrepreneurs*—who were actively involved in the bottom-up Europeanization process in Turkey. At the end of 2001, support for EU membership among the Turkish public exceeded 70 percent,[31] although these reforms were not

31. Ali Çarkoglu and Çigdem Kentmen, "Diagnosing Trends and Determinants in Public Support for Turkey's EU membership," *South European Society and Politics*, vol. 16, no. 3, (2011), pp. 365–379.

Table 2. Rates of Support for Turkey's EU Membership among the Turkish Public

Years	Positive	Negative
2004	62%	12%
2005	59%	20%
2006	44%	25%
2007	53%	25%
2008	42%	29%
2009	48%	26%
2010	47%	23%
2011	36%	33%
2012	30%	35%
2013	35%	34%
2014	43%	23%
2015	61%	11%

Source: Table created by the author based on Euro-barometer Standard Survey data.

simply an outcome of Turkey's desire to join the EU. The Europeanization process in Turkey tends to be interpreted as one of democratization, and from this perspective, the reform process in Turkey's Europeanization corresponded also to the demands of society for a more democratic and liberal political system.

Turkey tried to adopt the basic principles and norms of liberal democracy for the sake of its inclusion in the European order. Interestingly, as the Europeanization process stimulated democratic change in Turkey, the anti-European reactionary conservatives gained strength. As stated by Baç, opposition to the Europeanization process was organized politically around the religious vote in the 1950s with the Democratic Party; in the 1960s to a certain extent with the Justice Party (Adalet Partisi), and in the 1970s, 1980s and 1990s with the Nationalist Salvation (Milli Selamet Partisi), Welfare (Refah), Virtue (Fazilet) and Felicity (Saadet) parties.[32] The Justice and Development Party (AKP), with roots in the Islamist movement, came to power in 2002 with a more reformist stance than the more traditional Islamist party and appeared to be more receptive of the EU's demands for domestic change, transforming itself into one of the staunchest defenders of democratic rights and liberties, and an enthusiastic supporter of Turkey's entry into the

32. Müftüler Baç, *op.cit.*, pp. 17, 28.

EU.[33] The EU reforms also overlapped with the agenda of the AKP, which instrumentalized the promotion of EU accession to widen its support base towards the center and to anchor its political reforms aimed at curbing the influence of the Kemalists and the military. EU conditionality helped the AKP gain and hold political power.[34]

Keyman claims that "the AKP represents the socially conservative periphery that has demanded a share of power of the center," adding that this inclusion itself manifested greater democratization within the system. Moreover, the AKP's first term (2002–2007) brought Turkey closer to democratic consolidation as a result of the government implemented reforms in such areas as civil-military relations and the recognition Kurdish cultural rights.[35]

In December 2004, the European Council stated that with these reforms, Turkey had sufficiently fulfilled the Copenhagen political criteria to open accession negotiations with the EU on October 3, 2005. Since then, however, the speed of reforms has slowed in parallel to the increasingly dim perspective of membership after the EU's Turco-sceptic leaders offered Turkey a "special relationship," based on "privileged partnership" rather than "full EU membership," vetoing the opening of several chapters in Turkey's EU accession talks.[36]

The accession of Cyprus emerged as another obstacle during the accession negotiations, vetoing half a dozen chapters, including those related to the Judiciary and Fundamental Rights, Energy, and Education and Culture in Turkey's 2009 accession negotiations. A further eight chapters were frozen by the EU itself due to Turkey's non-implementation of the Additional Protocol extending the EU-Turkey Customs Union Agreement to Cyprus,[37] and no chapters have been opened since June 2010. Out of 35 chapters, 14 have been opened and 17 remain

---

33. Binnaz Toprak, "A Secular Democracy in the Muslim World: The Turkish Model," in Shireen Hunter and Huma Malik, eds., *Modernization, Democracy and Islam*, (Washington DC: Praeger and CSIS, 2005), pp. 277-293.

34. Tanja A. Börzel and Didem Soyaltin "Europeanization in Turkey: Stretching a Concept to Its Limits?" *Working Paper Freie Universitat Berlin-KFG The Transformative Power of Europe*, No. 36, (February 2012), p. 14.

35. Fuat Keyman and Sebnem Gümüşçü, *Democracy, Identity and Foreign Policy in Turkey: Hegemony through Transformation*, (Hampshire and New York: Palgrave Macmillan, 2014), pp. 48, 50.

36. Ünver Noi, *op. cit.*, p. 79.

37. Nathalie Tocci, *Turkey's European Future: Behind the Scenes of America's Influence on EU-Turkey Relations*, (New York and London: New York University Press, 2011), p. 121.

blocked, and Turkey froze its relations with the EU for the duration of the Cypriot Presidency in 2012.

Both internal and external developments have had a considerable impact on Turkey's democratization process, and have lessened the effectiveness of the EU's transformative power on Turkey owing to the lost ground in mutual trust; the decrease in enthusiasm in Turkey; and the fading attractiveness of the EU. The deceleration of accession negotiations between the EU and Turkey led to Turkish skepticism and has created an anti-EU backlash in the country. While support for the EU stood at 62 percent in 2004, it dropped to below 50 percent in 2009 and declined to its lowest level of 30 percent in 2012. In the same period, negative perceptions of the EU among the public has risen from 12 to 35 percent, which some have interpreted as "the adaptation process itself producing reverse reactions in perceptions."[38] At the same time, as argued in a report by the Turkish Economic and Social Studies Foundation (TESEV), the increasing self-confidence and expectations of Turkish society has sharpened its judgments about other societies while looking from a much more egalitarian perspective.[39] Moreover, the decreasing public support for EU membership makes it more difficult to mobilize the public in favor of implementing EU demands for reforms and the complicated tasks of *norm entrepreneurs*.

Since the AKP extended its power in the government by increasing its electoral support in its second term when the prospect for membership becoming less credible in the post-2005 period, the EU lost relevance for domestic institutional change. As Taspinar said, "the more power Erdogan won at the polls, the less interested he appeared in taking further reforms in human rights and freedom of expression."[40] The long-term hold onto power by one political party has been described as dominant-power system and politics,[41] and has the potential to hinder further democratization. This has in part been verified in Turkey's case, particularly during the third term of the AKP government. The fading

---

38. Etyen Mahçupyan, "Reflections on Turkey: Islamic Middle Classes at a Glance," *TESEV report*, (December 2014), p. 40

39. Ibid,, p. 40.

40. Ömer Taspinar, "Turkey: The New Model? in Robin Wright, ed., *The Islamists Are Coming: Who They Really Are?*" (Washington, DC: Woodrow Wilson Center Press, 2012), p. 128.

41. Thomas Carothers, "End of the Transition Paradigm," in Larry Diamond, Marc F. Plattner and Phillip J. Costopoulos, eds., *Debates on Democratization*, (Baltimore: Johns Hopkins University Press, 2010), p. 84.

support for EU membership in the Turkish public has further undermined the potential of using EU accession as a legitimization device.

Nevertheless, the adoption and implementation of domestic reforms continued in some areas after 2005. The Ankara criteria replaced the Copenhagen criteria. Turkish elites preferred "Europeanization à la carte"[42] in other words, picking and choosing from the EU policies to satisfy their constituencies and consolidate their political power.[43] Europeanization met greater resistance in some particular areas falling under the category of personal freedoms that did not fit in with the AKP's moral understanding along with issues that are likely to be securitized.

Modernization Theory

The second theory to be analyzed in terms of its impact on Turkey's democratization process is modernization theory. Before analyzing the directions of change in terms of democracy with a special focus on new Islamic middle class that has emerged over the last twenty years, the economic development and democracy relations based on modernization is analyzed in this section.

The roots of modernization theory, explaining the relationship between the sociology of religion and the development of the modern capitalist ethic, can be traced back to Max Weber's *Die Protestantische Ethik Und Der Geistdes Kapitalismus (1905)*. Weber argues that Protestantism constitutes an excellent breeding ground for capitalism, but argues at the same time that Protestant asceticism becomes a threat to itself.[44] Accordingly, industrious labor and consumption leads to an abundance that induces people to secularize their worldview; and modernization leads thus to such specific changes as industrialization, rationalization, secularization, and bureaucratization.[45]

The abundance resulting from these changes, particularly the secularizing influence of wealth, leads to less resistance to world temptations. Weber supports his argument by citing John Wesley, the founding

---

42. Börzel and Soyaltin, *op. cit.*, p. 16.

43. Ibid, p. 16.

44. Max Weber, *The Protestant Work Ethic and the Spirit of Capitalism*, (USA: Start Publishing LLC, 2012).

45. Dankwart A. Rustow, *A World of Nations: Problem of Political Modernization*. (Washington, D.C.: The Brookings Institution, 1967), p. 6.

father of Methodism: "I fear, wherever riches have increased, the essence of religion has decreased in the same proportion..."[46] This argument is supported also by John Calvin and Pieter de la Court, who claim that ordinary people only remain religious if they are poor.[47] According to this understanding, as capitalist culture develops, society becomes secularized.

The correlation between economic development and democracy was also highlighted by Seymour Martin Lipset, the famous scholar of Modernization Theory, in 1959. According to his general argument, "democracy is related to the state of economic development," increasing education, and the middle class, reducing inequality, and tempering the tendency of the lower class to political extremism. For Lipset, "economic development leads to positive social changes that tend to produce democracy, leading to a shift from tradition to secular-rational values."[48] His argument was reinforced by Kenneth A. Bollen and Robert W. Jackman in 1985, who argued that in the 1960s "the level of economic development has a pronounced effect on political democracy, even when other noneconomic factors are considered ... GNP is the dominant explanatory variable."[49]

According to sociologists Inglehart and Welzel, modernization increases the likelihood of the emergence of increasingly liberal and democratic political systems, since high levels of economic development tend to make people more tolerant and trusting, resulting in more emphasis on self-expression and more participation in decision-making.[50] Once the middle class becomes sufficiently large and articulate, it presses for liberal democracy, while industrialization leads to a shift from traditional to secular-rational values. Economic development is, indeed, linked strongly to pervasive shifts in the beliefs and motivations of people, and these shifts in turn change the role of religion, job motivation, human fertility rates, gender roles and sexual norms.[51]

46. Weber, *op. cit.*, p. 172.

47. Rustow, *op. cit.*, p. 5

48. Seymour Martin Lipset, *Political Man: The Social Bases of Politics*, (New York: Doubleday, 1960), pp. 31, 50.

49. Samuel P. Huntington, *The Third Wave: Democratization in the Late Twentieth Century*, (Norman: University of Oklohama Press, 1991), p. 60.

50. Ronald Inglehart and Christian Welzel, "How Development Leads to Democracy: What We Know About Democratization," *Foreign Affairs*, (March/ April 2009), p. 37.

51. Ibid., p. 39.

Modernization theorists underestimated the challenges faced by non-Western countries on the route to modernization.[52] Diamond argues that a different path to modernization may be the increasing trend towards the hybrid regimes like those found in Latin America, where elections are held, but none of the usual constitutional checks and balances exist.[53] Examples can also be found among the Islamic states of countries that "develop their own models of modernity, ones that value the role of reason and are pluralist, but also religious."[54]

Inglehart and Welzel (2005) emphasize that even though socioeconomic development tends to drive systematic changes in people's value and belief systems, the impact of cultural traditions does not simply disappear. Inglehart and Welzel (2005) suggest that industrialization is linked with one main process of cultural change, being the rise of secularization and bureaucratization, while the growth of postindustrial societies gives rise to another main process of cultural change that follows a different direction, being a growing emphasis on such values of self-expression as civil and political freedom or individual autonomy.[55] In the following section, the impact of modernization particularly the correlation between economic development and democracy is analyzed on Turkey's democratization process.

Modernization in Turkey and its Impacts on Democratization 1999–2015

The modernization of Turkey began with the establishment of the Republic as the primary goal of Atatürk, who wanted a modernized and secular Turkey that could compete with other countries at the highest level of contemporary civilization. The 1920s was a period of revolutionary reform in the constitutional and cultural spheres, embracing the

---

52. Andrew Linklater, "Globalization and the transformation of political community" in John Baylis, Steve Smith & Patricia Owens, eds., *The Globalization of World Politics*, (New York: Oxford University Press, 2011), pp. 540-558.

53. Larry Diamond, "Elections without Democracy: Thinking About Hybrid Regimes," *Journal of Democracy*, vol. 13, no. 2, (April 2002), p. 23.

54. Tamara Sonn, "Islam and Modernity: Are They Compatible?" in Sheeren Hunter and Huma Maliki, eds., *Modernization and Islam*, (Westport: Praeger, 2005), p. 80.

55. Ronald Inglehart and Christian Welzel, "Changing Mass Priorities: The Link Between Modernization and Democracy," *Perspectives on Politics*, 2010.

abolition of the Caliphate and the secularization of the legal system, although in the economic sphere, policies were far more conservative.[56]

The political reforms under the Westernization and modernization drive in the early years of the Republic, from 1923 to 1938, were adopted in order to make a break with the Ottoman past and to create a modern European state. Yet not everybody in Turkey shared that ideal, since Turkey's European aspirations was considered a project of the elite. As a consequence, the Turkish modernization process turned into a struggle between the Europe-oriented state elite and the conservative elements of Turkish society. The state in Turkish modernity assumed the capacity of transforming society from above, and planned import-substituting industrialization as the most appropriate path to development. National development based on rapid modernization and industrialization and the top down transformation of the society into a modern, industrial and civilized one was the ideology behind this state-centric Turkish modernization.[57]

The development of a strong private sector and a business elite, which led to a shift from former import-substitution policies to export-oriented growth and free-market economies, contributed also to Turkey's democratic consolidation in the 1980s. These developments also led to an expansion of communication networks such as the Internet, fax machines, television satellite dishes, cables and direct telephone lines, accompanied by a significant increase in the number of students studying abroad and in international travel. These changes have played an important role in opening Turkish citizens to international influence and the liberalization of the political system.[58]

Turkey's journey towards Richard Rosecrance's idea of a "trading state"[59] began under the leadership of Turgut Özal in the 1980s,[60] bringing capitalism to Turkey and liberalizing the Turkish economy,

---

56. William Hale, *The Political and Economic Development of Modern Turkey*, (London: Croom Helm, 1984), p. 153.

57. Keyman and Gümüşçü, *op. cit.*, p. 19.

58. Toprak, *op. cit.*, p. 289.

59. Richard Rosecrance, "The Rise of the Trading State: Commerce and Conquest in the Modern World," *American Journal of Sociology*, vol. 92, no. 3, (November 1986), pp. 709-711.

60. In the 1980s, Rosecrance argued that a "new trading world" was emerging, one that replacing a world characterized by a military-political and territorial system. Kemal Kirişçi, "The Transformation of Turkish Foreign Policy: The Rise of the Trading State," *New Perspectives on Turkey*, no. 40, 2009, pp. 29-57.

which in turn led to the growth of a new business elite and Turkey's trade relations with the outside world.[61] While this process was interrupted in the 1990s, it was reignited by the AKP with the growth of a tradition of conservative, traditional, rural and religious voters in Turkey that had reservations—to say the least—about the process of Europeanization.[62] This process not only led to a change in Turkey's national interests, determined in terms of national security with the addition of economic considerations, such as the need to trade, to expand export markets, and to attract and export foreign direct investment, but also managed to create its own middle class.[63] Since the AKP came to power in 2002, the Islamic portion of society has managed to create its own Muslim bourgeoisie in Anatolia. The urbanization of the prospering middle class has led to radical changes in the lifestyles of the majority of citizens, leading to new political demands and contributing to the AKP rise to power.

Turkey's economy enjoyed remarkable success in the 2002–2006 period, with growth averaging 7.2 percent. Since then, however, growth has slowed, dropping to 4.2 percent in 2013 and further to 2.9 percent in 2014. Per capita income increased to 10,500 USD in 2011 from 3,500 USD recorded in 2002, although the global crisis affected also Turkey as a result of the declining external demand and falling international capital flows. Growth rates in 2008 and 2009 were below the remarkable performance achieved between 2002 and 2007, however Turkey achieved a growth rate of 9.2 and 8.5 percent in 2010 and 2011 respectively. Turkey became the 17th largest economy in the world in 2012 with a GDP of around 800 billion USD.[64]

However, contrary to arguments of modernization theory, rather than creating secularization (as an outcome of modernization) that diminishes the religious congregation, this modernization has on the one hand expanded the congregation, and on the other, has altered the meaning of religiosity in Turkey. A research into the political and sociological evolution of Turkey conducted by the Turkish Economic and Social Studies Foundation (TESEV) revealed the perceptions, expectations, and demands of the rising Islamic middle class, and their influ-

---

61. Ibid. p. 33; Taspinar, *op. cit.*, p. 128.

62. Müftüler Baç, *op. cit.*, p. 28.

63. Kirisçi, *op. cit.*, p. 33.

64. Economic Outlook of Turkey, Ministry of Foreign Affairs, 2011, http://www.mfa.gov.tr/prospects-and-recent-developments-in-the-turkish-economy.en.mfa

ence in determining the policies of the AKP. The research indicated that the group that defined themselves as religious corresponded to the conservative middle class that supported the AKP, and had strengthened after the AKP came to power.[65]

The report identified a general positive perception about democracy, although what was understood by democracy also varied. For the majority of the participants, democracy implied the election of administrators by the majority, the decisions' being taken by the majority and the compliance of minorities with the norms of the majority. They noted that their freedoms had been restricted before, but come to feel freer during the term of the AKP government. The definition of freedom changes against attitudes not falling in line with Islam, and the freedom of others is recognized as legitimate, so long as the sensitivities of the Islamic segment of society are observed. This was particularly evident on the issue of the prohibition on the sale and advertising of alcohol.[66]

Every participant believed that a prime minister or a party leader must make decisions after consulting the people around him, in that consultation has an important place in Islam, being *sunna*; although some participants added that a strong leader must exert his authority in cases of indecisiveness. This view was supported by the analogy of home life one of the participant of survey: "If I am the leader of the family, I can then exert my authority without contradicting what I have said before."[67] This "atavistic approach" manifests itself in references to the Ottoman state related to various issues. For instance, one of the participants said:

> If there is no democracy, then there would be pressure, a social pressure. This would prohibit individuals from expressing their views, leading them into illegal organizations and activities. For this reason, democracy is a must; although one thing must be added: the Ottoman model can be acceptable. We like the Ottomans—

---

65. Mahçupyan, *op. cit.*, p. 45.

66. Mahçupyan, *op. cit.*, pp. 46, 47. In 2003, new laws banned all forms of advertising and promotion of alcoholic beverages, including promotions, sponsored activities, festivals and free giveaways. It also included limiting retail sales hours from 6 am to 10 pm, and banning student dormitories, health institutions, sports clubs, all sorts of education institutions and gas stations from selling alcohol. Applications for new licenses required a business permit from the local municipality and a tourism document from the Ministry of Culture and Tourism.

67. Ibid., p. 50.

why? It is a monarchy that allowed people to live the way they wanted, although it still was a monarchy ...[68]

The participants were ready give up their personal freedoms when the question was asked using the term "relinquishing one's freedom for the sake of social order" rather than "interference of the state in individual lives." There was a common understanding that sacrifice was one of the rules of society. Although democracy was viewed essentially as majoritarianism and the functions of state are expressed as introducing measures, frameworks, and limits on freedoms, balance is sought in the end, affirming "a relinquishment of freedoms is acceptable only to some extent."[69]

The perception of the Islamic middle class on the Gezi Park-related anti-government demonstrations paralleled the government one. The AKP government style and that of the Prime Minister was generally supported. In response to the claims of excessive police violence, the participants stated that the police had been better trained in recent years and had reduced violence in police stations. Another justification for their support of the government's approach to the Gezi Park protests was that the protestors were supporters of illegal organizations. Despite these views, it was emphasized that the Gezi Park protests were not managed well, although some of the participants viewed the Gezi Park protests as a plot by "external forces" aimed at hindering progress in Turkey.[70]

The most important finding of the report was that the "new middle class" that has flourished over the last 20–30 years has become stuck between the desire to change and adapt and/or to protect identity and moral values.[71] Some Turkish scholars have described them as "a blend of Islamic traditionalism and European Union norms,"[72] although it is too early to reach a concrete conclusion on this issue, since the evolution of this class, which emerged only 20 years ago, is continuing.

---

68. Ibid., pp. 50, 53.

69. Ibid., pp. 55, 7.

70. Ibid., p. 67.

71. Ibid. P. 73.

72. Hakan M. Yavuz, *Secularism and Muslim Democracy in Turkey*, (Cambridge: Cambridge University Press, 2010).

That said, in the current situation, we can say that the support for democracy among the Islamic segment of society is based on pragmatic and vital reasons, rather than being based on principles. Democracy is considered desirable, but not absolutely necessary for their inclusion in social life and for their adaptation to the modern world.[73] From this perspective, it would seem less likely that they could be convinced to push for further democratization, particularly in the more sensitive fields that do not fit the moral understanding of this class and their representatives in government, or in the fields that are accepted by this class as a threat to national security or a threat to the government that represents them. The reflection of economic development and the emergence of the Islamic middle class on the democratization process in Turkey showed the limits of the democratization process, which can be explained with Huntington's argument that "The relationship between economic development and democracy is complex and probably varies in time and space."[74]

Securitization

The third theory to be analyzed to identify its impacts on Turkey's democratization process is the securitization theory of the Copenhagen school. Before analyzing its impacts on the democratization process in Turkey for the 1999–2015 period, securitization theory is analyzed here in general terms.

According to securitization theory, security emerges only in communication between subjects, being both a social and inter-subjective construction. It rejects the traditionalist's case for restricting security to one sector that of state centric and identifies with the military powers of nation states. "It offers a constructivist operational method for distinguishing the process of securitization from that of politicization for understanding who can securitize what, and under what conditions."[75]

Wæver, drawing upon language theory, regards security as a *speech act*. He argues that "something is a security problem when the elites declare

73. Mahçupyan, *op. cit.*, p.19.

74. Samuel P. Huntington, *The Third Wave: Democratization in the Late Twentieth Century*, (Norman: University of Oklohama Press, 1991), p. 59.

75. Barry Buzan, Ole Waeever, and Jaap de Wilde, *Security: A New Framework for Analysis*. (London: Lynne Rienner Publishers, 1998), vii.

it to be so."[76] The elite must establish that there is a threat potentially existential and possible with relative advantages of security handling compared to non-securitized handling.[77] Discourse presenting something as an existential threat to a referent *object* does not itself create securitization, but it is a *securitizing act*, and, the issue can only become securitized if and when the *audience* accepts it as such. If no signs of such acceptance exist, the object is not actually being securitized.[78]

Securitization focuses on the transformation of certain issues into matters of security by an *actor*, and enables the use of extraordinary measures in the name of security. A securitization act has three components: *securitizing agent/actor, referent object* and *audience*. The *securitizing agents* are political leaders, bureaucrats, governments, lobbyists, and pressure groups that have the authority for security-speak.[79] They make *securitizing statements* that trigger the perception that referent objects are under threat. In this regard, there should be a referent *object* that is being threatened and that needs to be protected. Successful securitization is not decided by the *securitizer*, but by the audience of the security speech act.[80] In this regard, there should be an *audience* that is a target of the *securitization act*, and that needs to be persuaded and needs to accept that the issue as a threat to security. According to securitization theory, anyone can succeed in promoting something as a security problem through *speech acts*. If a subject is securitized, then it becomes possible to legitimize extraordinary measures to resolve the perceived problem, since the security speech-act calls for exceptionality by offering to handle the issue through extraordinary means, which may include breaking the normal political rules of the game, such as applying limitations on inviolable rights.[81]

Perception also plays an important role in the acceptance of an issue as a threat. The perceived image of the *issue* as an existential threat from which the referent *object* must be protected is one of the benefits of con-

---

76. Ole Wæver, Securitization and De-securitization, in *On Security*, Ronnie D. Lipschutz, ed., (New York: Columbia University Press, 1995), pp. 46-86.

77. Ole Wæver, "Politics, Security, Theory," *Security Dialogue*, vol. 42, no.4-5, (August-October 2011), pp. 465-480.

78. Buzan, Waeever and Wilde, *op. cit.*, p. 25.

79. Sinem Akgül Açikmese, "EU Conditionality and De-securitization Nexus in Turkey," *Southeast European and Black Sea Studies*, vol. 13, no. 3, 2013, pp. 303-323.

80. Buzan, Waeever and Wilde, *op. cit.*, p. 31.

81. Buzan, Waeever and Wilde, *op. cit.* pp. 25, 26.

structing a threat that facilitates the securitization of the object. In referring to a certain development as a security problem, the state can claim a special right. Power holders may always try to use instruments for the securitization of an issue to gain control over it.[82]

De-securitization, which is the opposite of securitization, can be observed in four forms: change through stabilization, replacement (a combination of one issue moving out of security while another is simultaneously securitized), re-articulation (de-securitizations that remove an issue from its securitized state by offering an active political solution to the threats, dangers and grievances in question), and silencing (when an issue disappears or fails to register in security discourse).[83] In the following section, the concepts of both securitization and de-securitization and their impacts on Turkey's democratization process are analyzed.

Securitization in Turkey and its Impacts on Democratization

Securitization is not a new concept for Turkey, being a country that had a highly securitized inward-looking foreign and security policy during the 1990s. Fear of loss of territory has long been one of the major aspects of Turkish security culture owing to the Treaty of Sevrés, that facilitated the partitioning of the territories of the Ottoman Empire among the European powers after World War I. Although the Treaty of Sevrés was rejected by Turkish national movement, and Lousanne Treaty that defines borders of modern Turkish Republic signed, this fear continued.

During the 1990s, the focus on national security shifted from external to internal threats.[84] The terrorist activities of the PKK (Kurdistan Workers' Party) a decade ago, identified as "a few terrorists,"[85] intensified in the 1990s. Securitization of separatism (the Kurdish issue) came to the agenda as a threat to the territorial integrity of Turkey. Bilgin explains this situation, "During the post-Cold War period that coincided with Turkey's struggle with the PKK and its application to join

---

82. Wæver, *op. cit.*, p. 54.

83. Lene Hansen, "Reconstructing De-securitisation: The Normative Political in the Copenhagen School Directions for How to Apply It," *Review of International Studies*, vol. 38, (July 2012), pp. 525-546.

84. Akgül Acikmese, *op. cit.*, p. 308.

85. Ibid., p. 308.

the EU, that sub-text of fear of loss of territory was turned into text in Turkey's security discourse."[86] In this regard, an atmosphere of "more security, less democracy" manifested itself in the implementation of exceptional suspensions of several democratic rights in Turkey.[87]

In the first half of the 2000s, however, Turkey's new outward-looking foreign policy deepened its relations with its neighbors, and made it a "model and order setter"[88] in the wider world. The economic boom and political success in combining democracy with Islam, and the freedoms enjoyed by the Turkish people due to the ongoing democratization process, had a considerable impact on the public perception. Moreover, changes in attitudes, along with the comments of the political elite, the AKP government, civil society and the media also changed the formerly inward-looking security policy, all having acted as agents in the move towards the de-securitization of the Kurdish issue. The EU accession prospect, in other words, the EU's conditionality, facilitated a process of de-securitization in Turkey, with its impact being noted with particular focus on the mainstream discourse of threats articulated as the "Kurdish issue" and "political Islam."[89]

However, this did not last too long. The unfavorable internal and external environment that emerged was more of a hindrance than an aid to the transformation. Moreover, the AKP's emerging moral agenda initiated to satisfy its supporters, including the Muslim middle class, paid little regard to the demands of the secularists, who perceived the agenda as an infringement of their personal freedoms. This led to polarization in society based in particular on the AKPs focus on its own constituencies and Europeanization *a la carte*—or pick and choose democracy.[90] This led to criticisms that the more power the AKP won at the polls, the less democratization featured on the agenda, resulting even in backward steps in this regard.

---

86. Pinar Bilgin, "Turkey's Changing Security Discourses: The Challenge of Globalisation," *European Journal of Political Research*, vol. 44, 2005, pp.175-201, p. 184.

87. Akgül Acikmese, *op. cit.*, p. 312.

88. Serhat Guvenç and Soli Özel, "Turkey: Model, Order-Setter, or Trade Partner?" in Nathalie Tocci, Elena Maestri, Soli Özel and Serhat Güvenç, Ideational and Material Power in the Mediterranean The role of Turkey and the gulf Cooperation Council, *Mediterranean Paper Series 2012*, June 2012.

89. Ibid., p. 303.

90. Börzel and Soyaltin, *op. cit.*, p. 16

All opposition acts were perceived as attempts at a *coup d'état*, aimed at destroying the AKP government. This led to discourses that portrayed any kind of opposition as a threat to the existence and success of the AKP in its New Turkey aspirations. This situation gained momentum after the corruption allegations of December 2013, which were seen as a political contest between Erdogan's circle within the AKP and their former long-term ally, the Gülen Movement. The government accused the Gülen Movement of exerting undue influence in state institutions, the police and the judiciary, and attempting to bring down the government.[91]

In order to eliminate the obstacles in the way of the drive for a New Turkey, legislative amendments were made. Arrangements were made to reappoint and/or remove from their positions judges, prosecutors, police, etc. that were considered as having a role in the organization defined as the "parallel state."[92] The military coup in Egypt had a significant impact on these developments, and discourse started to reflect a more populist conservative nationalism.

Furthermore, revealing some national secrets regarding the AKP's Syria policy by a prosecutor considered to be affiliated with Gülen Movement (later revealed also by some opposition journalists) brought the issue of transparency and accountability in democracies to the agenda. According to arguments that can be traced back to Immanuel Kant, public accountability allows democracies to implement efficient and successful foreign policies. Kant's argument on the institutions of consent has been utilized to extend the logic of accountability in democracies to foreign and security policy issues. According to Kant's argument, extortion occurs when states exaggerate or oversell foreign threats to society, whether through incomplete information or outright deception.[93]

Mill suggests that democracies are defined by the transmission of information to and among the public, through which informed citizens' consent is built. Civil society institutions or organizations promoting transparency, and a free press allows for open debate about the public

---

91. World Report (2015). *Events of 2014.* Human Rights Watch.

92. BBC, "Turkey's Erdogan Battles 'Parallel State' 17 December 2014, http://www.bbc.com/news/world-europe-30492348

93. Michael P. Colaresi, *Democracy Declassified: The Secrecy Dilemma in National Security,* (Oxford and New York: Oxford University Press, 2014), pp. 24, 28.

benefits and costs of competing policies.[94] The AKP's argument, rather, parallels that of Gabriel Almond and de Tocqueville, who claim that a democracy's lack of secrecy inhibits effectiveness by making potential enemies aware of vulnerabilities and weaknesses. The AKP accused the people who leaked information to the media of being traitors and of harming security. The secrecy dilemma, tensions between national security secrecy and government public accountability in democracies were discussed at even greater depth after security leaks in the United States by Chelsea Manning, Julian Assange and Edward Snowden sparked public debate about the issue, and the Turkish government used it to justify its argument even further.

The liberal theory of democratic foreign policy synthesizes the benefits of public accountability with the capacity for executive secrecy, rather than simply trading secrecy for accountability. Here, debates have been raised about the limits of transparency in democracies, related specifically to national security issues.[95] Through applied measures, the government impedes the ability or likelihood of the media holding government authorities to account or scrutinizing their activities.[96]

The government also labeled any kind of opposition as a *coup d'état* attempt orchestrated by foreign forces or an "interest lobby."[97] All acts of opposition were stigmatized as an act against the success of "New Turkey"[98] in discourse and in the speeches of political leaders. The political elite repeated this discourse constantly, stating that Turkey was under threat, so as to legitimize extraordinary measures to resolve the problems. The audience, particularly the supporters of the AKP, accepted this as a security threat and was ready to sacrifice freedoms for the greater good. Securitization followed by undemocratic restrictions were put in place to contain the threat. For instance, the homeland security bill came to the agenda after the wave of demonstrations against the government (Gezi Park protests) in May-June 2013 and after the Kurdish protests against government policies towards Kobani

---

94. Ibid.
95. Ibid., p. 24.
96. World Report, *op. cit.*, p. 549.
97. Joe Parkinson, "Dismay over Turkish Rates," January 12, 2012, The Wall Sreet Journal, http://www.wsj.com/articles/SB10001424052970204124204577154353478071244
98. Umut Uras, "Erdogan Promises a 'New Turkey'," 12 July 2014, *Aljazeera*, http://www.al-jazeera.com/news/middleeast/2014/07/erdogan-promises-new-turkey-20147127316609347.html

(Kobani demonstrations). Although the opposition parties warned that the bill would turn Turkey into a police state, the homeland security bill passed in Parliament, enhancing the powers of the police to search and detain and to use firearms, and increasing penalties against protestors. The bill breached the separation of powers of the legislative, executive and judicial branches of the state, bestowing governors with authority previously reserved for prosecutors and judges.[99] The potential effects of the ongoing Syrian conflict that gave the Kurds in Syria a territorial advantage in their fight against ISIS made the situation more complicated, seeming to have a securitization effect on the discourses of securitizing agents and their extraordinary measures.

Turkey's problems with regards to democracy and human rights preceded the AKP era, being a consequence of Turkey's conceptions of security. The security-first orientation of the state has long affected the observance of civil liberties and pluralism in the country, with secessionist Kurdish demands since the 1980s having a significant impact on the democratic and peaceful management of those demands by successive governments. Ethno-secessionist movements have been marked by hatred, numerous killings committed by all sides and by authoritarian practices,[100] and so the democratization process in Turkey can thus be referred to as de-securitization, since political reforms could only be possible through refraining from security speech acts and the passing of legislation on sensitive issues.[101] The conditions of EU membership were an important catalyst in Turkey's de-securitization, and the role of the EU in this regard was inevitable.[102]

The Democratic Opening Process (known also as the Kurdish Opening) that was initiated by the AKP in July 2009 paved the way for the de-securitization of Kurdish issue for a while, and also for resolving the issue in a democratic and peaceful way through the granting of several rights to Kurds, which led to negotiations and a truce in 2013. Yet external and internal developments and the securitization of the issue pre-

---

99. World Report, *op. cit.*.

100. Alfred Stepan, *Democracies in Danger*. (Baltimore: The Johns Hopkins University Press, 2009), p. 5.

101. Münevver Cebeci, "Democratization as De-securitization: the Case of Turkey", paper presented at the SGIR, *Sixth Pan-European Conference on International Relations*, "Making Sense of a Pluralist World", Turin, 2007.

102. Sinem Akgül Açikmese, "EU Conditionality and De-securitization Nexus in Turkey," *Southeast European and Black Sea Studies*, 2013 Vol. 13, No. 3, p. 303.

vented the continuation of the process, and saw even a reversal of some democratic achievements.[103] In brief, securitization aggravated the problems of democratization that had emerged since 2005 due to the slowdown of reforms and the reversal of already adopted reforms caused by the lack of internalization of norms and rules, as well as deficiencies in practice.

Conclusion

The Europeanization in Turkey that took place according to RCI logic led to domestic change, and provided political actors with new opportunities and constraints to pursue their goals. Yet this process entered a reverse cycle due to the absence or limited existence of the conditions to bring about any domestic change for further democratization.[104] Moreover, de-securitization within the domestic policy context has lost ground. This led to the emergence of distrust and intolerance in the society in which democracy is unlikely to survive.[105] Furthermore, the expected positive role of the Islamic middle class in Turkey's modernization and of course democratization process came to its limits owing to cultural factors playing a significant role on socio-economic development and its social and political consequences. The formation of the middle class, the tendency for secularization and the establishment of democratic mechanisms have occurred differently from the West, and so have yielded different results.[106] From an SI perspective of Europeanization, this can be interpreted as the EU not leading to domestic change, especially within the Islamic middle class, through socialization and a collective learning process, resulting in norm internalization on issues that contradict particularly their religiously sensitive issues.

---

103. The suicide bombing by members of the Islamic State of Iraq and Levant (ISIL) in the border town of Suruç on July 20, 2015, which killed 32 socialist youth activists of mostly ethnic Kurdish origin and wounded dozens more, and the subsequent terrorist attacks by the PKK and ISIL led Turkey to rethink its approach to both groups. The failure to establish a coalition government and the resulting early election promoted the securitization of the "Kurdish issue" followed by the suspension of Democratic Opening Process, and the declaration of a state of emergency in the southern provinces in response to the PKK's insurgency. Aylin Ünver Noi, "Turkey's Fight with ISIL and PKK: A Return to the 1990s?" Huffington Post, 2015 http://www.huffingtonpost.com/aylin-unver-noi/turkeys-fight-with-isil-a_b_8008904.html

104. Akgül Açikmese, *op. cit.*, p. 303.

105. Ibid., p. 305. Inglehart and Welzel, 2009, *op.cit.*, p. 47.

106. Mahçupyan, *op. cit.*, p. 9.

These changes in Turkey also altered its standing as an international role model, based on the economic development and freedom enjoyed by the people in the region during the first half of the AKP government's term in office. The challenges to democracy Turkey faces today also impacted upon both its foreign policy approach and economic growth, hindering its soft power. Turkey, since 2002, has been a blatant example of dominant-power politics, but the results of the June 2015 parliamentary election saw this picture change when the AKP lost its parliamentary majority, bringing an end to the single-party government. After the election, the political parties failed to form a new government, but a second election in November later that year resulted in the AKP regaining its majority in Parliament. Many argued that the securitization of the Kurdish issue had helped the AKP to have this outcome; yet the emerging picture of escalating terrorism blurs the hopes for a more democratic Turkey. Future developments will show us whether Turkey will have a chance to opt for either a liberal democracy or whether it will continue with its illiberal preferences.

The ongoing accession negotiations with the EU may still stimulate Turkey's return to democratization. Revival of the EU-Turkey relations following the refugee crisis indicated us the necessity for cooperation between Turkey and the EU. The EU's conditional positive incentives, normative pressure and persuasion will be much more effective than a suspension of relations, which did not help the democratization process in Turkey. An egalitarian approach helps both sides eliminate their differences and find commonalities, and Turkey, as a "trading state"[107] can benefit from advanced relations with the EU. The heyday of the Turkish economy has been left behind, and she has turned from an emerging market into a country that is faced with financial vulnerabilities. An upgraded customs union in which Turkey can benefit from free trade agreements with third countries may become a positive incentive that is more egalitarian than previous approaches, and has the potential to change the public's perception of the EU positively, and finally create the potential to stimulate political will towards a more democratic Turkey. We should not ignore that Turkey's Europeanization process had a significant impact on the de-securitization of certain issues, as well as the democratization process in Turkey, once a credible EU membership perspective was attained and continued in the 1999–2007 period. Turkey's economy enjoyed remarkable success in the 2002–2006 period,

---

107. Richard Rosecrance, *op. cit.*

with growth averaging 7.2 percent, and this coincided with Turkey's reform process and Turkey's increased soft power.

As former Deputy Prime Minister Ali Babacan said at the B20-World Bank Group meeting on *Towards a Global Steering Mechanism* held on April 17, 2015 at the IFC, "The rule of law and high quality democracy is at the essence of a predictable business environment."[108] A return to the democratization process is vital for the economic well-being of Turkey. Continuing the accession negotiations with a credible membership perspective and positive incentives by providing political actors with new opportunities may still have the potential to bring about liberal democratic tendencies rather than illiberal ones in Turkey; [109]and in turn, the transformation of Turkey may also have a positive impact on the EU's transformative power, which has lost ground in recent years.

---

108. Aylin Ünver Noi, "Turkey and Iran: From Competition to Cooperation?" Huffington Post, 2015,http://www.huffingtonpost.com/aylin-unver-noi/turkey-and-iran-from-comp_b_7127854.html

109. Merkel's visit to Turkey to discuss the Syrian refugee flows to Europe and visa liberalization talks are important steps.

Chapter Four

Challenges of Democracy in Serbia

Daniel Serwer

Serbia is the center of gravity of the Balkans. The largest of six former Yugoslav republics in population, it rivals Bulgaria, which is third in the region only to Romania and Greece. Landlocked, it is geographically central, bordering eight other countries: Croatia, Bosnia and Herzegovina, Montenegro, Kosovo, Macedonia, Bulgaria, Romania and Hungary. Only much larger countries have land borders with more neighbors (Brazil, China, Democratic Republic of the Congo and Russia). In GDP per capita at Purchasing Power Parity, according to 2015 IMF figures, Serbia is second only to Montenegro among Balkans countries not yet members of the European Union, despite a decade of war in the 1990s and lagging economic performance in the 2000s.

It would be too much to suggest that as goes Serbia, so goes the Balkans. Many countries in the Balkans progressed politically and economically while Serbia stagnated in the 1990s. But Serbia is an important player that has in the past generated more than its share of regional instability, conflict, economic disruption and displacement. Serbia matters.

A Decade of War and Autocracy

In the 1990s Serbia was at war much of the time. After the Berlin Wall fell, Yugoslavia flew apart with the secession of Slovenia (1990), Croatia (1991), Macedonia (1991) and Bosnia and Herzegovina (1992). Belgrade, which used the remnants of the Yugoslav National Army (JNA) to contest by military means all but the secession of Macedonia, was left with Montenegro in a rump Federal Republic of Yugoslavia, later rechristened the State Union of Serbia and Montenegro. Slobodan Milošević, a former Communist apparatchik, governed it as an elected autocrat whose popularity was based on his appeals to Serbian nationalism, his control of the main media outlets, support from the security services and crony capitalists, and his vicious treatment of rivals and dissenters.

The wars accompanying the secession of three of Yugoslav's republics ended in 1995, after NATO intervened against Serb forces in Bosnia and Herzegovina and brought Milošević to Dayton suing for peace. He had already faced a difficult challenge that spring, when Croatian forces took back from Serb control three of four UN Protected Areas. About two hundred thousand Croatian Serbs, who had lived in the Krajina (border) area of Croatia for hundreds of years, fled Croatia for Serbia, where they called for Milošević to step down in the wake of military disaster. He feared that the Bosnian Serbs, who numbered at least two if not three times as many, would likewise leave Bosnia as Federation (Bosniak and Croat) forces swept west and north in the summer of 1995 with Croatian support in the wake of NATO bombing of the Serb forces. The Bosnian Serb leader Radovan Karadzic was regarded at the time as a rival to Milošević in Belgrade. Milošević needed peace in Bosnia to protect his own hold on power in Serbia. He made that peace at Dayton.

He soon faced a challenge from within. Milošević blatantly falsified local election results in late 1996. For the first time, the Serbian opposition political parties and nongovernmental organizations took to the streets to protest through the winter, echoing previous protests in March 1991, when an opposition political party massed large numbers of protesters in Belgrade. Both protests fizzled when Milošević accommodated some of their demands, though not enough to allow a challenge to his own position. He was a master of the political tactics required to keep himself in power despite dramatic military losses and popular discontent.

The Autocrat Falls

Milošević's skills fell short a few years later in Kosovo. An Albanian-majority province nominally inside Serbia, it had a representative on Yugoslavia's collective presidency, like the six Yugoslav republics. Kosovo had enjoyed a wide range of self-governance until 1989, when Milošević ended its autonomy and put it under Belgrade's direct rule. The Albanians then established their own parallel institutions, including a presidency and parliament as well as health and education systems. Milošević's crackdowns on nonviolent protests and the subsequent violent insurgency in Kosovo attracted international attention by the late 1990s, even as he formed a government of national unity and narrowed the area of dissent allowed inside Serbia. An effort by the United States and the European Union to negotiate a political solution in France at the Rambouillet Chateau outside Paris in 1999 failed when Serbia refused to sign on.

Another war ensued. NATO, without United Nations Security Council authorization, undertook to prevent continuing expulsion of Albanians from Kosovo by bombing Serb forces as well as military and dual use infrastructure in both Kosovo and Serbia proper. The NATO/Yugoslavia war ended 78 days later with UN Security Council resolution 1244, which established UN administration of the province, promised a transition to democracy and foresaw an eventual decision on its political status. Milošević, faced with the prospect of irreversible damage to Serbia's infrastructure and economy, withdrew Serbian forces from Kosovo as NATO-led forces took charge.[1]

Serbs were unhappy with the outcome, which left the country in ruins and Kosovo outside Belgrade's control. Sporadic protests against Milošević broke out in the summer of 1999. His opposition controlled a number of local governments, which got preferential treatment from the European Union, in particular supplies of energy.[2] But by the summer of 2000, an opposition political coalition, formed to demand new elections, had split. Milošević thought he had the situation again under control and called early Yugoslav elections, with himself as a candidate for President. Confident of victory, if only because he could falsify votes, he made a fatal mistake: he allowed counting of votes at the polling places.[3]

Yugoslavia was no democracy, but it allowed opposition candidates as a useful safety valve for discontent. This time most of the opposition united behind the nationalist democrat Vojislav Koštunica, chosen over his somewhat less nationalist rival Zoran Đinđić because he had 'high positives' and 'low negatives.' Crucially, Serbian civil society also mounted a major effort, led by an organization called CeSID (the Cen-

---

1. Stephen T. Hosmer, *The Conflict Over Kosovo: Why Milosevic Decided to Settle When He Did*, (Santa Monica, CA: RAND Corporation, 2001)
http://www.rand.org/pubs/monograph_reports/MR1351.
2. "Commission Successfully Completes Energy for Democracy in Serbia," European Commission, May 25, 2000, accessed August 9, 2015,http://europa.eu/rapid/press-release_IP-00-527_en.htm.
3. Siniša Vuković, "Serbia: Moderation as a Double-Edged Sword," in I. William Zartman, ed., Arab Spring: Negotiation in the Shadow of the Intifadat, (Athens and London: the University of Georgia Press, 2015)

ter for Free Elections and Democracy), to verify the accuracy of the voting and counting. It communicated the results from polling places faster than the government's official election apparatus was able to do. It also blocked efforts to report and tabulate falsified votes from Kosovo. Koštunica had won, by a narrow margin.

Street demonstrations returned. The student-led Otpor (resistance movement), which had pressed for opposition unity, helped turn out millions of demonstrators in favor of acceptance of the election results. Milošević fell when those results were officially recognized. Serbia had delivered a democratic result, despite long odds. Its civil society deserved a lot of the credit.

Another Mostly Lost Decade

But the next decade would not fulfill the hopes of the street demonstrators or most Serbian civil society organizations. Serbia remained bogged down economically and politically. In the aftermath of Koštunica's Yugoslav electoral victory, his less nationalist and more pro-European rival Zoran Đinđić was elected Prime Minister of Serbia. He marshaled Milošević off to the International Criminal Tribunal for the former Yugoslavia (ICTY) in 2001 and showed signs of preparing to reform the security services. But Đinđić was assassinated in 2003, by people closely associated with both the security forces and organized crime. A dozen people have been convicted of this crime, but precisely who ordered the assassination and why is still not clear. Suspicions of high-level involvement persist.

Boris Tadić was elected President of Serbia in 2004 and served until 2012. Unquestionably democratic and European in general orientation, Tadić was also committed to maintaining Belgrade's claim to sovereignty over Kosovo and at the same time preparing for EU membership. Seeing him as their best hope, EU institutions in Brussels and the United States government backed him to the hilt. He launched (2005) and completed (2007) negotiations with the EU for a Stabilization and Association Agreement (interrupted however for a year because Belgrade was not cooperating sufficiently with the International Criminal Tribunal in The Hague) as well as negotiations for the Schengen visa waiver program, which came into force in 2009. Serbia also applied for EU membership in 2009. But none of these steps, other than the visa waiver program, had a serious impact on ordinary people's lives.

In the meanwhile, Tadić presided during the peaceful dissolution of the State Union of Serbia and Montenegro, after Montenegro voted for independence in a 2006 referendum. Tadić also presided during the rewriting the Serbian constitution and then Kosovo's independence, declared in 2008 over Serbian objections but in accordance with a plan prepared by a UN envoy.[4] Tadić's second term coincided with the global financial crisis and produced little for a Serbia no longer consumed by nationalist passions. Failure to meet the demand for jobs and prosperity resulted in Tadić's resounding defeat at the polls in 2012.

The 2006 rewriting of the Serbian constitution had particular significance for Kosovo and for Serbia's still young democracy, which was anxious not to be blamed for losing Kosovo and committed to maintaining sovereignty. The new constitution was prepared in an opaque process with no substantial public or parliamentary debate. It contains a preamble that appears to obligate the Serbian state to do everything it can to maintain sovereignty over Kosovo (and Metohija, a reference to Church lands in the province):

> Considering also that the Province of Kosovo and Metohija is an integral part of the territory of Serbia, that it has the status of a substantial autonomy within the sovereign state of Serbia and that from such status of the Province of Kosovo and Metohija follow constitutional obligations of all state bodies to uphold and protect the state interests of Serbia in Kosovo and Metohija in all internal and foreign political relations[5]

The referendum to approve this constitution had to meet a dual threshold: 50 percent of voters had to approve, and 50 percent of registered voters had to come to the polls. The second threshold was thought to be out of reach if the Kosovo Albanians were counted on the voter rolls and refused to vote, as they had for almost 20 years. They certainly would not go to the polls to enable Serbia to adopt a constitution that included the sovereign claim to Kosovo. Voting 'no' would,

---

4. Martti Ahtisaari, Report of the Special Envoy of the Secretary-General on Kosovo's Future Status, report, March 26, 2007, accessed July 16, 2015, http://www.unosek.org/docref/report-english.pdf.

5. "Constitution of The Republic of Serbia," World Intellectual Property Organization, September 30, 2006, accessed July 22, 2015, http://www.wipo.int/wipolex/en/text.jspC?file_id=191258.

ironically, have validated a constitution they disagreed with but could not defeat.

The dual threshold problem was solved, perniciously. Prime Minister Koštunica sent a letter to the UN administration in Kosovo asking to hold the referendum there. The UN did not respond. This provided him an excuse not to include the Kosovo Albanians on the voting register, thus depriving them of the option of blocking the new constitution by not voting. The international community nevertheless praised the process and accepted the results, which were mutually contradictory: the process demonstrated that Kosovo Albanians were no longer counted as Serbian citizens, but the outcome claimed they were. This bit of constitutional hypocrisy is still outstanding, although increasingly there is recognition in Serbia that the constitution will eventually have to be amended, for several reasons.[6]

Alternation in Power Brings Change

Serbia up to 2012 had witnessed only one democratic alternation, when opposition figures Koštunica and Đinđić came to power in Yugoslavia and Serbia, respectively in 2000 and 2001. When Đinđić's heir as head of the Democratic Party, Tadić, lost his bid for a third term in May 2012, Progressive Party leader Tomislav Nikolić came to power under the apt slogan "Let's Get Serbia Moving." Nikolić appointed Ivica Dačić, a holdover from Tadić's government, as prime (and interior) minister. Aleksandar Vučić, deputy leader of the Progressives and a disciple of Nikolić, served as deputy prime minister and defense minister. Nikolić, Dačić and Vučić all had origins on the pro- Milošević, nationalist side of Serbian politics: Nikolić and Vučić in the Radical Party and Dačić in Milošević's own Socialist Party.

This unlikely triumvirate has taken major steps in the European and democratic direction for Serbia in the wake of Tadić's uninspiring second term. The EU and U.S. actively encouraged this evolution, which has gone much further under the aegis of Serbs with strong nationalist credentials than under nominally less nationalist ones. While continuing to declare that it will not recognize Kosovo's unilateral declaration

---

6. The preamble is not the only problem, see "Opinion on the Constitution of Serbia," European Commission for Democracy through Law, March 19, 2007, accessed July 22, 2015, http://www.helsinki.org.rs/doc/Venice%20Commission%20on%20Serbian%20Constitution.pdf.

of independence, Belgrade has implicitly acknowledged that Serbia will not even try to re-establish Serbian authority in its former province, which could only be done by military and autocratic means.

The story of this evolution is essentially one of Serbian acceptance of "external incentives," building on a foundation of "social learning."[7] After Kosovo Serbs injured German peacekeepers in 2011 during a demonstration, Chancellor Merkel read Belgrade the riot act and insisted that it "normalize" relations with the Pristina authorities who had declared independence and were recognized by close to 100 sovereign states. Generated in part by the burdensome costs of maintaining German peacekeepers in Kosovo, Berlin's pressure, supported by the European Union and the United States, led to a series of technical agreements (on state documentation, Kosovo representation in regional organizations, telecommunications, electricity, border/boundary monitoring, etc.) and eventually to a political agreement in April 2013.[8] Serbia, it was made clear, would not progress further in its EU ambitions without making significant progress in normalizing relations with Kosovo, which also came under pressure to talk directly with Belgrade.[9]

In both countries, majorities identify as Europeans and want democracy. In Serbia, the political elite regards adoption of the *acquis communautaire* as essential to modernizing a state still mired in outmoded socialism. In Kosovo, adoption of the *acquis* is regarded as essential to building a state from the ground up in a country with limited technical capabilities and governing experience. While implementation of European standards is often lacking in both Belgrade and Pristina, politicians in both countries claim to adhere to European values and norms. They even compete in claiming to be more European than the other.

Neither the technical agreements nor the political agreement between Belgrade and Pristina have yet been fully implemented, but their implications are clear. Belgrade has accepted Pristina's constitu-

7. Frank Schimmelfennig and Ulrich Sedelmeier, "Governance by Conditionality: EU Rule Transfer to the Candidate Countries of Central and Eastern Europe," *Journal of European Public Policy*, 11:4, 661-679, http://dx.doi.org/10.1080/135017604200024889, accessed July 31, 2015.

8. Edita Tahiri, Brussels Agreement Implementation State of Play, report, March 23, 2015, accessed July 23, 2015, http://www.kryeministri-ks.net/repository/docs/Kosovo_Report_on_Implementation_of_Brussels_Agreements__230315-signed-signed.pdf.

9. Frank Schimmelfennig & Ulrich Sedelmeier (2004) Governance by Conditionality: EU Rule Transfer to the Candidate Countries of Central and Eastern Europe, Journal of European Public Policy, 11:4, 661-679, DOI:10.1080/1350176042000248089.

tional and judicial authority on the whole territory of Kosovo, including its four northern, Serb-majority municipalities, which it has been agreed will form with Serb-majority municipalities south of the Ibar an Association/Community provided for in the Ahtisaari plan. It has also accepted that Kosovo and Serbia will apply and qualify for European Union membership separately (and without hindering each other). This implies that Kosovo is sovereign, as only sovereign states can apply for EU membership. While Serbs in Kosovo remain citizens of Serbia, Kosovo Albanians do not in any practical sense. They generally travel on Kosovo passports, they do not vote in Serbian elections or pay taxes to the Serbian state.

The results in terms of progress towards the EU have been substantial, but more procedural than financial. The European Union rewarded Serbia for its agreements with Kosovo by giving Belgrade a date to begin accession negotiations. They were initiated in December 2015 with the opening of Chapter 35 on normalization with Kosovo and Chapter 32 on financial controls. Serbia had already begun receiving substantial pre-accession funding from the EU, totaling 1.4 billion euros from 2007 to 2013 (178.8 million euros in 2013). An additional 986 million euros in soft loans and grants was provided in 2014, in response to floods. Belgrade is slated to receive 1.5 billion euros in 2014-20, only a small increase over the previous allocation.[10] The bulk of the funding is explicitly intended to support implementation of the *acquis communautaire*. The EU has not generally linked particular funding to particular legislation or other Serbian actions, but the Commission makes its expectations clear in annual progress reports and frequent meetings. The amount of pre-accession assistance could increase or decrease depending on Serbia's needs and rate of progress as well as the European Commission's will and availability of funds.

Accession negotiations began in January 2014. Support for EU membership in Serbia remains around 60 percent, though it has drifted downwards in recent years. Serbia has begun to conform its laws and regulations to EU requirements, especially when it comes to the public administration, the transportation sector and the media law. EU conditionality remains effective on many issues, though implementation is

---

10. "Serbia Progress Report," European Commission, October 2014, pg. 4, accessed July 20, 2015, http://ec.europa.eu/enlargement/pdf/key_documents/2014/20140108-serbia-progress-report_en.pdf.

often spotty.[11] Many chapters of the *acquis* are not expected to cause big trouble for Belgrade, which is socialized to its technical requirements. The current Greek financial crisis may make Serbia leery of adopting the euro, but that has not been an issue so far since the Serbian dinar is free floating and Serbia is nowhere near fulfilling the macroeconomic criteria required to enter the euro-zone, whose members would not likely welcome Serbian membership in any event.

March 2014 elections confirmed Serbia's EU ambitions and brought Vučić's Progressives an absolute majority in parliament, making him prime minister. Thus the choice between Kosovo and the EU that stymied Tadić's presidency and slowed democratization has found at least a temporary resolution under Nikolić, Dačić and Vučić, all of whom came from the more nationalist and less democratic wing of Serbian politics. Serbia has progressed in many respects since the Milošević era. It is now in a position to claim that it is on the road to democracy and to a European future.

International Misalignment Persists

But that claim coexists with an attachment to non-alignment that is unique in the Balkans. Former Yugoslavia was a leader in the non-aligned movement during the Cold War. The habit persists in Belgrade. The parliament in 2007 declared Serbia militarily neutral, in pique at the impending Kosovo declaration of independence. While most Serbs want to join the EU, Belgrade traditionally has close ties with Moscow, with which it shares an Orthodox religion and Slavic language. Cultural heritage counts, especially in an era of contestation between East and West. Russia has significantly stepped up its opposition to EU and especially NATO enlargement in the wake of the Ukraine crisis. It exploits its close connections with more traditional and religious segments of Serbian society to weigh against Serbia's all too obvious inclination to move westward. Despite that, Prime Minister Vučić claims Serbia has made a strategic choice for Europe and democracy, while President Nikolić continues to court Moscow more than Washington.

---

11. Bodo Weber and Kurt Bassuener, "Analyzing the EC Serbia Progress ReportsUseful Tool or Tactical Whitewash?," Democratization Policy Council, June 23, 2015, accessed July 22, 2015, http%3A%2F%2Fwww.democratizationpolicy.org%2Fanalyzing-the-ec-serbia-progress-reports-useful-tool-or-tactical-whitewash-.

Non-alignment lost its real meaning for most of the world more than 25 years ago, with the fall of the Berlin wall and the collapse of the Soviet Union. All the other countries of the Balkans have opted unequivocally for Brussels, leaving Serbia surrounded by EU and NATO members and aspirants. Several maintain good bilateral relations with Russia, even while joining in Ukraine-related sanctions. Serbia has refused to do that, avowedly because it would receive no EU compensation, in contrast to EU member states. But some more nationalist Serbs certainly sympathize with Russia's stated aim of protecting Russian speakers in neighboring states, which is analogous to an objective that Serbia pursued aggressively (often on equally false pretenses) during the breakup of Yugoslavia.

Serbia's disappointment in Russian cancellation of the South Stream natural gas pipeline, on which Belgrade had invested both financial and diplomatic capital, has however led to some reappraisal of the wisdom of relying too heavily on Moscow for energy production. The main near term alternative, heavily favored by the United States, is the Trans-Adriatic Pipeline, which would deliver Azerbaijani gas to Serbia via Italy. Prime Minister Vučić has declared himself ready and willing to reduce dependence on Russian gas.[12]

The question now is what else would encourage and enable Serbia to take further steps away from its traditional "non-aligned" stance and persistent attachment to an increasingly autocratic Russia, towards a more in-depth commitment to European Union accession, democratic values and possible NATO membership.

Priority Internal Reforms

The road ahead to EU membership is still long. While Serbia's electoral mechanisms appear to function correctly, it is just beginning to reform its laws and administrative capabilities in conformity with the *acquis communautaire*, economic growth has been slow and fiscal imbalances are high, even if tax revenues and exports are increasing. Minority protection is imperfect, especially for Roma as well as for gays and lesbians, but progress is visible.

---

12. Dusan Stojanovic and Jovana Gec, "Premier: Serbia Ready to Reduce Dependence on Russian Gas," The New York Times, May 27, 2015, accessed July 22, 2015, http://www.nytimes.com/aponline/2015/05/28/world/europe/ap-eu-serbia-us.html?_r=0.

Serbia remains laggard in three key areas, all of which go beyond the technical requirements of the *acquis*: security sector reform, media freedom and rule of law. It needs to up its game in all three.

It is widely believed that the successful removal of Milošević in 2000 was achieved in part through a pact, tacit or explicit, between at least some leaders of the political opposition, in particular future prime minister Zoran Đinđić, and elements of the security forces, which apparently agreed not to protect Milošević in exchange for at least an implication they would not be held accountable for their behavior during his regime. The result was hesitation in reforming the security services, including not only the army but also the police and intelligence services. After Đinđić's assassination, a special operations unit was disbanded but there was even more reason to hesitate in reforming the rest, for fear of stirring a hornets' nest. Progress since then has been sporadic at best, driven largely by international pressure to cooperate with the International Criminal Tribunal for the former Yugoslavia and Serbia's membership in Partnership for Peace, achieved before the declaration of neutrality.[13] The net result has been slow adaptation of the security services to civilian control but little high-level accountability for past abuses. As Serbia for now is not expected to join NATO and internal pressure for reform is weak, the EU accession process will need to play a far stronger role than usual in its security sector reform.[14]

The media issue is not formal censorship but rather informal pressures and even self-censorship, often exercised through politically-appointed editors and fear of losing contracts for valuable government advertizing. In addition, politicians in Serbia, including the current prime minister, frequently attack the medium and even the journalist, not only the message, sometimes rousing extremists to violence against government critics.[15] Fear cows many outlets into submission—memories of what happened to media moguls who resisted Milošević's dominance are still fresh.[16] Serbian media need more diversified rev-

---

13. "The Missing Link: Security Sector Reform, 'Military Neutrality' and EU Integration in Serbia," Center for Euro-Atlantic Studies and Democratization Policy Council, November 2014, accessed August 9, 2015, http://ceas-serbia.org/root/prilozi/CEAS-DPC-Study-Missing-Link-SSR-military-neutrality-Serbia-EU-integration.pdf.

14. Ibid.

15. "Serbia Progress Report," European Commission, October 2014, pg. 4, accessed July 20, 2015, http://ec.europa.eu/enlargement/pdf/key_documents/2014/20140108-serbia-progress-report_en.pdf, pg. 46.

16. Kemal Kurspahić, *Prime Time Crime: Balkan Media in War and Peace* (Washington, DC: United States Institute of Peace Press, 2003).

enue streams and less intimidation by government officials in order to feel free to criticize without fear of retaliation.

Rule of law in Serbia suffers three chronic ailments: slowness, lack of professionalism and political influence. Commercial disputes can drag on for decades. Appointment of judges and prosecutors is politicized. Previous efforts at reform have failed. High-level corruption cases are rarely pursued and the fight against organized crime is lagging, even though the government now takes a hard rhetorical line in public on corruption. Tycoons and higher level war criminals are too often protected from prosecution. One of the prime suspects in the murder of the Bytyqi brothers, American Kosovars killed in 1999 by Serbian security forces, is a member of the prime minister's political party and serves on its executive board.[17] Nongovernmental organizations have accused the Serbian Army chief of staff of war crimes they say units under his command committed in Kosovo.[18] Prosecutors rarely pursue such high level cases. The courts need to be liberated from political constraints and encouraged to pursue malfeasance whenever and wherever it occurs, provided they follow proper procedures.

Interconnectedness is Important

Serbia is heavily dependent on Russian natural gas as well as Russian investment and technology for exploitation of its own gas and oil resources. This dependence will increase as Serbia's own domestic reserves are depleted. It needs alternatives. Theoretical long-term options, in addition to Azerbaijani gas via the Trans-Adriatic pipeline, include gas from Qatar, Libya, Croatia, Israel and Cyprus. Any of these could put Serbia in a much better position to resist Russian pressure on issues like Ukraine. Several of these options would benefit from resuscitation of the Krk pipeline from Croatia, a proposition under study in several countries.[19]

---

17. Marija Ristic, "Serbia's Broken Promises Over US Albanians' Murders," Balkan Insight, July 20, 2015, accessed July 23, 2015, http://www.balkaninsight.com/en/article/bytyqi-case-a-decade-long-brocken-promises-1.

18. Marija Ristic, "Natasa Kandic: Serbia's Bloodstained Army Boss Must Go," Balkan Insight, February 10, 2010, accessed July 23, 2015, http://www.balkaninsight.com/en/article/natasa-kandic-serbia-s-bloodstained-army-boss-must-go.

19. Sven Milekic, "Croatia to Include Serbia in Gas Pipeline Project," Balkan Insight, February 11, 2015, accessed August 6, 2015, http://www.balkaninsight.com/en/article/croatia-to-include-serbia-into-gas-pipeline-network.

While located in the heart of the Balkans, Serbia is still not well connected, especially to the Mediterranean. While many in Serbia and Montenegro may object, the quickest and easiest fix would be to complete the Durres/Pristina road through Kosovo to the southern Serbian town of Nis. This project, which the European Union is committed in principle to financing, faces obvious political difficulties, as it would be the first major new infrastructure linking Kosovo and Serbia since their 1990s warfare.[20] But it would provide serious economic benefits to both countries and go a long way to healing old wounds.

Also important would be economic cooperation between border/boundary communities in the two countries. Vital for this is an agreement on identification documents that would allow easy transit, like those in use between the U.S. and Mexico as well as the U.S. and Canada. It is difficult, however, to move in that direction without clarity and precision about where the boundary/border lies. It has not been formally agreed or demarcated, though there appear to be no serious disputes about where it lies. One can look long and hard for two countries without a demarcated border that have good relations. Demarcation of the Kosovo/Macedonia border led to a rapid improvement of relations between Skopje and Pristina, despite Kosovar objections that the line had been agreed with Belgrade prior to independence. Kosovo and Montenegro have recently completed demarcation of their border. The time has come for Belgrade and Pristina to begin technical preparations for border/boundary demarcation.

Military Posture Needs to Continue Shifting

Serbia is a member of NATO's Partnership for Peace and enjoys active cooperation with the Ohio National Guard. It has signed a NATO Individual Partnership Action Plan, participates in NATO military exercises and contributes to UN peacekeeping.[21] But unlike other Balkan militaries, Serbia's army has not deployed with NATO or US forces. That would be an important step in cementing Serbia's relations with the

---

20. "Western Balkans 6 Meeting in Brussels," European Commission Press Release Database, April 21, 2015, accessed August 10, 2015, http://europa.eu/rapid/press-release_STATEMENT-15-4826_en.htm?locale=en.

21. Fred Stern, "Serbia's Growing Role As a UN Peacekeeping Contributor," DipNote, March 9, 2014, accessed September 7, 2015, http://blogs.state.gov/stories/2014/03/09/serbia-s-growing-role-un-peacekeeping-troop-contributor.

West, one that Macedonia, for example, has taken by deploying embedded in the Vermont National Guard in Afghanistan. The Serbian Army medical corps is good and prepared for an operational deployment of this sort. War deployments are happily hard to come by these days, but a natural disaster deployment embedded with the Americans (or vice versa) could be a step in the right direction, especially if the Serbs bring their own helicopters (always in short supply) to the venture.

A NATO Membership Action Plan for Serbia is another possibility, albeit one that Moscow would resist, along with portions of Serbia's population committed to neutrality or nonalignment. But it could happen if Belgrade wants it. Once fully qualified Montenegro, which has received an invitation, enters the Alliance, and especially if former neutrals Sweden and Finland were to apply, it would make no strategic sense for Serbia to remain outside. Nonalignment really is going out of fashion.

Serbia has a southern military base on the border with Kosovo (Jug) that it might like to make available to NATO for exercises. So long as these are open to participation by the Kosovo armed forces, that idea might be a positive contribution to regional security. But Serbia's Defense Ministry and Chief of Staff still need to engage constructively, as neighbors normally do, with Kosovo's Security Force and its Ministry.

Regional Issues

When it comes to regional security, Serbia has particularly important roles to play in Bosnia and Herzegovina as well as Kosovo, both of which have Serb populations whose welfare Belgrade rightly values. Most concrete issues with Croatia have been resolved, but bilateral relations wax and wane, often over differing perceptions of what happened between Croats and Serbs during World War II and in Croatia's retaking of Serb-held territory in 1995.

In Bosnia and Herzegovina, Milorad Dodik has long led Republika Srpska, the Serb-dominated 49 percent of the country. His political ambitions are tied to independence for his entity. It will not happen, not least because it would leave in central Bosnia a rump Islamic Republic that neither Serbia nor Croatia would find a compatible neighbor. Nor would Serbia risk endangering its EU accession process by recognizing an independent Republika Srpska. But even without secession, Dodik's pursuit of his nationalist project has rendered the Bosnian state pretty much nonfunctional. At this writing, he is blocking a Bosnian commitment to reform of the labor market that the EU sees as vital. This is just his latest attempt to put a spoke in Sarajevo's wheel.

What is needed from Serbia is a clear break with Dodik. July 2015 marked the 20th anniversary of the Srebrenica massacre of more than 8000 Muslim men and boys by Serb forces in eastern Bosnia. There was no better occasion for Vučić to renounce his past nationalist excesses.[22] It was also an opportunity for Serbia to say it profoundly regrets the genocidal act perpetrated in its name and wants Bosnia's Serbs to repair the damage by helping to build a Bosnian state capable of providing equal rights and economic opportunity for all its citizens. Vučić failed to take advantage of that opportunity. He continued the practice of his predecessors of refusing to call what happened at Srebrenica "genocide." Angry people throwing stones chased him from the 20th anniversary commemoration, making the needed break with Dodik more rather than less difficult for him.

In Kosovo, the issue for the moment is nitty gritty. Mediated by the EU, Belgrade and Pristina have reached both a broad agreement of principles, including application of the Kosovo constitution on all its territory, and specific technical agreements. They have also reached agreement in principle on forming a Serb Association of Municipalities inside Kosovo, which will be able to cooperate with Belgrade within the limits of Kosovo law (and is still very controversial in Pristina). Fully implementing the agreements would be helpful both to Serbia in its pursuit of EU membership and to Kosovo in its pursuit of a visa waiver from Brussels. The process will be long and drawn out, but external incentives will continue to function.

Serbia will need some day to face the issue of accepting Kosovo as a sovereign state and establishing some sort of diplomatic relations with it. The easiest way would be for Serbia to drop its objection to UN membership for Kosovo, followed by exchange of diplomatic representatives with the rank of ambassador (liaison officers have already been exchanged). One or more of the 23 EU members who already recognize Kosovo will surely block Serbia's membership if it fails to resolve this issue.

---

22. Miloš Ćirić, "Contexts Don't Burn," Pescanik.net, June 1, 2015, accessed July 22, 2015, http://pescanik.net/contexts-dont-burn/.

While Belgrade appears to have decided to postpone formal acceptance of Kosovo's sovereignty until late in its EU accession process, there is a good reason to face it sooner rather than later: Kosovo is designing its security forces, which in the absence of recognition will have to be significantly stronger than might be needed if the two countries had truly normalized their relationship, including by exchange of ambassadors.[23] NATO forces in Kosovo now number under 5000 and likely will decline further by 2020. As they are drawn down, recognition (or at least admission of Kosovo to the UN) and diplomatic relations at some level could reduce Kosovo's security requirements as well as Serbia's, saving both countries a bundle.

Conclusion

Serbia is proud of its long history, which it traces to 14th century Kosovo and earlier. Unfortunately that history also includes an inept monarchy between the world wars, several more recent decades of Communist mismanagement under Tito as well as a decade of autocratic rule and military misadventures under Milošević. It needs now to tend to its democratic future, which is gradually coming into clearer focus. The next decade or more will be devoted to qualifying for EU membership. Both the country's current leadership and its people are committed to that goal and appear ready for many of the domestic reforms required. Serbia has put off the difficult question of explicitly accepting Kosovo as a sovereign state, but once the benefits of EU membership are more proximate even that is unlikely to prove an insurmountable challenge.

Whether the door will be open when Serbia is ready to enter the EU is not however clear. Euro-skepticism is plaguing many EU members, fed by the euro crisis that has engulfed Greece and the dramatic influx of Middle Eastern and African migrants from around the Mediterranean. The EU, much like Serbia, is aging and declining demographically. While the logic of the situation favors revitalizing Europe by opening its doors to both young migrants and neighboring countries with a European tradition, there is no guarantee that will happen. The

---

23. Kosovar Center For Security Studies, "Destination NATO: Kosovo's Alternatives towards NATO Membership," accessed 2015, http://www.qkss.org/repository/docs/Destination_NATO_Kosovos_Alternatives_towards_NATO_Membership_556716.pdf.

last challenge for democracy Serbia will inevitably face will be convincing the public in EU member states, all 28 of which will have to ratify the accession treaty, that Serbian membership should be welcomed, not shunned.

Chapter Five

Challenges of Democracy
in Bosnia and Herzegovina

Sasha Toperich and Mak Kamenica

Twenty years have passed since the Dayton Peace Accords stopped the war in Bosnia and Herzegovina (BiH). Since then, the reconciliation and the nation building process have had many ups and downs. The member states of the Peace Implementation Council (PIC), an international body in charge of implementing the Dayton Peace Agreement for Bosnia and Herzegovina, often disagreed on priorities for the international community in this country. The Office of the High Representative (OHR) that was mandated under Article II of Annex 10 of the Dayton Peace Agreements to monitor the implementation of the peace settlement lost its efficiency in recent years, passing the torch to the EU Special Representative in BiH and the EU Delegation to BiH. After 9/11, the United States faced a new set of national security threats and problems around the globe, leaving to the EU the leading role in BiH. But the EU was faced with a set of new problems as well: the crisis in Ukraine, Mediterranean migration, Greek debt uncertainty, economic crises, and lack of steam for further EU enlargement.

These new realities made the focus on unfinished business in BiH scattered. It resulted in a set of EU political inconsistencies in BiH, along with the rise of corruption and political anarchy in BiH. The country's progress towards EU membership was slow and insignificant. In February 2015, violent demonstrations alerted local politicians and the international community (IC) alike, both recognizing the need to engage more strongly in BiH. With several unsuccessful attempts to make BiH a more functional state through efforts to implement constitutional reforms in the country, the EU has launched a robust socio-economic reform plan accepted by BiH. If BiH successfully implements socio-economic reforms, it may indeed have better internal conditions to engage in political and institutional reforms and create a more functional country. Social and economic reforms will not address the Sejdic-Finci ruling at this point in time, an issue that BiH politicians could not resolve after debating it for four years. EU membership without the implementation of the European Court on Human Rights ruling is simply not possible. Washington is strongly backing newly EU initiated social-economic reforms, but with many failed efforts in the past, caution is highly present.

What does the framework for reforms include? Will the effort, even if successfully implemented, achieve a better life for ordinary citizens, and create a more prosperous, politically stable country? Clearly there are fewer and fewer fans cheering for BiH, and maybe this time, local politicians got the memo. Engaging strongly in and implementing the socio-economic reforms may well be the last serious chance for BiH to catch the rest of the Western Balkans in the EU integration process. This chapter gives perspective on BiH's unique European journey.

From 1945 To 1995

Before its dissolution, the Socialist Federal Republic of Yugoslavia (SFRJ) consisted of six federal republics (Slovenia, Croatia, Bosnia and Herzegovina, Serbia, Montenegro, and Macedonia), and two autonomies (Vojvodina and Kosovo). The Communist Party was the only party ruling the country from its formal inception in 1943 to Marshal Josip Tito's death in 1980. The role of the Communist Party was cemented in the 1946 Constitution and its influence grew proportionally since then, creating a very centralized system that ruled the country for almost four decades. The process of decentralization slowly began in the 1970s. After Tito's death in 1980, the country was ruled by a collective Presidency comprising eight members, one from each republic and one from each of the two autonomies. The Presidency chairmanship rotated every twelve months. Fifty years of one-party rule left a deep mark on the development of democracy in the countries of the former Yugoslavia. The dissolution of Yugoslavia began in the 1990s only to descend into brutal wars, ethnic cleansing, genocide, waves of refugees and hundreds of thousands dead and missing. In BiH, the General Framework Agreement for Peace was reached at the Wright-Patterson Air Force Base near Dayton, Ohio, United States on November 21st 1995, known as the Dayton Peace Accords.

Achieving peace in BiH at Dayton was a major international effort, successfully led by then-U.S. Secretary of State Warren Christopher and Accord's chief architect Richard Holbrooke with EU Special Representative Carl Bildt and Russian First Deputy Foreign Minister Igor Ivanov as two Co-Chairmen The main participants from the region were Alija Izetbegovic, President of Bosnia and Herzegovina and Muhamed Sacirbey, Foreign Minister of Bosnia and Herzegovina; Franjo Tudjman, President of Croatia; Slobodan Milosevic, President of the Federal Republic of Yugoslavia (representing Bosnian Serbs' interests, in the absence of Bosnian Serb leader Radovan Karadzic). U.S. General Wesley Clark, later NATO Supreme Allied Commander Europe; Pauline Neville-Jones, head of the UK team, and Colonel Arundell David Leakey from the UK military; and Paul Williams of the Public International Law & Policy Group that served as the legal counsel to the Bosnian government delegation.[1]

The full agreement was signed in Paris on December 14th 1995, witnessed by Bill Clinton, U.S. President; John Major, UK Prime Minister; Jacques Chirac, President of France; Helmut Kohl, German Chancellor, and Viktor Chernomyrdin, Russian Prime Minister.

Political Scene from 1995 to the Present

Political leaders of post-war BiH are the inherited former Yugoslavian Communist Party political elites, suddenly 'transformed' into 'democratic,' 'pluralistic' leaders, and ethnic community dominant political party elites pursuing nationalist agendas. Interestingly enough, in the last twenty years of peace in BiH, almost all large political parties split up into two or more smaller political parties, creating antagonisms beyond the capacity to be resolved by such a small country. The platforms of all political parties are very similar. All of them profess joining the EU as matter of national interest, promising more jobs, justice, prosperity and reforms. Yet, immersed in the melting pot of day-to-day politics, and with such a complex constitutional structure, real progress on these promises is very slow. It often happens that one political party is represented not only both in power and in the opposition, depending where they had enough votes to join the ruling coalition and where they didn't, but also on what are the current fabrics of personal relations between political leaders, who changes their "firm alliances" in no time. The underlying interest of all political parties is to be the one that sets

---

1. https://en.wikipedia.org/wiki/Dayton_Agreement.

all the rules, gaining money, control, and power. This makes it very difficult for voters to really vote for change.

Democracy under the Most Complex Political System in the World

The Dayton Peace Accords stopped the war but also created arguably the world's most complicated political system, comprising a tripartite Presidency (Bosniak, Serb, and Croat members of the Presidency rotating the chairmanship every eight months), a Council of Ministers (at the state level), two entities (Federation of BiH and Republika Srpska), one district (Brcko), and municipalities. In the Federation of Bosnia and Herzegovina, in addition to these layers of administration, ten cantons were created. Annex 10 of the Dayton Peace Accords provided a legal basis for the creation of the Office of the High Representative (OHR) and for the High Representative to oversee the civilian implementation of the Dayton Agreement. The OHR also serves to represent the countries involved in the implementation of the Dayton Agreement through the Peace Implementation Council (PIC). At its 1997 meeting in Bonn, the PIC agreed to grant further substantial powers to avoid delays and obstructions by local politicians in implementation of the Dayton agreement. Hence, the small country of 3.8 million started its post-war building of democracy with fourteen governments and parliaments, 150 ministers, and all together, over 350 elected officials.

Candidates for the Presidency are, on an ethnic basis, self-defined and they can only be from within the three constitutive peoples. "Others," or minority representatives, are not eligible to run for the Presidency, a disqualification of a large percentage of the population seriously at odds with the very foundation of democracy.

As an example, following the general elections held on October 3rd 2010 that produced a fragmented political landscape, the country waited eighteen months before a ruling coalition and parliamentary majority was formed. Political crises spread to local levels as well and within the complex Federal entity, where political leaders need to agree not only on ministerial appointments for the government of the Federation of BiH, but also on the ministerial appointments for all ten cantons within the Federation of BiH. Political elites need to agree also on which political party controls seats in the administration of which public company, as the main financial source for funding both party and installing loyal party members to their helms. Appointment of crucial positions in the justice and security apparatus also took a long time and plenty of negotiation, not because political leaders look for independent, professional, appropriate people for the jobs, but rather for politically suitable and "controlled" individuals that will serve as an added mechanism to fight their opponents. Depending how much and with how many political parties the "victory cake" has to be shared with, that takes much time to agree vertically on every position. Add to this that the national balance of power must be honored to represent each of the three ethnic groups in equal proportion, such processes can and most of the time do take a long time. After months of dysfunction and arguments about legality, the short-lived government of the Federation collapsed in February 2013, creating a major political stalemate that lasted until the following general elections held on October 12th 2014.

The legislative branch of the government also has mechanisms to stall progress. Any proposed decision of the Parliamentary Assembly of BiH in the House of Peoples could be declared destructive to the Bosniak, Croat, or Serb peoples' vital national interest by a majority vote of delegates from the respective ethnic group. In such a case, the Speaker of the House of Peoples will immediately convene a Joint Commission consisting of three delegates, one Bosniak, one Croat, and one Serb, in an attempt to resolve the issue. If the Commission fails to resolve the issue within five days, the case will be transferred to the Constitutional Court of BiH that will review the issue under emergency procedure.

Politicians in BiH learned fast and well all the legal loopholes in the Dayton Accords, and have almost never failed to use them both when their national interest were indeed in question, and more often, when their own political (read: financial) interests were in question. Dayton Peace Accords were ad-hoc designed to bring peace, stop suffering and destruction, and start healing and reconstruction process in the country. It was understood twenty years ago, and so much more today that constitutional reform is desperately needed.

In addition, in 2006, representatives of the Jewish and Roma minorities in BiH, Jakob Finci and Dervo Sejdic, sued Bosnia and Herzegovina at the European Court of Human Rights in Strasbourg as under the Dayton Peace Accord, they were not eligible to be candidates for either the Presidency of BiH or for the House of Peoples of the Parliament of Bosnia and Herzegovina.[2] (Under Annex IV of the Dayton Peace Accord only members of three ethnic groups—Bosniak, Serb, and Croat—can be considered candidates for these offices.) Contributing to their victory in December of 2009 at the European Court in Strasbourg were also Article 2 that guarantees human rights and liberties applying European Convention on Human Rights as the priority towards any other legislations. BiH is yet to implement Strasbourg's ruling because political parties cannot agree on how to make room for minorities to take active part in political life in BiH. In 2012, the EU made resolution of the so-called Sejdic-Finci ruling a pre-condition for country to sign and activate a Stabilization and Association Agreement (SAA) with the EU, but pushed the issue aside after last general elections in BiH in 2014.

Constitutional Reforms

In the past twenty years, after the signing of the Dayton Peace Accords, several attempts were made to improve the constitutional framework in BiH. In post-Dayton negotiations on constitutional reforms, all political parties in BiH were engaged. The international community supported the efforts, but insisted on local ownership and local political consensus for the country's future. Discussions amongst political parties in BiH reflected growing seeds of democracy but they have failed to produce any concrete breakthrough.

The first such major effort was initiated in 2005, commonly referred to as the April Package. On April 26th 2006, it fell short by only two votes of winning the needed two-thirds majority in the Parliament. For more than a year, representatives from across the political spectrum developed amendments to clarify ethnic, individual, and minority rights, along with the mechanism to protect the famous "vital national interest" of constituent peoples. Amendments also included reforms to strengthen government, redefining (strengthening) powers of the prime minister and reducing duties for the Presidency. Paul Williams, of the Public International Law & Policy Group, also helped the process.

In the autumn of 2009, the EU and U.S. initiated another effort to kick-start the constitutional changes, the so-called "Butmir process" launched by then-U.S. Deputy Secretary of State James Steinberg and Spanish Foreign Minister Miguel Angel Moratinos, with the hope of

---

2. Council of Europe, http://www.coe.org.rs/eng/news_sr_eng/?conid=1545.

paving the way for the Office of the High Representative (OHR) in BiH to be closed and an EU office to take over the leading role on behalf of the international community initiating the SAA process to set the country finally towards its EU path.

Unlike the April Package process that was thoroughly prepared and carefully crafted, the Butmir Process was exactly the opposite. It was ill-prepared, exposing divisions within the international community and, at the end, it created a depressive political mood and sense of desperation.

Realizing the Federation's troubling political landscape could continuously produce political crises and thus destabilize the country, the U.S. Embassy in Sarajevo initiated and coordinated locally owned debates, mobilizing grassroots organizations, students, academics, and civil society organizations throughout the Federation to draft proposals for constitutional reform in order to create a more functional and economically sustainable and less bureaucratic entity. From this effort, an expert group was formed that produced around 180 recommendations, among them: to delete the "Others" from the Constitution and instead state alongside the three constituent peoples there should be a reference to "those who do not declare themselves members of constituent peoples or members of national minorities"; to scrap the entity presidency and strengthen the position of the Speaker of the Parliament and that of the Prime Minister; to cut number of lawmakers in the assembly. Reduction of the number of the cantons or their total abolition was discussed. On June 24th 2013, the Federation Parliament accepted the expert group's proposal for constitution change as the basis for further work, yet to the present day no serious political effort and result-striving debate on this crucial issue has taken place in the Federal Parliament.

EU Inconsistency

In 2003, the European Commission conducted a so-called feasibility study for the SAA, outlining 16 priority areas that needed progress before the SAA would commence. In 2005 the OHR mandated conditionality for BiH to implement police reform if it were allowed to start SAA negotiations with the EU. No other countries of the former Yugoslavia received such a condition from the EU. Also, there were no EU standards as to how to organize the police force.[3] After three years

---

3. http://www.crisisgroup.org/en/regions/europe/balkans/bosnia-herzegovina/164-bosnias-stalled-police-reform-no-progress-no-eu.aspx.

of endless negotiations, in 2008 police reform was pushed aside after the OHR accepted cosmetic changes.

The SAA was initiated on December 4th 2007, and was signed on June 16th 2008 but 32 months passed before it was ratified by all EU member states. (France ratified it last, in February 2011.) The SAA had to be suspended again before it could enter into full force;in 2009, BiH was found to be in violation of the European Convention on Human Rights in the famous Sejdic-Finci lawsuit.

For a full four years, political leaders discussed but could not find any solution to the European Court ruling; this continues to the very present day. The EU's inconsistency was once again visible in the European Commission enlargement strategy published on October 14th 2009 where it stated that the EU would not consider BiH's application for EU membership until the OHR is closed, only to soften that prerequisite at the EU General Affairs Council meeting in December 2009 stating: "The EU will not be position to consider an application for membership until the OHR transition to a reinforced EU presence is decided."

BiH made some positive steps towards EU candidacy status, namely by adopting a census law and reaching a political agreement on immovable defense property. With mixed signals from Brussels on ways to move forward and a lack of implementation of Sejdic-Finci by local politicians, a breakthrough never happened, even after the EU General Affairs Council concluded "satisfactory implementation of the Interim Agreement, as a whole."

Discontent for lack of any progress and economic stagnation produced by the entrenched political elite in BiH culminated in violent demonstrations in February 2014, with attacks on government buildings. People demanded jobs and progress. Realizing the political conditionality will not unblock the stalemate, in late 2014, a British-German initiative came to life, later to be endorsed by the entire international community. It focuses on socio-economic reforms in BiH.[4]

On March 16th 2015, foreign ministers from the 28 EU member states agreed that the SAA between BiH and the EU should enter into force. Some critics argue that the EU has yet again been inconsistent by pushing aside addressing the European Court demand for implementa-

---

4. http://www.balkaninsight.com/en/article/uk-germany-propose-bosnia-s-renewed-eu-perspective.

tion of Sejdic-Finci ruling, but after six years of inaction this may well be a positive strategic and concrete breakthrough.

Reform Agenda for 2015—2018

The Council of Ministers of BiH, government of the Federation of BiH, government of Republika Srpska, and the governments of all ten cantons in the Federation of BiH and Brcko District have jointly declared and recognized the urgent need to initiate economic recovery processes and modernization of the economy to strengthen sustainable, efficient, socially just and stable economic growth. Governments also recognized the urgent need to create new jobs, to increase and reorganize (better distribute) welfare benefits, and to create a sustainable and just social environment. Officials also acknowledged awareness that these reforms are crucial for BiH to receive EU candidacy status. Priorities foreseen in this reform agenda were already discussed with international financial institutions, and they should serve as the foundation for negotiations for individual programs for financial and technical assistance from the international financial institutions and the EU, as well as other partners and donors that would possibly be willing to support the reform effort.

The reform agenda is closely tied with new EU goals for the Western Balkans' economic development and is in accordance with the EU program for economic reforms intended to establish macroeconomic stability and encourage growth and competitiveness. The set of mid-term priorities includes fiscal consolidation to gradually reduce the budget deficit and reduce public debt. BiH has committed to a three years fiscal consolidation program and will sign arrangements with the International Monetary Fund, The World Bank, and the European Commission to secure financial support. In order for fiscal reform to succeed, BiH will have to carry out structural reforms: reform in the public administration sector and in policies for public sector job recruitment; improvements to the business climate and competitiveness; restructuring publicly-owned companies; reform in the welfare sector; reform in the health sector; and reform in the rule of law. Fiscal consolidation will be implemented by increasing the tax income and tax base expansion with reduction of gray economy and various tax reliefs along with the improvement of the tax authority performance efficiency. Tax increases will be considered if these measures fail to produce results by the end of 2015.

Officials in BiH also recognized the need to significantly reduce government administration and government spending and improve efficiency. It is necessary to implement the reduction of burden on labor by reducing contributions for health insurance, but it is also necessary to provide additional revenue and budget funds to cover the losses that will be incurred due to the reduction in the contribution rate. It will be necessary to determine the total wage bill and all current expenditures at all levels of government, which cannot be increased regardless of the growth in tax revenues. Measures to improve tax collection will be actively implemented. This will include efforts to share information between the four tax administrations and acceptance of access audits and inspections based on risk, all in accordance with the constitutional system and the responsibilities of each of the tax agency in the framework of the concluded Memorandum of Cooperation, as well as increasing efforts to collect unpaid tax debts. E-services for VAT and income tax will be introduced.

Governments of the entities, cantons and Brcko District will seek financial and technical assistance from the World Bank to implement the reform of the health sector. Reform implies resolution of debts of the health sector, the introduction of the treasury system and the definition of new models and sources of funding, with the precise standardization of the network of health care institutions. The World Bank will look through the DPL program to provide technical and financial support for the reorganization of the health sector. Entity and cantonal governments and Brcko District will use these means for the settlement of arrears in the health sector (in particular the contribution) by the end of 2015. In parallel, the authorities in BiH will support an increase in excise taxes on tobacco and alcohol, which will be the direct revenues of the Fund for Health Insurance and health insurance funds in the Federation and the cantons and the Brcko District by the end of 2015.

Further growth and prosperity must be based on attracting investment. There is a need to improve competitiveness by eliminating the well-known and documented obstacle to investments. In addition, there is a need to unify the ground for investment by removing hidden subsidies and other forms of assistance to many large enterprises and improving bankruptcy procedures and extension activities to address the problems with some of the non-viable companies. In addition, there are inconsistencies and complexity of the regulatory framework and tax systems, which is the main problem for potential investors in the economy, accompanied by high administrative barriers.

Business environment reforms will include: FBiH, the cantons, and Brcko District passing new laws on corporations and foreign direct investment including simplification and automation of business registration; speeding up the procedures for obtaining building permits and electricity connections; exports' continued inspections reforms and the strengthening of national quality control, harmonized according to EU requirements; and examination of the feasibility of implementing fiscally sustainable public-private partnerships and achieving greater private sector participation in infrastructure development. All levels of government will prepare and publish a comprehensive list of para-fiscal levies in order to ensure their transparency and reduction in accordance with the division of responsibilities.

Officials in BiH also recognized the need for better laws and practices for the protection of investors, including improvement in corporate governance, strengthened risk management practices in order to improve access to finance (especially for new companies), better protection of minority shareholders and a more efficient framework for insolvency by changing the bankruptcy law that would introduce new pre-bankruptcy proceedings, with the objective of financial restructuring of the debtor to avoid bankruptcy and preserve jobs but also unable continued performance of the core business of the company. Both entities, cantons, and Brcko District will revise their bankruptcy legislation in order to shorten the bankruptcy proceedings. FBiH will be introducing Commercial Courts as well.

Public enterprises will be divided into viable (with minor or major needs for restructuring) and unviable lists, with the envisaged publication of a list of such companies. These lists will form the basis for a comprehensive program of restructuring and privatization program or liquidation in the medium term. Government entities, cantons, and Brcko District will seek financial and technical assistance from the World Bank to prepare and to implement public enterprise restructuring program. Special attention will be given to the restructuring of the railways (in both entities), and coal (in the Federation), which implies reorganization. The drafting preliminary plans in order to prepare BiH Telecom for partial privatization in FBiH.

To improve trade, governments will ensure the implementation of the new law on customs policy to simplify customs processing and reduce administrative requirements.

Social protection systems will be reformed (in consultation with the World Bank and the IMF), including improved targeting of social protection that is not financed by contributions. Reform will also establish centralized databases of all social benefits users in the FBiH and the cantons. Reform efforts will aim to encourage members to be active participants in the economy, and with the protection and enhancement of social assistance for those who need it most. The Federation and the cantonal assurance systems must be placed on a solid financial footing as follows: freezing the cost of privileged pensions and reducing the option of early retirement for risk occupations, and the introduction of reasonable penalties for early retirement and bonuses for later retirement, in order to prolong the effective retirement age and introduction of sustainable indexing income. The audit work of verifying the eligibility of existing customers will be accelerated throughout the Federation and the cantons to strengthen the legal framework for improving the audit process. Reforms will accelerate the implementation of pension reforms under the new law on pensions in FBiH.

FBiH and the cantons will seek World Bank assistance in resolving the issue of unpaid obligations to the social fund from employment. In RS, the government will examine the need to reform the pension system parameters. Both entities, cantons, and the Brcko District will vigorously work on drafting the scheme for voluntary retirement. FBiH and the cantons will work to introduce necessary legislation, while RS will continue with activities on the establishment of the first voluntary pension fund.

A judicial system reform action plan for 2014–2018 will be adopted, to establish effective prevention of corruption and conflicts of interest in the judiciary; increase professionalism and integrity by stipulating objective criteria for the appointment of judicial functions and the adoption of measures for the integrity of the entire judicial system in BiH; strengthen the disciplinary accountability of judicial functions by adopting new rules of disciplinary proceedings and the introduction of new disciplinary measures. Courts will have to make decisions within a reasonable time and to consider the possibility that the municipal cases are resolved out of court. Procedure for the sale of seized property and enhance the role of judicial executors in order to reduce the burden on the courts in enforcement proceedings must be improved. Rule of law institutions will adhere to the highest standards of integrity and adequate measures will be in place at all levels of government to ensure preventing corruption and sanctions effectively applied. The fight against serious crime and corruption, in addition to effective investigation, prosecution and conviction will also be based on more solid legal and institutional framework governing the seizure of property, money laundering, and returns at all levels of government. In addition to the strategies adopted to combat terrorism in BiH, accompanying action plans will be completed with operational agreement with Europol in order to ensure a two-way flow of confidential information about crime between BiH and the Member States. Improvement of the flow of information between police and prosecutors can be achieved by increasing the efficiency of data exchange system, and adoption of the new strategy of integrated border management ensuring better cooperation between all related agencies and across its borders with harmonization of legislation on civilian possession of weapons.

All levels of government will draw up new laws on civil servants and employees, with the help of the World Bank and SIGMA, that would facilitate the reform of public administration and introduce greater flexibility of working arrangements. These laws will be adopted soon after the adoption of new labor laws in the entities, cantons and Brcko District. Candidates for employment in the civil service will be assessed on the basis of pre-determined eligibility criteria and the results of tests of competence and administrative bodies to ensure the employment of the best ranked candidates

The Council of Ministers of BiH, entity and cantonal governments and Brcko District will impose restrictions on employment in public administration until revised personnel systems are adopted and implemented. The total wage bill in the public sector will be frozen until the adoption of the revised wage setting system, based on values.

Publication of decisions on appeals in public procurement procedures (as a legal obligation) will be of central importance to ensure transparency in procurement procedures, decision-making on complaints and ensured public access to the decisions of the procurement review body. It will be given full support for the successful implementation of activities related to the census of population, households and apartments, with full respect for the provisions of the list, by-laws and European statistical standards in census activities.

Conclusion

After the last European Parliament elections held in May 2014, Brussels pushed back on further EU enlargement. Greece's economic crisis, challenges of undocumented immigration in the Mediterranean, and the crises in Ukraine are but a few reasons for it. The EU also recognized some recently accepted member states were not entirely ready to be admitted to full membership and that they may cause further instability within the Union. It also became evident that it is difficult to export rules and norms, especially with such diverse cultures and religions throughout the European continent. Bosnia and Herzegovina must look forward and work hard to implement initiated reforms in order to bring the country to the EU's doorstep. The recently adopted new labor law in FBiH is an optimistic sign. The decision by the government of FBiH to privatize several public companies is another. To keep the current momentum, the EU and the U.S. should speak with a unified voice, seconded by civil society groups in BiH, to get everyone breathing for a change—something that is long past due for the citizens of BiH.

Part III

Challenges of Democracy
in the Neighborhood
of the European Union

Chapter Six

Rethinking the European Union's Neighborhood Policy

Michael Leigh

The European Union engaged in a year-long review, culminating in November 2015, of the European Neighborhood Policy (ENP), which it developed over the last decade with a view to strengthening stability and encouraging reform in sixteen countries in Eastern Europe, the Southern Caucasus, North Africa, and the Levant.[1] The review asked fundamental questions about whether the policy should be maintained at all and, if so, what adjustments should be made to it. In launching the review, the European Commission and the High Representative for Foreign Affairs and Security Policy, Federica Mogherini, implicitly acknowledged that the ENP had failed in its goal of building a ring of well governed states around the EU and that more effective policies were needed in future.

Many countries covered by the ENP are even more unstable today than they were a decade ago. The ENP was the proximate (though not the underlying) cause of the series of events beginning in November 2013 that led to the tense standoff with Russia over Ukraine. The ENP raised hopes in neighboring countries but failed to deliver expected benefits. It has brought the EU little or no increased influence in the areas covered by the policy while complicating efforts to achieve a new strategic balance in Europe.

Efforts under the ENP to export the EU's preferred model of society, in the absence of convincing incentives, have not worked. Cumbersome procedures bearing the Brussels hallmark have little meaning in coun-

---

1. European Commission, Communication from the Commission to the Council and the European Parliament, *Wider Europe—Neighbourhood: A New Framework for Relations with our Eastern and Southern Neighbours*, COM (2003) 104 final, Brussels, 11 March. European Commission, European External Action Service 2015. Joint Consultation Paper, *Towards a New European Neighbourhood Policy*, JOIN (2015) 6 final, Brussels, 3 April. Joint Communication to the European Parliament, the Council, the European Economic and Social Committee and the Committee of the Regions, *Review of the European Neighbourhood Policy* JOIN (2015) 50 final, Brussels, 18 November, 2015.

tries facing life-threatening challenges. In any event, the ENP's values-based approach has received scant support from the EU's own member states, which give priority to their own perceived national interests concerning security, trade, investment and access to resources, paying only lip service to common EU initiatives such as the ENP.

How, for example, can the European Commission expect to nudge Egypt toward more democratic practices when a member state sells it state-of-the-art military equipment without a hint of political conditionality? Will the Baku government listen to civil rights strictures from Brussels when the country plays an essential role in the EU's efforts to diversify energy resources away from Russia?

Despite increasing awareness of such shortcomings, the existing framework will be difficult to change significantly. The ENP represents a compromise among the twenty-eight member states. It balances the concerns of Italy, Spain and other southern Member States about North Africa and the Middle East with those of Poland, the Baltic States, the Nordic countries and other EU members in northern, Central and Eastern Europe about Russia. Both sets of Member States are engrossed in their particular geopolitical preoccupations.

This may be changing, somewhat, as a result of the influx of asylum seekers into the EU from its southern neighborhood and the efforts to achieve an EU-wide arrangement for accommodating them. This situation should oblige northern member states, the destination of choice for most asylum seekers, to give greater support to efforts to contain the explosion of violent extremism in North Africa and the Middle East. Failure to nurture stability and democracy, the avowed goal of the ENP, in these areas, before and after the Arab uprisings, created fertile ground for extremists and contributed to the refugee crisis as well as the spread of violent extremism.

The gravity of the situation should encourage Member States to go beyond bland references to "differentiation" and "mutual ownership" in the ENP review and to commit themselves to policies better adjusted to current realities. Most of these policies lie outside the existing ENP framework in areas like migration, security, energy, and infrastructure as well as poverty alleviation and humanitarian support. Such policies should be pursued vigorously on their own merits, without tying them to an unwieldy mechanism that has little meaning in the countries concerned.

Eastern Europe, North Africa and the Middle East are crucial to any effort by the EU to exercise real political influence beyond its own borders. Effective and joined up policies would tackle migration pressures and violent extremism at their source and help check the growing radicalization of young people within the EU itself. There will never be a common foreign and security policy, worthy of the name, unless the EU manages to act effectively in the part of the world where its potential influence is greatest.[2]

No Political or Geographical Logic

The single ENP framework for sixteen diverse national settings each facing their own existential challenges accentuates process rather than impact and effectiveness. In future there should not be a single framework covering the East and the South.[3] Instead policies should be devised for each country individually. The current geographical scope is both extensive and restrictive. It is arbitrary and follows no coherent policy or geographic logic. The countries included are not all terrestrial or maritime neighbors of the EU. Several pose challenges that are shared with countries outside the ENP, for example, Syria (ENP) and Iraq, Libya (ENP) and Mali, Azerbaijan (ENP) and Turkmenistan.

Policies need to be developed that address the concrete challenges for the EU posed by these countries without creating artificial divisions among them. Key migration issues related to Libya or Syria need to be treated in conjunction with policies for Eritrea, Iraq, Mali, Niger, Sudan, and other countries of origin. Energy policies toward Azerbaijan need to take into account decisions by other possible providers of gas to be transported through the Southern Corridor. The same ministers, officials, committees, working groups etc. that are concerned with Iraq should also address Syria. The ENP framework creates an unnecessary and unhelpful barrier between countries posing related challenges to the EU. These problems are too serious to be consigned to a few

---

2. The present chapter develops arguments put forward in Michael Leigh, *The European Neighbourhood Policy: A Suitable Case for Treatment*, in Sieglinde Gstöhl and Erwan Lannon, eds., *The Neighbours of the European Union's Neighbours: Diplomatic and Geopolitical Dimensions beyond the European Neighbourhood Policy*, (Ashgate, 2015) and Michael Leigh, *A New Strategy for Europe's Neighbourhood*, German Marshall Fund of the United States, September 2014

3. Those covered by the ENP are Algeria, Armenia, Azerbaijan, Belarus (suspended in practice), Egypt, Georgia, Israel, Jordan, Lebanon, Libya, Moldova, Morocco, the Palestinian Authority, Syria, Tunisia, Ukraine.

phrases in a report noting that 'the neighbors of the neighbors' also deserve attention.

Ineffective Policy Instruments

The ENP's main policy instruments, developed first under the 'Eastern partnership' and then extended, in principle at least, to North Africa and the Levant, are a new generation of Association Agreements (AAs), incorporating Deep and Comprehensive Free Trade Agreements (DCF-TAs).[4] DCFTAs have been concluded with Georgia, Moldova and Ukraine and are under negotiation with Morocco. Initial conversations have been held with Egypt and Jordan. Provisional application of the agreement with Ukraine was postponed until 1 January 2016 as part of efforts to find a peaceful solution to the Ukraine crisis.

In any event, such agreements are entirely inappropriate for most of the countries to which they are addressed. They are more ambitious than the 'Europe agreements,' which were concluded with the Czech Republic, Poland, Hungary and other countries in Central and Eastern Europe that were preparing for EU membership.[5] These countries had, of their own volition, undertaken fundamental reforms designed to bring about their 'return to Europe.' By contrast, the countries covered by the ENP have demonstrated no such determination and, despite the nominal eligibility of European countries for membership, lack a realistic prospect of one day joining the EU. Full scale regulatory convergence with the EU is not high on their priority list anyway, in light of more pressing preoccupations. An EU foreign minister told the author that there is no prospect that the countries concerned will fulfill the majority of obligations imposed by the DCFTAs within the foreseeable future.

Many of these countries are extremely poor (the GDPs per capita of Ukraine and Morocco, for example, are close to that of Bolivia, expressed in current US dollars) and they have fundamental develop-

---

4. European Commission, Communication from the Commission to the European Parliament and the Council, *Eastern Partnership*, COM (2008) 823/4, Brussels, 3 December; See, for example, European Commission 2013. *EU-Ukraine Deep and Comprehensive Free Trade Area*, April 2013

5. The Europe Agreements were association agreements between the EU and its member states and the Central and Eastern European countries that joined the EU in 2004/2007. They formed the legal framework for the accession process of these countries to the EU.

ment needs.[6] Some face grave solvability and liquidity problems. Several of these countries suffer from critical political and sectarian conflicts, state failure, dysfunctional democracy, authoritarian rule, corruption, clientalism, transnational terrorism, secessionist wars supported by outside powers, and other problems which cannot be addressed or mitigated within the AA-DCFTA framework.

Despite their asymmetric structure, DCFTAs offer few immediate trade benefits. Many products are still treated by the EU as sensitive. Regulatory convergence, especially regarding health and safety, is a precondition for exports of many products to the EU. North African countries would benefit from real market openings by the EU for the few (largely agricultural) products in which they have a comparative advantage. The economies of several neighboring countries are dominated by agricultural products, energy or raw materials. DCFTAs offer few advantages to such countries and are enormously demanding in terms of negotiation, ratification, and implementation.

These agreements were put forward without a clear vision of their ultimate goals or a detailed assessment of their wider impact. The decision of former Ukrainian President Viktor Yanukovych not to sign the AA-DCFTA with the EU was the proximate (not the ultimate) cause for the Maidan demonstrations in Kiev, the flight of Yanukovych to Russia, and subsequent devastating events. President Vladimir Putin has targeted the AA-DCFTAs as proof of nefarious Western policies to suborn former Soviet states and has obliged Armenia to back off from signing its agreement with the EU.

Under these circumstances, and given that similar agreements have been concluded with Moldova and Georgia and that preparations or negotiations have begun with Morocco, Egypt and Jordan, it will be awkward for the EU to change course. Yet change course it must. Otherwise the EU will be burdened for years ahead with unwieldy and ineffective agreements that are good for speeches and resounding Council of Ministers conclusions but little else.

The notion of an 'Association Agreement' is hard to abandon in midstream, especially under Russian pressure. But the scope of each agree-

---

6. All three countries had GDPs per capita of just over $3,000 in 2010-2014, expressed in current US dollars, though Morocco and Ukraine come in considerably higher and above Bolivia expressed in purchasing power parity, World Bank, http://data.worldbank.org/indicator/NY.GDP.PCAP.CD

ment should be highly differentiated country-by-country. There is no need to make these agreements comprehensive, covering virtually all aspects of the acquis. Approximation with the acquis—the main thrust of the AAs-DCFTAs—is very low on the list of challenges facing these countries. Regulatory convergence could be limited initially to requirements affecting products and services actually traded between the two sides. The EU should give up any aspiration to remake these countries in its own image.

Action Plans That Do Not Work

"Action Plans," containing priorities for each country stipulated by the EU, after consultations, figure prominently in the ENP.[7] They are loosely adapted from the earlier "Accession Partnerships" with countries preparing for EU membership.[8] They are entirely inappropriate for countries that are not on a path toward membership. They are sovereign states and the EU cannot impose reforms on them.

Over a decade, the governments of ENP countries have signed up to Action Plans that they had no intention or capacity to implement. Action Plans should now be dispensed with in favor of trade and assistance arrangements matching their real needs, capacities and intentions. Outside efforts to bring about change will not succeed unless rulers and citizens in these countries genuinely wish to embrace EU values and regulatory regimes. This problem is too fundamental to be glossed over by a mere change in terminology.

Pitfalls of Working with Civil Society

The EU has in the past sought to work with civil society, especially in countries where governments are disinclined to embrace Brussels initiatives. This may give encouragement to proponents of democratic change but needs to be undertaken with caution. It can be counter-productive for the EU to appear, inadvertently, to be associated with illegal activities, however much the laws in question fly in the face of values which west Europeans cherish. Nascent NGOs in partner countries

---

7. Actions Plans can be found at: http://eeas.europa.eu/enp/documents/action-plans/index_en.htm.

8. Associations Partnerships are explained at: http://ec.europa.eu/enlargement/policy/glossary/terms/accession-partnership_en.htm.

may be de-legitimized if their very existence depends on financial support from the EU. It may often be better for the EU to support unobtrusively European NGOs that cooperate with corresponding bodies in the countries concerned.

No *locus standi* for Intrusive Progress Reports

Until 2015, the EU produced detailed annual "progress" reports on countries covered by the "ENP", as it does on countries preparing for EU membership.[9] However such reports have no constraining effects on ENP countries; indeed, they may appear to them as interference in their internal affairs.

The time, effort and resources that go into these reports are disproportionate to any practical benefits which they may offer. Instead, the Commission and European External Action Service could, in the future, report on situations arising that have real political or economic significance for the member states. There is no need to be bound by a reporting calendar or by an annual 'package' that mimics regular reports on countries that are actually preparing for membership.

Assistance Should Focus on Urgent Needs

Economic, technical and financial cooperation with each country should relate to its specific needs and capacities as well as EU interests. There is little to be gained by seeking to cover all aspects of the acquis with each partner country. There is no need to be comprehensive in the approach to cooperation. Instead a very limited number of priority issues should jointly be identified with each government, if possible extending the consultation to stakeholders beyond the authorities themselves. Cooperation projects should then focus on those areas where concrete progress can be made in the short to medium term.

In practice each partner country has a limited number of urgent needs and priority areas, which should be the focus of attention. For example, Jordan and Lebanon have overwhelmingly urgent needs linked to the large number of refugees within their borders from Syria and Iraq. This poses demands that cannot be met locally on the education

---

9. The last such reports, published on 25 March 2015, can be found at: http://eeas.europa.eu/enp/documents/progress-reports/index_en.htm.

system, energy supply, and public finances. Libya, where no single authority is in control of the national territory, manifestly cannot cope with the influx of refugees and asylum seekers, or with criminal gangs trafficking them to Europe in perilous conditions. The Moroccan economy needs diversifying, the taxation system should be made more progressive, and employment creation schemes are required in certain parts of the country. Ukraine is facing critical solvability and liquidity problems and a significant part of its economic base has been destroyed by violent Russian-sponsored intervention.

Against this background, a pragmatic approach is needed to choosing priorities and developing tools for cooperation. Macro-economic stability, poverty alleviation, institution building, the fight against corruption, strengthening the efficiency and independence of the judicial system and the enforceability of contracts should be among the top priorities.

For each country a limited number of priorities should be established commensurate with (a) its most pressing needs, (b) the resources that the EU is able to mobilize to address the issues concerned and (c) the member states' willingness to lend their full support to EU efforts through bilateral initiatives.

A Tangle of Overlapping Policies

The EU has developed many overlapping policy frameworks which apply, at least in principle, to countries neighboring the EU: Barcelona Declaration, Euro-Mediterranean Partnership, European Neighborhood Policy, Union for the Mediterranean, Partnership for Democracy and Shared Prosperity, Eastern Partnership, Black Sea Synergy, European Security Strategy, Common Foreign and Security Policy, Common Security and Defense Policy, etc. This multiplicity of initiatives creates confusion and operational difficulties. It is perplexing for the United States, Canada, Norway and other countries seeking to work together with the EU.

In June 2015, the EU's highest body, the European Council, asked the High Representative to produce a new "Global Strategy for Foreign and Security Policy" by summer 2016.[10] Yet the European Neighbor-

---

10. European External Action Service, *Global Strategy to steer EU external action in an increasingly connected, contested and complex world*, 30 March 2015. http://eeas.europa.eu/top_stories/2015/150627_eu_global_strategy_en.htm.

hood Policy review, covering the area of the world where the EU could most expect to exercise influence, appeared earlier in November 2015, no doubt through an accident of timing. To be sure, the new take on the EU's security strategy will subsume the results of the ENP review. But an observer from outside the Brussels beltway might well conclude that there is a problem of coordination, at the very least, and that the EU devotes far too much time to paper strategies while burning issues require urgent attention. The EU would do better to eschew grand strategies in favor of well thought-out initiatives with real impact and effectiveness before it is too late.

EU Advocacy of Multilateral Cooperation

The EU often considers that it has a particular vocation to promote multilateral cooperation, for example through regional trade agreements. However the countries concerned trade relatively little with each other and generally do not consider that they have much to gain from such cooperation in terms of the transfer of technology, management experience or capital. Multilateral cooperation, in its different forms, should be approached in a pragmatic case-by-case manner. Its success depends on genuine commitment by the countries concerned to cooperate. No effort should be made to impose multilateral cooperation from outside or to make this a condition for providing assistance or opening markets.

EU Efforts to Promote Religious Freedom

EU efforts to promote religious freedom and to protect religious minorities form part of its policies toward neighboring countries and beyond.[11] Guidelines on "the promotion and protection of freedom of religion or belief" were adopted by the Council in June 2013.[12] The Council's conclusions and guidelines established a mechanism for prodding reluctant countries toward guaranteeing religious freedom and for supporting persecuted minorities. They also recognize the importance of freedom *from* religion, i.e. the right not to hold a religious brief.

---

11. This section draws on Michael Leigh, *Religious Freedom in the European Union and its Southern Neighbourhood*, in *Faith, Freedom and Foreign Policy: Challenges for the Transatlantic Community*, Transatlantic Academy, Washington DC, April 2015

12. Adopted by the Foreign Affairs Council meeting, Luxembourg (June 24, 2013)

The guidelines champion the universal character of the freedom of religion, based on the relevant international conventions. They call for the withdrawal of financial assistance and other benefits from a country if religious freedom is violated. Full implementation of these guidelines requires political will, something urged by the Foreign Affairs Committee of the European Parliament in its 2014 Annual Report on Human Rights.[13]

Until now, the EU's promotion of religious freedom has been largely declaratory. Its effectiveness will be judged by the degree to which it guides action by EU institutions and member states and by its impact in the countries directly concerned. The full commitment of member states is particularly important. However, member states are reluctant to withhold financial assistance from strategically important countries that interfere with religious freedom.

Efforts by EU institutions to promote fundamental rights and freedoms, including the freedom of religion, lose credibility if member states ignore agreed conditionality and pursue business as usual, impelled by security or commercial considerations. At the same time, the failure of European countries to take resolute action when religious and ethnic minorities in their neighborhood are subjected to persecution on an unprecedented scale, calls into question the value of the EU's ponderous procedural approach to the problem.

The willingness of some EU countries to accept in particular Christian asylum seekers from war-torn countries further blurs the EU's proclaimed commitment to universal values. The confusion of the EU's message is exacerbated by its relative inaction following the displacement of one and half million eastern Christians in Syria and Iraq and the singling out of Christians for execution by terrorist groups in Libya and Kenya in 2015.

A fundamental re-think of the EU's approach to the promotion of religious freedom and the protection of religious minorities should be included in the current policy reviews, which are underway.

---

13. European Parliament Committee of Foreign Affairs, "Draft Report on the Annual Report on Human Rights and Democracy in the World 2013, and the European Union's Policy on the Matter," (November 28, 2014) 2014/2216 (INI).

European Values Face Competition

Societies in countries covered by the ENP do not necessarily share or give priority to 'European values.' Yet the ENP was founded on the principle of commitment to shared values. In 2008, for example, the responsible member of the European Commission told a meeting in the European Parliament that the ENP "is based on a privileged relationship through which we draw our partners closer and closer, building upon common commitments and shared values."[14] In practice, however, values founded on ethno-nationalism, religion, including intolerant, sectarian forms of religion, or social conservatism, and actively promoted by outside powers, are today prevalent in many of these societies.

Russia, China, Iran, the Gulf States and Turkey, whose agendas differ significantly from the EU's, are active influences in the EU's neighborhood. In several cases, they offer far greater finance than the EU, in the form of grants or loans, often linked to specific investment projects. Such support usually comes without western-style political conditionality. Strings may be attached but they are linked to goals that have little to do with the values promoted by the EU. In reviewing the ENP, member states need to take into account the fact that the EU is now only one of several outside powers competing for influence in adjoining countries. Governments and companies in the member states have long since adapted to this new reality. It is time for the Brussels institutions to catch up with their members.

More for More?

This maxim has been invoked many times as expressing the EU's approach to political relations and especially to financial assistance.[15] It implies that the more a country is ready to implement commitments to goals based on European values, the more financial support the EU will

---

14. Benita Ferrero-Waldner, European Commissioner for External Relations and European Neighborhood Policy, http://europa.eu/rapid/press-release_SPEECH-08-306_en.htm?locale=en

15. For example the "Partnership for Democracy and Shared Prosperity", introduced in March 2011 after the first Arab uprisings, described the initiative as "an incentive-based approach based on more differentiation ("more for more"): those that go further and faster with reforms will be able to count on greater support from the EU." Brussels, 8.3.2011 COM (2011) 200 final Joint Communication to the European Council, the European Parliament, The Council, The European Economic and Social Committee and the Committee of the Regions, "A Partnership for Democracy and Shared Prosperity with the southern Mediterranean."

be ready to offer. However this is not an effective operational strategy for a number of reasons:

    a. "Closer integration" with the EU based on "shared values" is not a viable option for most of the countries concerned.

    b. The amounts of grant assistance available from the EU pale into insignificance compared with assistance from the Gulf States to countries covered by "ENP South."

    c. Russia, China, Turkey, Iran, and the Gulf States do not impose political conditionality in the financial support that they provide. As noted above, any strings they attach are linked to an entirely different agenda from the EU's.

    d. Incremental increases in the relatively small amounts of assistance provided by the EU in response to the implementation of specific reforms do not offer a sufficient incentive to most "ENP countries."

    e. Member States do not practice "more for more" in their bilateral relations with these countries.

    f. The EU and its Member States often provide "more for less" in engaging with these countries for reasons related to security, trade, or access to energy.

Instead of patchily enforced political conditionality, the EU could undertake dialogues with neighboring countries on democracy, human rights, and rule of law issues, as it does with certain other international trade partners. It must expect give and take in such dialogues, with the light sometimes shined on shortcomings in the EU itself. However, experience suggests that this approach is more effective than implausible carrot and stick methodologies.

In a broader sense, the EU can indeed expect to develop closer links with countries with which it has more in common, be this shared values, security and commercial interests or traditional ties. But 'more for more' is not a sound guide for European policy-makers. Despite its catchy appeal, it should be given up in favor of balanced and realistic policies toward each country in the EU's vicinity.

A Membership Perspective for Neighboring Countries?

Political leaders in some EU member states, especially Poland and the Baltic countries, often advocate an EU 'accession perspective' for Ukraine, Georgia and other eastern neighborhood countries. This is intended as encouragement for reforms and for those who seek a more decisive break with Russia. Yet it is misleading to encourage these countries to pursue internal reforms in the expectation that this will earn them a place in the queue to become EU members. In reality, there is unlikely to be a consensus among the 28 member states to offer such a perspective for the foreseeable future. Even existing candidates for membership, like Turkey, Serbia or Albania, will not join the EU during the present decade, if at all.

Armenia, Belarus, Georgia, Moldova and Ukraine, as European states, are generally considered eligible in principle for EU membership under Article 49 of the Treaty on European Union. However, given their very limited progress made in meeting the criteria for membership as well as the current geopolitical, economic and financial conjuncture in Europe, the issue of eventual membership does not arise at present. It is confusing to suggest to these countries that they might be offered such a perspective in the future and that they should work toward it, considering the manifest lack of consensus among EU member states to move in this direction.

If Not Now, When?

The ENP review demonstrates that the current leadership in Brussels has understood the need for change in the EU's approach to its neighborhood and is seeking suggestions from diverse stakeholders as to the future direction of policy. This is a welcome development even if overshadowed by the parallel lengthy review of the EU's foreign and security strategy that is scheduled for summer 2016.

There are two principal risks associated with this exercise. The first is that the ENP review will not be pushed far enough. More of the same, with genuflections to 'differentiation' and 'mutual ownership,' will not help to address urgent problems including poverty, violent extremism, and migration, which pose major challenges *now*. The second is that it will remain a paper exercise. Yet the EU and its member states cannot afford institutional inertia when facing challenges of the magnitude of those unleashed by the Arab uprisings and by failed or partial transitions to the East. The dangers involved could grow considerably in the years ahead and increasingly affect the EU itself. The EU must not fiddle while Rome burns.

The ENP review should reconcile the traditional interest-based policies pursued by member states and the values-based approach that they have delegated to EU institutions. This dual approach may be defended as a kind of 'good cop, bad cop' strategy, but a decade's experience suggests that it reduces the EU's overall credibility and just does not work. Trade, investment, and security, including energy security, need to be moved to the forefront of the ENP, or rather its successor policies. The promotion of democracy, the rule of law and human rights need to be included more visibly in bilateral national policies if, indeed, the member states consider these important in relations with neighboring countries. A more joined-up approach is essential in future.

Above all, though, the EU and its member states will need to act quickly and pragmatically in a variety of fields beyond the ENP if grave problems to the East and the South are not to threaten security and stability in Europe itself. The diverse initiatives required do not fit into pre-conceived administrative categories that correspond with departmental responsibilities in Brussels. Instead of clinging to familiar but ineffective policy frameworks, the Commission and the European External Action Service should set out clearly concrete priorities for the months and years ahead. They should use their influence to coordinate the necessary response by the Brussels institutions and the member states, accepting that the member states will continue to reserve major foreign policy and security decisions to themselves.

The 2015-2016 policy reviews provide an opportunity to move away from the false comfort of high sounding strategies toward pragmatic initiatives with greater impact and effectiveness. The member states should seize this opportunity without waiting to be further overwhelmed by events.

Chapter Seven

Challenges of Democracy in the Caucasus

Alexander Sokolowski

In assessing the challenges and potential pathways for democracy building in the South Caucasus, we confront great and increasing variation across Armenia, Azerbaijan and Georgia. While *geography* often prompts scholars and analysts to consider these three countries together, *topography* (namely, the mountains that separate them) has rendered them distinct in a number of ways. Each country possesses its own rich ethnic, linguistic, historical, religious, and cultural traditions. And the post-Soviet development of their respective political systems is no exception—diverging in three distinct paths, particularly over the last decade. For considering post-Soviet democratization in the South Caucasus, mountains matter. While seven decades of Soviet rule have instilled certain commonalities in the political systems of these three countries, the collapse of the Soviet Union has allowed for the potential re-emergence of separate political trajectories.

Given these distinct and divergent pathways, those seeking to encourage democratization in these three countries should be ready to seek and take advantage of *different kinds of openings for forward movement where they exist and emerge* in these three distinct contexts.

Against the backdrop of varying contexts, however, there remains one central and common challenge that all three countries must address if they are to become consolidated democracies: building and sustaining institutions, processes, and public attitudes that reliably check executive authority. Across most of post-Soviet Eurasia, the emergence of predominant networks of political and economic elites has meant that political power has consistently become consolidated in executive branches and ruling parties.[1]

The thoughts presented here are those of the author and not necessarily those of USAID or of the U.S. Government.

1. Henry Hale, *Patronal Politics: Eurasian Regime Dynamics in Comparative Perspective*, (New York: Cambridge University Press, 2015).

Common Background Challenges for Democracy Building in the South Caucasus

Before considering the varying challenges and opportunities for democratization—and thus further European integration—in each country, it is also important to briefly consider a number of common background challenges that these three countries face.

Very Limited Experience with Democratic Institutions before Independence in 1991

Each of the three countries has had some limited experience with democracy during the post-World War I/pre-Soviet period with parliamentary republics that existed from 1918 to 1920 (Armenia and Azerbaijan) and 1918 to 1921 (Georgia). These bright spots just under a century ago are not insignificant, in that they provide a historical point of reference, to which democratizers in each country can point and try to learn from. Yet, these brief periods are clearly exceptions to much longer periods of authoritarian or totalitarian forms of government in the Caucasus. This very limited democratic tradition should prepare us for a potentially longer road towards democratic consolidation for the Caucasus region overall. A single 'good' election or even 'breakthrough' election will not be enough to transform the complex sets of institutions, practices, procedures, behaviors, and attitudes that support and sustain consolidated democracies.[2] Instead, that will require changes in patterns of behavior by a wide range of stakeholders over an extended period of time.

Disputes over Boundaries and over who is a Member of the Political Community

Dankwart Rustow's well-known 1970 article on 'transitions to democracy' posits that the overall agreement on the limits political community is important for the formation of democracy.[3] Of course, all three Caucasus countries unfortunately have had serious territorial disputes, including most notably Nagorno-Karabagh, Abkhazia, and South Ossetia. And while Armenia and Azerbaijan are highly ethnically

---

2. Juan Linz and Alfred Stepan, *Problems of Democratic Transition and Consolidation* (Baltimore: Johns Hopkins University Press, 1996).

3. Dankwart Rustow, "Transitions to Democracy: Towards a Dynamic Model," *Comparative Politics*, vol. 2, April 1970, pp. 337-363.

homogenous, Georgia also has significant ethnic minorities, most notably Armenians and Azeris concentrated in Samske-Javakheti and Kvemo-Kartli respectively. Although these disputes and issues related to ethnic minorities would not seem to, in and of themselves, be insurmountable challenges for democratic development, they certainly provide challenges in that they push some to focus on security and territorial claims, rather than on the character of internal governance.

Wars and Perceived Threats from Neighbors

These kinds of security threats make it easier for some to make the specious argument that democratization is a luxury that can come later—once the imminent existential threat or pressure is gone. More broadly, each of the three Caucasus countries must deal with the challenge of being small states, bordering much larger, more powerful and more populous countries. Given that there is also a history of conflict and domination with countries such as Russia, Iran, and Turkey, this has tended to create a sense of distrust of these neighbors. This factor could also contribute to a prioritization of short-term security over democratic reform.

Relatively Small Middle Classes

Seymour Martin Lipset[4] and Jurgen Habermas[5] both made well-known arguments on the importance of a certain level of socio-economic development for the development of democracy. The combination of leisure time, social interaction, education, and financial resources among a certain segment of the population all contribute to a demand for democracy. Yet all three countries still have relatively small middle classes and under-developed economies. If we accept the logic of these arguments, this should also make us potentially more cautious about the near-term potential for consolidated democracy in these countries until their economies and societies develop further.

---

4. Seymour Martin Lipset, "Some Social Requisites of Democracy: Economic Development and Political Legitimacy," *American Political Science Review*, vol. 53, No. 1 (March 1959), pp. 69-105.

5. Jurgen Habermas, *The Structural Transformation of the Public Sphere* (Cambridge, MA: MIT Press, 1989).

Wide Disparities between the Center and the Periphery within *these Countries*

Communities outside capitals and major cities are often the ones where it is most difficult for democratic institutions and processes to take root and thrive. Under-developed local economies make it less likely that the active political party structures, civic organizations, business associations, and independent media outlets, which are so important for resilient political systems, will emerge and be sustained. If most of Georgia, Armenia and Azerbaijan looked like Tbilisi, Yerevan, and Baku, the background conditions for democratic strengthening would be considerably more promising. However, the combination of the collapsed Soviet-era industries and underdeveloped agriculturally-based economies has left the much of the peripheries of these countries far less economically prosperous than the centers. When outlying areas are more financially dependent on the 'center,' this increases the likelihood that patronage networks and clientelism will dominate regional and local politics.

Relatively Low Levels of Political Trust

In all three countries, there is little trust that political disagreements between those in power and those in the opposition will not escalate into more existential threats. Even if ideological or policy differences may appear modest, political polarization is high. There is little trust that political competition will not quickly devolve into struggle for political survival and/or for freedom from potential criminal charges. Indeed, in the post-Soviet South Caucasus, political leaders have often faced criminal charges—both opposition leaders and former government officials. In other cases, there is outright rejection of the legitimacy or legality of political adversaries. With the stakes so high in political competition, this makes political actors less willing to accept the institutionalized uncertainty of outcomes that characterizes truly democratic systems.[6]

Lack of Trust in Political Institutions

According to data from the Caucasus Barometer survey from 2014, in none of the three countries does public support for political parties run above 14 percent. For NGOs, the figure does not surpass 24 per-

---

6. Adam Przeworsky, *Democracy and the Market* (New York: Cambridge University Press, 1991) pp. 12-13.

cent. Public trust in the courts did not exceed one-third of those surveyed.[7] So citizens of the Caucasus do not seem to trust in many key democratic institutions. While this result is not surprising, given the weakness of those institutions, such low levels of public trust may indicate apathy and cynicism that may make democratic reform more difficult. This lack of trust in political institutions among citizens in turn also leads to comparatively high levels of corruption, which also undermines democratic development. Of the three Caucasus countries, only Georgia scores in the moderate range for corruption, according to Transparency International's Corruption Perceptions Index, with Armenia and Azerbaijan receiving much lower scores.[8]

Current Situational Challenges for Democracy Building in the South Caucasus

In addition to the 'background' conditions mentioned above, which complicate the prospects for democratization in the Caucasus, a set of more immediate, 'situational' and external factors pose new challenges for the adoption of democratic institutions, processes, and values in the region. That is, internal political development has also been affected by current external influences and the choice between West and East. More specifically, the choice between greater economic, political and security integration with Europe, with Russia, or a more independent path all have profound consequences for the pace and strength of democratization.

Fading Attractiveness of Western Norms

Certain democratic norms, standards, and rules set by Euro-Atlantic institutions and countries have lost some of their luster and can seem to be in tension with traditional values. In the broad sense, the European Union has had a 'normative draw' over the countries of the former Soviet Union. As Manners has argued, the EU's normative power has been based on norms that are centered around peace, democracy, liberty, rule of law, and human rights.[9] The attractiveness of democracy,

---

7. *2013 Caucasus Barometer*, July 7, 2014, Caucasus Research Resource Centers (CRRC).

8. Transparency International, *Corruption Perceptions Index 2014*. For 2014, Armenia and Azerbaijan scores (out of a possible 100) were 37 and 29, respectively. Georgia received a score of 52 out of 100. http://www.transparency.org/cpi2014/results.

9. Ian Manners, "Normative Power Europe: A Contradiction in Terms?" *Journal of Common Market Studies*, vol.40, no 2 (2002) pp. 235-58, p. 242.

rule of law and human rights was initially quite strong across the former Soviet Union in the early 1990s, but it has lessened to varying degrees across the region since that time, as democracy has been sometimes associated with the chaos of the 1990s. Still, all three Caucasus countries continue to speak in favor of democracy as their model for their further political development. Recently, all three Caucasus countries signed onto the Riga Declaration of May 2015, in which all Eastern Partnership (EaP) countries reaffirmed their commitment to "strengthen democracy, rule of law, human rights, and fundamental freedoms..."[10] As the polities of Caucasus have confronted the real challenges that adopting these democratic processes, institutions, and norms entail, and the prospect of accession into European institutions has seemed more distant, the normative power of the EU has been diminished to varying degrees. Its power has remained strongest in Georgia, which has been the most steadfast in its European aspirations and weakest in Azerbaijan, which has been increasingly adopting an independent path.

In addition, norms of broad *inclusion*, such as broader inclusion for ethnic minorities and women may strike some citizens of these countries as a turning away from long-held traditions or cultural or religious views. Meeting European Union standards, even when the people of a country want to enjoy the levels of prosperity they associate with the EU, can be cast as an abandonment of 'traditional national values.' This can make democracy seem 'externally imposed.' Although standards for full inclusion have moved relatively rapidly in Europe since the 1960s, they appear not to have evolved quite as rapidly in the former Soviet countries, including the Caucasus. For example, in Georgia and Armenia, the occasional tensions between traditional/national and 'European' values have emerged on issues raised by the national churches in each country. Given the high level of trust citizens in these countries have put in their respective religious institutions,[11] this difference in views on human rights issues between the church and international institutions may complicate or slow their broad acceptance.

---

10. Eastern Partnership, "Joint Declaration of the Eastern Partnership Summit" (Riga, 21-22 May 2015), p. 1. http://www.consilium.europa.eu/en/meetings/international-summit/2015/05/21-22/.

11. In all three Caucasus countries, trust in religious institutions has been very high. According to the 2013 Caucasus Barometer, trust in religious institutions was ranked the higher than any other in Armenia and Georgia (with 76% and 82% respectively fully or somewhat trusting. In Azerbaijan, it ranked third behind the president and the army (with 57% fully or somewhat trusting.) *2013 Caucasus Barometer*, July 7, 2014, Caucasus Research Resource Centers (CRRC).

Uncertainty about Belonging to the Euro-Atlantic Community

A sense of uncertainty about when and whether they will be fully welcomed into the Euro-Atlantic community is another challenge of democracy in the region. All three countries have expressed, at one time or another, frustration at not being more welcomed by Western countries into Euro-Atlantic institutions. Georgia has been the most forward-leaning in pushing for rapid inclusion into NATO and the European Union, signing an Association Agreement with the EU in June 2014. It still remains unclear when Georgia will ultimately be asked to join the EU and when it will join NATO.

Armenia and Azerbaijan have also both sought clearer and more encouraging signals of partnership and integration with the West. Even as Armenia has decided to sign on to the Eurasian Economic Union, it has sought to maintain a dialogue and closer ties with the EU and the US.[12] While Azerbaijan appears to have chosen a more independent path for its foreign policy,[13] it has for several years sought a closer more strategic relationship with the US and Europe. Clear assurances and timelines generally have not been forthcoming. While this is due to the fact that these three countries—especially Azerbaijan and Armenia— have not met the conditions for membership in these institutions, the less-than-clear pathway and timeline to integration in these institutions likely diminishes the motivation for carrying out the democratic reforms and legal changes necessary to gain membership. More recent economic and financial crises (Greece) and migrant crises may also send the signal to these countries that acceleration towards EU integration is not likely any time soon.

Greater engagement, specificity and clarity on standards and timelines from the Euro-Atlantic community could represent important steps to reassure these countries that the democratic reforms needed for European integration will in fact ultimately yield other rewards. The signals sent to Georgia, which is furthest along both in its democratic development and its commitment to Europeanization, will also be particularly important for demonstrating that progress on democratic standards yields dividends towards further integration.

---

12. Sergey Minasyan, "Armenia Keeps on Balancing—Between the European Union and the Eurasian Economic Union," *PONARS Eurasia Policy Memo*, no. 377 (August 2015).

13. Thomas De Waal, "Azerbaijan Doesn't Want to Be Western," *Foreign Affairs*, September 26, 2014. https://www.foreignaffairs.com/articles/russia-fsu/2014-09-26/azerbaijan-doesnt-want-be-western.

A New, More Assertive Posture from their Northern Neighbor

These countries also confront new concerns about how Russia will respond not only the foreign policy choices they make (as seen in Ukraine), but also the choices of their internal political systems. Resolute moves towards more open and competitive political systems could prompt disapproval or a negative response from Russia. Russia has expressed strong concern about 'color revolutions,' not only at home, but also potential color revolutions in Azerbaijan and Armenia, and of course the Rose Revolution in Georgia. For example, Russian government officials and several Russian-based media outlets saw the electricity protests in Yerevan ('Electric Yerevan') in mid-2015 as another possible 'Maidan.'[14] Russian Prime Minister Medvedev recently stated, "We are closely watching what is happening in Armenia because you are our neighbor, ally and close state, and we are certainly not indifferent to how events unfold in a friendly country."[15]

Russia also is making more proactive and direct efforts to influence media environments in other countries, which may impact the ability of those countries to successfully pursue a more democratic path. For example, Russia attempted to open a branch of the pro-Russian Sputnik radio station in Georgia in 2014.[16] These media outlets have often sought to discredit democracy-building efforts supported by Western donors and NGOs as illicit conspiracies to de-stabilize these political systems.

Taken together, this set of factors should lead us to conceive of democratization in the South Caucasus as a complex, challenging, and longer-term endeavor that may be significantly affected by a broad range of both external and internal actors. Consequently, those supporting democratization in the Caucasus will need to be realistic, patient, yet determined in supporting that effort.

---

14. For example, see "Armenian protests resemble Ukrainian Maidan coup scenario - Russian MP," RT.com, June 24, 2015. https://www.rt.com/politics/269392-russian-senator-armenia-unrest/.

15. Emil Danielyan, "Russian, Armenian PMs Discuss Yerevan Protests," *Radio Liberty*, July 9, 2015. http://www.armenialiberty.org/content/article/27119140.html.

16. "Radio Appendage of "Russia Today" Appears in Georgia," Georgi Menabde, *Eurasia Daily Monitor*, vol: 11, issue: 207 November 19, 2014. http://www.jamestown.org/programs/edm/single/?tx_ttnews%5Btt_news%5D=43097&cHash=c58e7a9057787507d35001d5aebc2ede#.VVVTG-usaJU.

Country Cases: Challenges and Opportunities

Having considered several common factors, which affect the prospects for democratization in the South Caucasus, this section will briefly outline the specific, varying opportunities and challenges present in each of the three countries of Georgia, Armenia, and Azerbaijan.

Georgia

Georgia has been the strongest performer on democratic development in the Caucasus, and the one that has clearly made the most progress to date. Benchmarking indices for democratic governance clearly show Georgia as the most advanced on democracy in the Caucasus. For example, Georgia's scores in Freedom House's the global *Freedom in the World* survey and in the regional *Nations In Transit* survey are the best in the region.[17] Georgia also receives the highest ranking and scores of the three in the Economist Intelligence Unit Democracy Index.[18] Georgia is also the clear leader among the three in the World Bank's Worldwide Governance Indicators, particular in the aggregate indicators for Voice and Accountability, Government Effectiveness, and the Rule of Law.[19] Having noted that, Georgia still has much to do to consolidate its democratic institutions, and significant setbacks, detours, or even derailments are possible.

Importantly, Georgia has undergone two peaceful political transitions since the Shevardnadze era. These are the 'Rose Revolution' in 2003/2004 and the transfer from the United National Movement (UNM) to the 'Georgian Dream' Coalition in 2012/2013. The 'Rose Revolution' was extra-constitutional, but peaceful; the transfer of power in 2012/2013 was both constitutional and peaceful. While one can

---

17. Freedom House's *Freedom in the World* survey reports Georgia's 2015 overall freedom rating (which measures events in 2014) as a 3.0 (on a 1 to 7 scale, with 7 being the worst.) Armenia's corresponding score is a 4.5. Azerbaijan's"freedom score" for the same year is a 6.0. Freedom House, Freedom in the World 2015, https://freedomhouse.org/report/freedom-world/freedom-world-2015#.VavyIIusaJX.

18. For 2014, Georgia received a score of 5.82, while Armenia received a 4.13 and Azerbaijan received a 2.83 (out of a possible 10.00). Economist Intelligence Unit, *Democracy Index 2014*, "Democracy and its Discontents." http://www.eiu.com/public/topical_report.aspx?campaignid=Democracy0115.

19. World Bank Institute, Worldwide Governance Indicators 2013, http://info.worldbank.org/governance/wgi/index.aspx#countryReports.

debate whether the specific changes in leadership during those two periods of transition were in and of themselves positive, those studying democratization have viewed the peaceful and constitutional transfers of power from one ruling group to another as a sign of institutionalization and resilience of a democratic political system. If one considers Samuel Huntington's 'two turnover test,'[20] then it is reasonable to conclude that Georgia has made significant progress on the path towards the institutionalization of democracy since 2003. In Georgia, perhaps due in part to the turnover of power, there has been significant dynamism and reform of the political system on a number of fronts, but there are still significant challenges and real possibilities for regression. The recent controversies over Rustavi-2 and political polarization surrounding it are examples of these ongoing challenges and threats.

Positive Developments. As we consider the current situation in Georgia, we observe the following set of recent developments that would seem to indicate factors of strength and continued forward momentum towards the maturation and consolidation of its democratic institutions.

A Set of Talented and Influential Non-governmental Organizations. Georgia's democratic trajectory has been significantly buttressed and safe-guarded at key moments by a group of publicly minded civic organizations that have served to provide crucial oversight and checks on executive branch authority in that country. Groups such as the Georgian Young Lawyers Association (GYLA), the International Society for Fair Elections and Democracy (ISFED), Transparency International Georgia, New Generation New Initiative (NGNI), Public Movement for Multinational Georgia (PMMG), United Nations Association of Georgia (UNAG) and others have been led by energetic, intelligent, and articulate young Georgians who have made a real difference in engaging Georgia's governments in serious dialogue and helping to "keep the government honest" on a range of issues from elections to corruption to the rule of law. It is also important to note that this group of NGOs would not have been nearly as influential and consequential for maintaining Georgia's democratic path without government officials who have taken them seriously and consistently have been willing to engage with them substantively in dialogue on key issues.

---

20. Samuel Huntington, *The Third Wave* (Norman: University of Oklahoma Press, 1991), pp. 266-267.

Centers for Civic Engagement (CCEs). These centers, established during the Saakashvili/UNM period, serve as hubs for civic activity, political activism, and the free flow of information in Georgia's regions. These centers, now ten in number, have helped create greater opportunities for greater citizen, party, and NGO engagement throughout much of Georgia's regions.[21] In doing so, these centers have helped establish better conditions for strengthening the fabric of democracy in Georgia's periphery—mentioned above as a particular challenge in the context of the South Caucasus.

The Ombudsman's Office (Public Defender's Office). Georgia's Public Defender's Office has evolved in recent years from what had been more of a politicized 'one-person show' into an institution, with greater staff and enhanced capacities for representing and defending citizens' interests.[22] The office has been playing a constructive role in mediating between society and the government by speaking out and preparing reports on a range of issues, from child protection, to persons with disabilities, to human rights.

An Increased Commitment to Open Government. An enhanced commitment to more transparent and accessible government began under during President Saakashvili's tenure, and it has continued under the Georgian Dream coalition. Georgia's current Open Government Partnership (OGP) Action Plan is ambitious and substantive, with 27 different commitments across four major areas, including "improving public services, increasing public integrity, more effectively managing public resources, and creating safer communities."[23]

Civil Service Reform. While the government of Georgia opted against embarking on civil service reform under President Saakashvili and the UNM, the current government has decided to move decisively in this direction. The reform was launched initially through a concept in July of 2014 and made official through a decree in November 2014.[24] This reform will hopefully enhance the competence, professionalism and

21. See http://www.cce.ge/portal/alias__CCE/tabid__4593/default.aspx.

22. See the Georgian Public Defender's website, particularly the description of its structure at http://www.ombudsman.ge/en/about-us/struqtura/departamentebi.

23. *Open Government Partnership Action Plan of Georgia 2014-2015*, http://www.opengovpartnership.org/sites/default/files/OGP%20Georgia%20AP%202014-2015_eng_0.pdf.

24. Government of Georgia, Decree ? 627, Dated 19 November 2014 , Tbilisi, "On the Approval of the Civil Service Reform Concept and Some Other Related Measures," csb.gov.ge/uploads/627.pdf.

continuity of Georgian public administration and lessen the politicized character of the bureaucracy.

Judicial Reform. This reform will allow for the formation of the High Council of Justice through secret ballot, increasing the independence of judges' representatives on the council. Given past controversies over judicial independence in Georgia, and concerns about possible selective justice or politically motivated prosecutions, measures towards strengthening judicial independence represent important positive steps.

Decentralization. Georgia has recently moved to establish 11 self-governing cities. When added to Tbilisi (which had already has its own local self-government and directly elected mayor) that makes 12 self-governing cities nationwide. Allowing for greater spheres of political autonomy and decision-making at local levels has the potential to add a new dimension to Georgia's democratic system and give citizens an enhanced and more direct voice in how their cities are run. Both of these developments would enhance the resilience and stability of Georgia's democratic system.

Challenges/Concerns

Fragility of the Political Party System. The ruling Georgian Dream's organizational development—or that of its key constituent parts—remains uncertain. Georgian Dream's organizational coherence still appears to rely heavily on former Prime Minister Bidzina Ivanishvili, who no longer holds any formal public office or party leadership position. It also remains unclear if Georgian Dream will be able to develop a coherent ideological focus that will have strong roots in key segments of Georgian society or if it will fall into a 'party of power' syndrome—serving largely as a focal point for elites and other constituent seeking access to power, patronage, financial resources, and career opportunities. The core of the former ruling party, United National Movement, remains in place as an opposition counterweight and alternative to Georgian Dream, but it is unclear how the party may reinvent itself and stem further erosion of its support among the electorate. Second, ongoing debates and potential changes to the electoral system, which fundamentally affect political competition and the character of political party systems,[25] add a degree of uncertainty to the party system. In addition,

---

25. Giovanni Sartori, *Comparative Constitutional Engineering: An Inquiry into Structures, Incentives, and Outcomes* (New York: New York University Press, 1997). See also Sartori's *Parties and Party Systems* (Cambridge: Cambridge University Press, 1976).

party politics in Georgia remain highly polarized and marked by the fundamental distrust noted in the first part of this chapter. That polarization and distrust, if it somehow escalates, loom as ongoing potential threats to derail other gains that have been made towards democratic consolidation. Recent controversy over the media sphere also shows how the issue of ownership of a television channel can increase political polarization, and raise controversy over issue having to do with the balance in the information environment, due process, and property rights.

Getting Lustration Right. Georgia's political system currently faces an important challenge associated with its recent transfer of power. Georgia's current government, judiciary and society must seek to balance real concerns about the alleged past criminal behavior of former government officials with scrupulously ensuring due process of law for all, to avoid the perception of politically motivated prosecutions and score-settling. Perceptions of score settling or of using the judicial system as a political instrument to weaken political adversaries could have the potential to exacerbate the problem of a lack of political trust, referred to in earlier sections of this chapter. The transparency and procedural correctness of the manner in which any prosecutions against former government officials are handled will be critically important for Georgia, not only to reduce polarization, but for building broader confidence in its judicial institutions.

Ensuring a Positive Environment for Civil Society Engagement with Government and for Civil Liberties. While Georgia has begun to develop a clear pattern of substantive and often constructive dialogue between its government and civil society, some concerning signs have emerged in 2015. Some NGOs in Georgia have raised alarm bells about recent negative statements made by the former Prime Minister regarding civic organizations.[26]

Armenia

Armenia has shown less dynamism than Georgia in its democratic development, and its scores in benchmarking surveys on democratization show little movement over the last decade. There have been some mildly encouraging signs in Armenia over the last few years that are worth considering. For example, Armenia's overall Democracy Score in

---

26. See "NGOs Slam" "Informal Ruler" Ivanishvili's" "Threatening" Remarks," Civil Georgia, Feb 2, 2015. http://www.civil.ge/eng/article.php?id=28018

Freedom House's *Nations In Transit* index has improved modestly in the period from 2011 to 2015 (from a 5.43 to a 5.36).[27] The development of civil society has been a leading sector, while the rule of law, corruption, and electoral processes have been the spheres with the greatest remaining challenges. Armenia receives similar scores from the Economist Intelligence Unit's 2014 Democracy Index, 4.13 (out of a possible 10.00) and is ranked 113 out of 167 countries.[28]

Armenia has not undergone the same level of democratic political competition and elite rotation that Georgia has, and the ruling Republican Party of Armenia has been the leading political force for well over a decade. During its post-Soviet period, Armenia has demonstrated a combination of what appears to be limited and episodic political contestation with the concentration of power in the ruling party and the executive—what Henry Hale has called the construction of a "single pyramid system."[29] Also, in contrast to Georgia, post-election protests in 2008 led to violence and ten fatalities, raising the sense of high stakes and distrust in the sphere of political competition.

Still, the country has shown significant and often surprising levels of pluralism and political contestation. For example, opposition candidate Raffi Hovanissyan won nearly 40 percent of the vote in the presidential election in 2013. Although some have perceived Armenia's pluralism to be largely circumscribed to narrow elite competition,[30] in 2015, the 'Electric Yerevan' protests demonstrated the re-emergence and renewed influence of Armenian civil society. Notably, the government of Armenia has also clearly articulated further openness as a goal and embarked on some areas of democratic reform. A key question will be if it follows through on those reforms and makes progress in those areas in which it has faced criticism for insufficient freedom, such as judicial independence, media freedom, and fair political competition.

---

27. Freedom House, *2015 Nations In Transit*, Report for Armenia. https://freedomhouse.org/report/nations-transit/2015/armenia.

28. Economist Intelligence Unit, *Democracy Index 2014*, "Democracy and its Discontents." http://www.eiu.com/public/topical_report.aspx?campaignid=Democracy0115.

29. Henry Hale, *Patronal Politics: Eurasian Regime Dynamics in Comparative Perspective*, (New York: Cambridge University Press, 2015) p. 355, p. 64.

30. Alexander Iskandaryan, "From Totalitarianism via Elitist Pluralism: Whither Armenia?" in *Armenia's Foreign and Domestic Politics: Development Trends* (Yerevan: Caucasus Institute, 2013) pp. 48-54.

Positive Developments

De-Centralization/ Local Self-Governance. The government of Armenia has shown some positive movement on de-centralization, which could provide for more responsive and representative government at the local level, but much remains to be done, and the jury is still out on the broader implications of these plans. Reforms have entered the first phase of territorial and administrative consolidation of communities, which will potentially allow for the more efficient and effective provision of services to the local level. If this succeeds, this consolidation may pave the way for the transfer of greater authorities from the regional (*marz*) level to the local/municipal level. The hope is that these reforms will engender energy and channels for grass-roots participation reforms from below. The government of Armenia has enlisted the help of international donors on developing a strategy for decentralization. It has worked with USAID, the Germans (GIZ), the Swiss (SDC), and the World Bank to form a steering committee to oversee the reforms and potentially to provide technical assistance on implementation.

Anti-Corruption/ Open Government. The government has a new anti-corruption strategy under development in spring 2016. It has also formed a new anti-corruption council.[31] Admittedly, the formation of the new council has been met with some skepticism by NGOs, and to date, no non-governmental groups have joined the new council.[32] Having joined the Open Government Partnership (OGP) in September 2011, Armenia has carried out its second OGP Action Plan, which makes a number of positive steps in improving governmental transparency.[33] It also has legislation and plans for improving Freedom of Information.

Civil Society Development and Activism. Civic activity has been another relatively bright spot in Armenia, especially in terms of helping civil society to become more active at the community level and in its interaction with local governments. In contrast to some other Eurasian countries, generally positive NGO legislation has been in the works. In 2015, peaceful protests in the center of Yerevan in response to increases in electric utility rates ('Electric Yerevan' protests) were an indicator of

---

31. "Armenia PM Says Anti-corruption Council will Work Transparently," February 25, 2015. *www.news.am.* http://news.am/eng/news/254392.html.

32. Marianna Grigoryan, "Armenia: Doubts Abound on Anti-Corruption Initiative," *EurasiaNet.org*, May 5, 2015. http://www.eurasianet.org/node/73311.

33. "Open Government Partnership Second Action Plan for the Government of Armenia (2014-2016)," http://www.gov.am/u_files/file/bkg%20angl.pdf.

strong and growing civil society activism and a willingness to organize to defend citizen interests. While these protests resulted in some clashes with police, the protests did not lead to widespread or sustained violence or a brutal crackdown.

Challenges/Concerns

Concentration of Power in the Executive. The greatest longstanding and ongoing concern for Armenia's further democratization is the strong centralization of power in the hands of the executive and the ruling party, and limits on a level playing field for political competition and debate. While the government continues to articulate a readiness for reform, openness, and pluralism, its ongoing political predominance puts democratization on less certain footing than if political competition and the distribution of political power were greater.[34] Proposed constitutional reforms may potentially begin to address this issue, if and only if they work to create opportunities for the further distribution of, and checks on, political authority.

Recent shifts in party politics over the last year, specifically the struggle between the president and the former head of Prosperous Armenia Gagik Tsarukian, raise concerns about the possible further consolidation of power in Armenia. When Prosperous Armenia, which had traditionally cooperated with the ruling Republican Party, moved into strong opposition to the government in the fall of 2014, participating in protests with the Armenian National Congress and Heritage parties[35], this evoked a reaction from the pro-governmental side. In early 2015, members of Prosperous Armenia were arrested[36] and the president directly criticized Tsarukian and said he should leave politics. Tsarukian's decision to resign from his leadership post in Prosperous Armenia and to exit from politics in March 2015 has been interpreted by many political observers as an indication of the government's ability to sideline challengers to its political predominance.[37]

---

34. For example, see Alexander Iskandaryan, "Armenia: Stagnation at Its Utmost," *Caucasus Analytical Digest*, No. 76 (September 7, 2015) pp. 2-6.

35. RFE/RL, "Thousands Rally In Yerevan," *RFE/RL*, October 11, 2014. http://www.rferl.org/content/armenia-protest-/26631897.html.

36. "A Number of Prosperous Armenia Party Members Arrested," *Civilnet.AM*, February 17, 2015. http://civilnet.am/2015/02/17/a-number-of-prosperous-armenia-party-members-arrested/#.VbVV1YusaJU.

37. RFE/RL Armenian Service, "Embattled Armenian Party's Leader Quits Amid Pressure," *RFE/RL*, March 5, 2015. http://www.rferl.org/content/embattled-armenian-partys-leader-quits-amid-pressure/26883852.html.

Navigating Constitutional Reform. Second, the politicization of the issue of constitutional reform looms as a contentious and polarizing issue. There is a clear lack of trust of the part of the opposition that this set of reforms will not simply be used to extend the President's hold on power through a new position as Prime Minister or Speaker of Parliament. Still, it is possible that constitutional reform could bring greater powers to the government and the parliament, which might create opportunities for a broader circle of actors to engage meaningfully on policy issues.

Arrests of Radical Opposition Party Members. The government's arrest of radical political opposition members, who had called for the removal of the current government, in the spring of 2015 was also of concern for the potential for political pluralism.[38] More encouragingly, these figures were later released.

Azerbaijan

Azerbaijan remains the most challenging case for political liberalization and democratization in the region. Its scores on democratic performance from benchmarking indices Freedom House, Economist Intelligence Unit, World Bank Institute, and Transparency International all indicate fundamental challenges on democratic performance in virtually all areas, even with regard to basic freedoms.[39] Of additional concern is Azerbaijan's substantial decline in democratic freedoms over the last dozen years. Azerbaijan's scores in *Nations In Transit* have declined by over 1.25 points (on a scale of 1 to 7) since 2003.[40]

Positive Developments

Despite the very difficult environment in Azerbaijan for independent civic activity over the last few years, there have been areas and initiatives in Azerbaijan that have shown some promise, at least for stimulating meaningful civic activity at the grass-roots level. If the trend on political

38. Gohar Abrahamyan, "Protest Against Protest: Radical Group to Rally on April 24 despite Arrests," *Armenia Now*, April 8, 2015. http://www.armenianow.com/news/politics/62161/founding_parliament_party_zhirayr_sefilyan_zaruhi_postanjyan.

39. Freedom House's *Freedom in the World* survey reports Azerbaijan's "freedom score" for the calendar year of 2014 as 6.0. Freedom House, Freedom in the World 2015, https://freedomhouse.org/report/freedom-world/freedom-world-2015#.VavyIIusaJX.

40. Azerbaijan's overall democracy score in 2003 was 5.46. Its score for 2015 is 6.75. See https://freedomhouse.org/report/nations-transit/2015/azerbaijan.

liberalization were to begin to shift in a more positive direction, these are areas from which some momentum might be built.

Monitoring and Adapting to the Legal Enabling Environment for Civil Society. The non-governmental organization ICNL has worked with local partners to advise scores of NGOs on how to continue their work by complying with new more restrictive laws and regulations for NGOs in Azerbaijan. As NGOs better adapt to new requirements, their ability to survive and push for constructive change is enhanced.

Community Development. Some past initiatives have worked to help citizens to understand how it is possible to effect real and constructive changes at the community level through grass-roots, community-drive initiatives. For example, the Social Economic Development Activity (SEDA), run by East-West Management Institute, with the support of USAID and in cooperation with the government of Azerbaijan, has worked to support such community development projects in the regions of Azerbaijan since 2011.[41]

Women's Political Participation. There has also been incremental success in encouraging broader engagement and inclusion of women in political processes. For example, Counterpart International has worked to empower women to participate more in political processes and to raise awareness about women's participation and issues of importance to women.[42] By working against gender discrimination, providing leadership skills to women, and working to make the political environment more inclusive to women, this initiative may help to begin to create more favorable conditions for democratization and human rights over the longer term.

Transparency and Anti-Corruption. Another encouraging area of activities has been that of NGOs and citizens working together to promote government transparency and to take steps towards combating corruption. The Azerbaijan Partnership for Transparency (APT), which brings together a coalition of five NGOs has worked to promote government openness, responsiveness, and accountability through policy development, monitoring, and outreach since 2012.[43] While corruption is a

---

41. See http://ewmi.org/SEDA,

42. This Counterpart International project has been with the support of USAID. For more on the Women's Political Participation project, see http://www.counterpart.org/our-work/projects/womens-participation-program-in-azerbaijan

43. This project is led by Transparency Azerbaijan, with the support of USAID. See http://transparency.az/eng/apt/.

deeply complex and challenging problem in Azerbaijan, and this effort alone cannot singlehandedly shift the tide, efforts like it may hold the seeds to eventual progress over the longer term when other structural factors improve.

Challenges/Concerns

Continuing Closing Space for Civic Activity. Since 2008, the legal and regulatory environment for NGOs has become more difficult in Azerbaijan. Many international NGOs have had difficult years in Azerbaijan in 2014 and 2015, and several other NGOs have faced harassment. Two prominent democracy-promotion groups, NDI and IREX, felt the need to end their programs in Azerbaijan because of legal cases brought against them by the government.[44] The OSCE coordinator, which had also had a mandate to engage on civil society issues, was also asked to leave the country in July 2015.[45] The worsening situation with NGOs also started to jeopardize Azerbaijan's participation in the Open Government Partnership (OGP).[46]

Worsening Situation on Human Rights. The US Department of State's most recent Human Rights Report for Azerbaijan points to broad range of problems concerning fundamental freedoms and documents the cases of individuals considered to have been incarcerated for their civic activity.[47] Non-governmental human rights organizations have also issued reported on the full set of serious issues in Azerbaijan.[48] In addition, the rock group U2 raised the issue of Azerbaijan's political prisoners during

---

44. For IREX, see "IREX Stops Activity in Azerbaijan," *Contact.az*, October 8, 2014. www.contact.az/docs/2014/Politics/100800092722en.htm#.VbWGlYusaJUhttp://www.contact.az/docs/2014/Politics/100800092722en.htm#.VbWGlYusaJU. For NDI, see "NDI Office in Baku is Officially Closed." Contact.az, July 2, 2014.

45. See "OSCE Project Coordinator in Baku discontinues its operations in Azerbaijan," http://www.osce.org/secretariat/170146; See also Carl Schreck, "Azerbaijan Orders OSCE To Close Baku Office," *RFE/RL, June 5, 2015.* http://www.rferl.org/content/article/27055923.html.

46. "OGP Agrees Azerbaijan Harassing Civil Society," *Freedominfo.org*, May 18, 2015. http://www.freedominfo.org/2015/05/ogp-agrees-azerbaijan-harassing-civil-society/.

47. US Department of State's Bureau of Democracy and Human Rights and Labor, "Country Reports on Human Rights Practices for 2014: Azerbaijan," http://www.state.gov/j/drl/rls/hrrpt/humanrightsreport/#wrapper.

48. For example, see Human Rights Watch, *World Report 2015: Azerbaijan*, https://www.hrw.org/world-report/2015/country-chapters/azerbaijan; Also, see *Amnesty International Report 2014/2015*. https://www.amnesty.org/en/countries/europe-and-central-asia/azerbaijan/report-azerbaijan/.

its 2015 concert tour.[49] One somewhat encouraging development has been the release of human rights activists Leyla and Arif Yunus, based on health considerations, in late 2015.

Lack of Enabling Environment for Fair Political Competition. The previous two issues, closing civic space and insufficient respect for fundamental freedoms and human rights, lead to a situation in which fair political competition is simply is not feasible. Substantial progress on fundamental freedoms of association, assembly, and expression, combined with a freer civic life will necessary for that. The decision that Azerbaijan would not host monitors from the OSCE/ODIHR for parliamentary elections in the fall of 2015 was another discouraging sign for the possibility of objective, third party oversight of the electoral process.

Conclusion

Considering the common, longstanding and current situational challenges facing all three countries, and the country-specific concerns and constraints for Georgia, Armenia, and Azerbaijan, one should not expect dramatic breakthroughs, rapid transformations, or even uninterrupted linear improvement on democratization in the South Caucasus in the near term. Progress is on democracy building is much more likely to be protracted and incremental, episodic, uneven, and with occasional or even sustained setbacks. Like the mountain roads of the Caucasus, progress on democracy in the region is likely to be winding and long, with unexpected dips, ascents, and turns. External pressures, and measures taken based on perceived external threats or opportunities, can be expected to play significant roles in affecting the internal political development of all three countries. Perceptions of opportunities and timelines of Euro-Atlantic integration, acceptance of European values and adaptation with traditional ones, and measures taken by their Northern neighbor will all likely affect the pace of democratic change.

Progress on democratization will ultimately come as the people and governments of the South Caucasus recognize that democracy is the path most likely to lead to the stability, security, and prosperity of each of their countries. A successful strategy in facilitating that process—

---

49. "Rock Star Bono Speaks Out For Political Prisoners In Azerbaijan," *RFE/RL*, June 16, 2015, http://www.rferl.org/media/video/azerbaijan-baku-rights-bono-u2/27075011.html.

both for the citizens of these countries and members of the international community—will likely entail context-specific, targeted, determined and persistent engagement in helping to strengthen the institutions, processes, and values that engage, limit and check executive authority.

Chapter Eight

Challenges Of Democracy: Corruption

Shaazka Beyerle

On almost any given day, corruption is in the headlines, often out-raging citizens not only around the world but also in the European Union (EU) and neighboring countries. In many instances they are using their votes or grass-roots people power for justice, accountability and democracy. This chapter will examine the linkages between corruption, authoritarianism and violent conflict, their legacy in Europe and its neighboring countries, and implications for European democracy and security. One often overlooked but essential source of anti-corruption clout is the grass-roots, organized in nonviolent movements and campaigns. The second part of this chapter will provide a systemic conceptualization of corruption along with a conceptual grounding of people power. It will examine how citizens wield this form of pressure. Recent evidence-based research on such bottom-up civic initiatives will be cited. People power and citizen mobilization can build democracy from the bottom-up, and in the process, are redefining both our understanding and practice of democracy.

European Snapshots

People who failed to prevent this embezzlement, people who failed to find criminals, people who failed to find where the money is, people who failed to seize this money-of course they don't inspire any trust among the public.[1]

—Stanislav Pavlovsky, Dignity and Truth Movement, Moldova
(former judge, European Court of Human Rights)

I came here hoping that something will change, that we will manage to return democracy to Macedonia. I hope it is not too late for that.[2]

—Julija Krsteva, Protester, Macedonia

---

1. Rayhan Demytrie, BBC News, September 14, 2015, http://www.bbc.com/news/world-europe-34244341.
2. Sinisa Jakov Marusic, Balkan Insight, May 17, 15, http://www.balkaninsight.com/en/article/macedonia-braces-for-big-anti-government-protest.

Beyond their opposition to austerity [Manuela Carmena, Ada Colau], they share a belief in the public good and an understanding of democracy as a system that shouldn't be left to the whims of so-called professionals... The new mottos are confluencia and transparencia: people and parties joining forces in order to end the corrupt, paternalistic politics of backroom deals, self-enrichment, and hacer la vista gorda ("turning a blind eye").[3]

—Bécquer Seguín and Sebastiaan Faber, on the May 2015 Spanish local and regional elections

In tiny Moldova, lawyers, former parliamentarians and officials, journalists and civic activists formed the Dignity and Truth movement during winter 2015, after $1 billion vanished from the country's major banks. Meanwhile in Macedonia, citizens across the contentious ethnic divide have been mobilizing since spring 2015 over a wire-tapping and election-rigging scandal. They added pressure on the intransigent prime minister, who agreed to a political deal on new elections and reforms, facilitated by EU officials.

Back in the EU, also in May of that year, local and regional elections heralded the end of Spanish politics as usual. Two new parties—*Podemos* (We Can) on the left of the political spectrum and *Ciudadanos* (Citizens), on the right-made stunning gains. Both emerged out of civic mobilizations against austerity, inequality and corruption, including but not limited to the *Indignados* (The Outraged) movement. Over in the UK, the latest cash-for-access scandal erupted, after two Members of Parliament (and former foreign secretaries), were secretly filmed offering their services for money to journalists posing as representatives of a foreign company.[4] In September 2015, just after the House of Commons Standards Committee absolved them of wrongdoing, stating that "there was no breach of the rules on paid lobbying," some of its members divulged that they had misgivings about the decision.[5] "It is probably true that

---

3. Bécquer Seguín and Sebastiaan Faber, "In Spain's Seismic Elections, 'It's the Victory of David Over Goliath,'" *The Nation*, May 26, 2015 http://www.thenation.com/article/spains-seismic-elections-its-victory-david-over-goliath/.

4. Malcom Rifkind (Tory) and Jack Straw (Labour) were suspended from their political parties. Rifkind resigned from office while Jack Straw did not run in the May 7, 2015 elections; Anoosh Chakelian, "Lobbying Sting: Jack Straw and Malcom Rifkind Suspended from Their Parties," New Statesman, February 23, 2015, http://www.newstatesman.com/politics/2015/02/lobbying-sting-jack-straw-and-malcolm-rifkind-suspended-their-parties.

5. Peter Dominiczak, Claire Newell, Edward Malnick, and Christopher Hope, "MPs who 'Cleared' Jack Straw and Sir Malcolm Rifkind Reveal 'Misgivings'," *The Telegraph*, September 17, 2015, http://www.telegraph.co.uk/news/investigations/11873070/MPs-who-cleared-Jack-Straw-and-Sir-Malcolm-Rifkind-reveal-misgivings.html.

they [Straw and Rifkind] did not break the rules—and therefore we have got a problem with the rules," conceded a member.[6]

That same month the BBC ran a story on a leaked report conducted by Kroll, a financial investigations company. Moldova's missing $1 billion was traced to Fortuna United LP (limited partnership), with an address in a run-down apartment north of Edinburgh. It is composed of two Seychelles companies, whose directors happen to own Royston Business Consultancy, which set up Fortuna United and is at the same location. Contacted by the news service, one of the directors declared, "I don't have anything to worry about. I didn't commit fraud myself or my partner didn't do it. We comply with all the regulations."[7] As these latter two cases reveal, countries perceived as relatively clean on some corruption measures look very different when one examines illicit financial flows, money laundering, and permissible abuses of power for private gain.

Corruption and the Democracy-Accoutability Deficit

There are no corruption-free zones in Europe. We are not doing enough. That's true for all member states.[8]

—Cecilia Malmström, EU Commissioner for Home Affairs

The above stories are snapshots of the corruption challenges and threats facing the EU and surrounding countries. Recent research and opinion polls add to this less than rosy picture. Corruption is eroding the public's trust in their political systems, governments, and institutions, from the EU down to their national and municipal levels. Transparency International's 2013 Global Corruption Barometer found that across Europe and neighboring countries, political parties, a core pillar of democratic systems, are perceived to be among the institutions most affected by graft and abuse.[9] They included Bosnia and Herzegovina, Croatia, the Czech Republic, Estonia, France, Finland, Germany,

---

6. Ibid.

7. Tim Whewell, File on 4, BBC, October 7, 2015, http://www.bbc.com/news/magazine-34445201.

8. Ian Traynor, "There Are No Corruption-Free Zones in Europe, Commissioner Claims," *The Guardian*, February 3, 2104, http://www.theguardian.com/world/2014/feb/03/european-union-corruption-bribery-sleaze.

9. A total of 114,000 people were surveyed in 107 countries.

Figure 1. Transparency International's 2015 Corruption Perceptions Index

Greece, Hungary, Italy, Latvia, Macedonia, Norway, Portugal, Romania, Slovenia, Spain, Switzerland, Turkey, and the United Kingdom.[10]

When it comes to perceptions of public sector graft, one finds a large range across the EU and periphery, from the least corrupt to some abysmal performers (Figure 1).

The 2015 Edelman Trust Barometer, which measures public trust in the institutions of government, media, NGOs and business in 27 countries spanning the globe, found that nearly two-thirds are now "Distrusters" among the general online population. This included France, Germany, Ireland, Italy, Poland, Russia, Spain, Sweden, Turkey, and the UK.[11]

A landmark 2014 European Commission Anti-Corruption Report echoed these results. It concluded:

> Provoked by the crisis, social protests have targeted not only economic and social policies, but also the integrity and accountability of

---

10. Transparency International 2013 Global Corruption Barometer, October 14, 2015, http://www.transparency.org/gcb2013/.

11. 2015 Edelman Trust Barometer, October 11, 2015, http://www.edelman.com/insights/intellectual-property/2015-edelman-trust-barometer/.

political elites. High-profile scandals associated with corruption, misuse of public funds or unethical behavior by politicians have contributed to public discontent and mistrust of the political system.[12]

Malfeasance is also hurting taxpayers, socio-economic development, and the provision of public services. The European Commission report found that corruption cost taxpayers around 120 billion euros per year, the equivalent of the EU's annual budget. While member states have most of the necessary institutions and legal instruments essential to prevent and combat corruption, measures taken by countries are uneven, genuine political will is often lacking, and public procurement is particularly vulnerable.[13] A 2013 study by the European Research Centre for Anti-corruption and State-building also found that in 20 out of 27 member states (before Croatia's accession), "government favoritism was the rule rather than the exception."[14] Even education is not immune. According to the Council of Europe, widespread corruption exists in this sector, it is found in mature EU democracies, and it touches all levels of education.[15]

Transparency International has also assessed corruption risks in ten EU institutions, including the European Commission, European Parliament, Council of Ministers, and the European Council. It found that these bodies are susceptible to corruption because of loopholes and lax enforcement of ethics, transparency and financial control rules.[16] The report concluded that "failure to make full and proper use of existing controls will not reassure a public that are skeptical of the commitment of politicians and bureaucrats to a more open and ethical style of government."[17]

Public opinion corroborates these findings. A Eurobarometer survey, released along with the report, found that 76 percent of Europeans

---

12. Report from the Commission to the Council and the European Parliament: *EU Anti-Corruption Report* (Brussels: European Commission, February 2, 2014), 8.

13. Report from the Commission to the Council and the European Parliament, Ibid.

14. Alina Mingiu-Pippidi, "The Good, the Bad, and the Ugly: Controlling Corruption in the European Union," Working Paper No. 35, European Research Centre for Anti-Corruption and State-Building, April 2013, 21.

15. Snežana Samardžić-Marković, "New Ethical Approach to Combat Widespread Corruption in Education," *New Eastern Europe*, September 7, 2015, http://neurope.eu/article/new-ethical-approach-to-combat-widespread-corruption-in-education/.

16. Transparency International EU Office, "First EU Integrity Report Highlights Risks of Corruption in European Institutions," Press Release, April 24, 2014.

17. Transparency International EU Office, "The European Union Integrity System," 2014, p. 9.

believe that corruption is widespread and 56 percent said that the level in their country increased since 2011. Overall, the majority of respondents stated that corruption exists in EU institutions, in their national public institutions (70%), and in their local or regional public institutions (77%). Over half of EU respondents agreed that bribery and the abuse of positions of power are widespread among politicians (national, regional and local levels) (56%) and among political parties (59%).[18]

Corruption, Authoritarianism and Violent Conflict: A European Legacy

Corruption and Authoritarianism

> Corruption may be a scourge for the ordinary people, but it is a vital governing tool for authoritarian regimes.[19]

> —Minxin Pei

Corruption is one of the most pernicious legacies of authoritarianism. The two go hand in hand. At its core, corruption involves abuse of power, impunity and unaccountability of powerholders, which is the embodiment of dictatorships. Autocrats and cronies thwart or inhibit rule of law and transparency, not only in the government and overall state, but in other sectors they influence or control, such as the economy, education, and media. They exploit natural resources and construct economic entities to enrich themselves, their families and other elites.

Autocrats understand well that their grip on power is not absolute. Corruption is a means through which they can rule and sustain control. It is used to buy and maintain loyalties from various pillars in society, from security forces to the bureaucracy, business, media, and sometimes minority ethnic groups and organized religion. In such regimes, powerholders also turn a blind eye to corruption, allowing self-enrichment from the office clerk all the way up to ministers. It is yet another method, indirect in this case, to sustain support.[20] On the other hand, fabricated accusa-

---

18. Special Eurobarometer 397, European Commission, Directorate-General for Home Affairs, February 2014.

19. Minxin Pei, "Government by Corruption," *Forbes*, January 22, 2009, http://www.forbes.com/2009/01/22/corruption-government-dictatorship-biz-corruption09-cx_mp_0122pei.html

20. Shaazka Beyerle, "People Power Versus the Corruption, Impunity, Authoritarian Nexus," in Matthew Burrows and Maria Stephan, eds., *Is Authoritarianism Staging a Comeback?* (Washington, DC: Atlantic Council).

tions of corruption are often used to neutralize political competitors inside the regime, reformers, honest officials, political opponents, investigative journalists, civil society groups, human rights activists and organizers of nonviolent movements and campaigns. Over time, corruption can often become entrenched in the system in an escalating spiral, as more and more is needed to secure loyalty, support and riches for the regime. Taken to an extreme, such governments can become kleptocracies.[21]

Then again, corruption is the Achilles heel of authoritarians. It can lead to their downfall. Not only does graft and abuse erode their legitimacy, it rots their regimes from the inside out. It can enrich and strengthen competing political elites, who seek to usurp those in power.[22] As time goes by, this stimulates greater and deeper discontent among the populace, which ultimately can lead to nonviolent uprisings or tragically to violent conflict.[23] Some perceptive authoritarian regimes understand this dynamic. President Xi Jinping of China professed, "A great deal of facts tell us that the worse corruption becomes the only outcome will be the end of the party and the end of the state! We must be vigilant."[24]

The second paradox concerns the capacity of autocracies to fight graft and abuse. Even if there is some degree of political will at the top, when corruption is endemic, oppressive rulers cannot rein it in, let alone stamp it out. Yet, they fear one of the strongest forces against malfeasance—an empowered and active citizenry. A Chinese saying, attributed to a former top leader, encapsulates the dilemma: "Corruption will kill the party; fighting corruption will kill it too."[25]

Corruption and Violent Conflict

War economies are built on corruption as the parties in conflict rely on criminal syndicates, fraud and bribery to grease the wheels of the supply chain...[26]

—Cheyanne Scharbatke-Church and Kirby Reiling

21. Sarah Chayes, *Thieves of State: Why Corruption Threatens Global Security* (New York: Norton, 2015).

22. Kanybek Nur-tegin and Hans Czap, "Corruption: Democracy, Autocracy and Political Stability," *Economic Analysis and Policy* 42, no. 1, March 2012.

23. Beyerle, Ibid.

24. "China's Xi Warns of Unrest if Graft not Tackled," Reuters, November 18, 2012.

25. Pei, op. cit.

26. Cheyanne Scharbatke-Church and Kirby Reiling, "Lilies That Fester: Seeds of Corruption and Peacebuilding," *New Routes Journal of Peace Research and Action*, Vol. 14, no. 3-4 (2009), p. 3.

Violent conflict and corruption are intimately linked. Malfeasance is an enabler and sometimes the mechanism through which militaries, paramilitaries, non-state insurgents, and organized crime raise money, shift illicit finances across borders, purchase arms and supplies, and many other activities. A vicious cycle can develop, whereby more and more corruption is needed in order to maintain the conflict, which is perpetuated as warring groups begin to plunder resources or engage in illicit activities not only to fight but ultimately to enrich themselves.[27] Consequently, when the killing ends, corruption does not evaporate.

One reason stems from its systemic nature. Systems of graft and abuse that developed during the violent conflict tend to reconfigure. The vested interests previously benefitting from corruption adapt to the new reality and find new sources of illicit enrichment from the plethora of international funds pouring in for reconstruction and development, state building, and humanitarian aid.[28] A second reason is that many of the principal actors involved in the fighting retain influence and power after its cessation (often with the support of international actors). The Balkans is an example of such outcomes. For instance, mafia entities in Bosnia and Kosovo sought to tie up their power by gaining control over political and local economic processes.[29]

Implications for European Democracy and Security

Once one takes into consideration Europe's recent experiences with authoritarianism and violent conflict, the challenges that corruption is posing to democracy, powerholder accountability, and state-building are not surprising. Prior to joining the EU, the recent histories of many member states were strewn with violent strife, coups d'état, and/or dictatorships (military or communist), including Bulgaria, Croatia, Cyprus, Czech Republic, Estonia, Greece, Hungary, Latvia, Lithuania, Poland, Portugal, Romania, Slovakia, Slovenia and Spain. Neighboring countries experienced similar convulsions, from Albania to Georgia, Moldova,

---

27. "Same Old Story: A Background Study on Natural Resources in the Democratic Republic of Congo," *Global Witness*, June 2004, 5, http://www.globalwitness.org/media_library_detail.php/118/en/same_old_story

28. Shaazka Beyerle, "Civil Resistance and the Corruption-Conflict Nexus," *Journal of Sociology and Social Welfare*, special issue on "Perspectives on Peace, Conflict and War," vol. 38, no. 2.

29. Karen Ballentine and Heiko Nitzschke, "The Political Economy of Civil War and Conflict Transformation," (Berlin: Berghof Research Centre for Constructive Conflict Management, April 2005), http://www.berghof-handbook.net/documents/publications/dialogue3_ballentine_nitzschke.pdf .

Russia, Turkey and Ukraine. The Balkans suffered a double-whammy following the disintegration of Yugoslavia, ethnic cleansing, war, and the emergence of Bosnia and Herzegovina, Kosovo, Macedonia, Montenegro, and Serbia. Taken together, the majority of these countries are also the ones found to have significant corruption challenges.

The implications are sobering. Corruption and self-serving political elites are undermining the quality of democracy in the European Union, and its consolidation and resilience among neighboring nations. EU citizens are losing trust in electoral politics. Intolerance and ultra-nationalism are moving into the political sphere. During the 2014 European Parliament elections, anti-immigration parties won 140 of the 751 seats. Some existing governments are turning ominously authoritarian, such as Hungary, and potentially now in Poland, given the Law and Justice Party's efforts to change the Constitutional Courts and ultimately the Constitution. Over the weekend of November 12, 2015, the new Committee to Defend Democracy rallied thousands in cities across the country.[30] Similar forces can be seen in the candidate, potential candidate states and neighboring countries of the EU, where corruption is eroding the rule of law and the legitimacy of governments. The Turkish government is backtracking, in light of media crackdowns and ongoing efforts both before and after the November 2015 elections for constitutional changes to increase presidential powers. Relatively new democracies are weakened by malfeasant political parties. Citizens may now have the right to vote but their choices are often limited and abysmal.

Corruption also hampers the capacity of new democracies to provide basic public services. Transparency International's 2013 Global Corruption Barometer found that Albanians and Serbs cited medical and health services as the institutions most affected by corruption.[31] By 2015, the former health minister of Ukraine estimated that at a minimum 30-40% of the medicine budget is stolen, while equipment is bought at inflated prices, and then sometimes not even used.[32]

Thus, it is citizens who often bear the brunt of graft and abuse, and many are trying to leave. In addition to the heart wrenching exodus to

---

30. http:/www.telegraph.co.uk/news/worldnews/europe/Poland/12047373/Opposition-demostrations-as-Poland-faces-constitutional-crisis.html.

31. Transparency International website, October 14, 2015, http://www.transparency.org/gcb2013/results.

32. Oliver Bullough, "Welcome to the Most Corrupt Nation in Europe," *The Guardian*, February 6, 2015.

the EU from Syria, Libya and beyond, a mass migration from the Balkans is also headed in the same direction. A Friedrich Ebert Foundation survey found that among 14-to-29-year-olds, almost two-thirds want to leave Albania, and over half from Kosovo and Macedonia.[33] According to a SpiegelOnline report, from January to August 2015, 29,323 Albanians, 5,514 Macedonians, 2,425 Montenegrins, and 11,642 Serbians applied for asylum in Germany. Over 100,000 Kosovars left the new country from about September 2014–August 2015.[34] A clique of corrupt politicians is seen to hold top government positions, jobs in the oversized public administration are said to go to their relatives and supporters, and profits from shady deals are difficult to trace. "They have lost all confidence in their young democracies, and they dream of a better life," state the authors.[35] It should be noted that these figures don't include those who cross the borders without a legal status.

Finally, corruption is directly and indirectly impacting the European security landscape with geopolitical ramifications. The following two cases are illustrative of its cascading effect.

Moldova. An October 2015 Associated Press investigation detailed how criminal networks in the country, with possible Russian ties, have been trying to sell radioactive material to violent extremist groups in the Middle East. Over five years, a Moldovan police-FBI sting operation uncovered cross-border smuggling with Russia and Ukraine, uranium possibly coming from the melted-down Chernobyl reactor, and an offer to secure a visa for a buyer interested in attack helicopters, armored personnel carriers, dirty bomb plans, and radioactive material.[36] "The developments represent the fulfillment of a long-feared scenario in which organized crime gangs are trying to link up with groups such as the Islamic State and al-Qaida-both of which have made clear their ambition to use weapons of mass destruction," concludes the report.

Then there is Moldova's 1 billion dollars, discussed earlier in this chapter. There are indications that politicians from the ruling pro-Europe

33. Susanne Koebl, Katrin Kuntz and Walter Mayr, "What is Driving the Balkan Exodus," *Spiegel Online*, August 26, 2015, http://www.spiegel.de/international/europe/western-balkan-exodus-puts-pressure-on-germany-and-eu-a-1049274.html.

34. Ibid.

35. Ibid.

36. Desmond Butler and Vadim Ghirda, "AP Investigation: Nuclear Black Market Seeks IS Extremists," Associated Press, October 7, 2015, http://bigstory.ap.org/article/9f77a17c001f4cf3baeb28990b0d92eb/ap-investigation-nuclear-smugglers-sought-terrorist-buyers.

coalition were involved in the theft.[37] The disgraced government is seen as turning a blind-eye to corruption, paying lip-service to combatting it, and being too close to oligarchs.[38] The Dignity and Truth Movement, though pro-Europe in perspective, is demanding the government's resignation and early elections. Could this herald a victory for pro-Russian opposition parties linked to their own set of oligarchs? Perhaps, if enough citizens want to punish the present group in power or simply want them out. The geopolitical consequences for Europe and beyond are grave.

Ukraine. While graft and impunity have plagued the country since its independence from the Soviet Union in 1991, there is a consensus that it drastically increased during Viktor Yanukovych's rule. The most prominent elements are malfeasance in the police and judiciary, as well as state and regulatory capture throughout the public sector at all levels.[39] A 2015 National Integrity System report on the country concluded that "corruption remains a systemic problem in Ukraine on all levels of public administration."[40] Others simply say that corruption is the system.

Following the onset of the violent, pro-Russian separatist conflict in eastern Ukraine, another harsh reality set in. Corruption had seeped into all levels of the military, undermining its capabilities and putting soldiers at even greater risk in the battlefield. How does this play out on the ground? Essential equipment, such as body armor, has been found to be sub-standard. New recruits have not been given adequate supplies. Families have had to spend approximately 2000 U.S. dollars to properly equip their loved ones before sending them off to the frontlines, while others spend the money on bribes to avoid combat.[41] Soldiers report that supplies, food, equipment and parcels from home are stolen, and army command demand bribes for treatment of combat wounds.[42] Even

37. Piotr Oleksy, "The Moldovan Indignados," *New Eastern Europe*, June 4, 2015, http://www.neweasterneurope.eu/articles-and-commentary/1616-the-moldovan-indignados.

38. Judy Dempsey, "Waiting for a New Moldova," *Judy Dempsey's Strategic Europe*, Carnegie Europe, September 10, 2015.

39. Andrew McDevitt. *The State of Corruption: Armenia, Azerbaijan, Georgia, Moldova and Ukraine* (Berlin: Transparency International, 2015).

40. "Ukraine: Fight against Graft Inhibited by Government Influence on Anti-corruption Institutions," Transparency International-Ukraine, August 2015.

41. Aleksandr Lapko, "Ukraine's Own Worst Enemy: In War Time Corruption in Ukraine Can Be Deadly," *New York Times*, October 7, 2014.

42. Clement Ch, *Corruption: The Achilles Heel of Ukrainian Army*, Euromaidan Press, October 6, 2014; Alya Shandra, "Ukrainian Soldiers are Casualties of Corrupt Army," Euromaidan Press, April 30, 2015, http://euromaidanpress.com/2015/04/30/ukrainian-soldiers-are-casualties-of-corrupt-army/.

more disturbing, there are allegations that some high ranking officers sold information about a unit's movements and positions to Russians.[43] Transparency International-UK's 2013 Government Defence Anti-Corruption Index gave Ukraine a D+. Russia got an even worse grade, D-.[44] Presumably the separatists are not much better. If the Ukrainian military could clean up its act, it could well gain a strategic advantage.

A Systemic Definition Of Corruption

The most commonly used definitions of corruption are: "the abuse of entrusted power for private gain" and "the abuse of public office for private gain."[45] They do encompass the phenomenon, but there are some limitations to them. First, corruption is not merely a collection of interactions between a corruptor and a corruptee (willing or unwilling). Second, the abuse of power is not limited to private gain, but also transpires for political gain or collective benefits for a third party, entity, group, or sector, for example, state security forces, political parties, businesses, financial services, and unions. Third, as evident in the EU and neighboring countries, corruption also occurs in the economic realm and among non-state sectors in society.

In practice, corruption functions as a system of power abuse involving a tangled web of relationships, some obvious and many others hidden. One also needs to take into consideration that within this system are long-standing interests wanting to sustain the venal status quo. They will often resort to lawsuits, intimidation, violence and even murder to thwart anti-graft efforts and stop reformers, integrity champions, investigative journalists, and activists. Thus, my preferred definition of corruption is:

> a system of abuse of entrusted power for private, collective, or political gain-often involving a complex, intertwined set of relationships, some obvious, others hidden, with established vested interests, that

---

43. Ibid.

44. Transparency International UK Defence and Security Program website, October 14, 2015, http://www.defenceindex.org/.

45. "Frequently Asked Questions about Corruption," Transparency International website, http://www.transparency.org/news_room/faq/corruption_faq; Daniel Kaufmann, "Ten Myths about Governance and Corruption," *Finance and Development*, 41 (September 2005), http://www.imf.org/external/pubs/ft/fandd/2005/09/index.htm.

can operate vertically within an institution or horizontally cut across political, economic and social spheres in a society or transnationally.[46]

Malfeasance and impunity can also be viewed from a bottom-up perspective, through the experiences of regular people. "Where corruption is endemic, it is the poorest that pay the highest price," observed Laurence Cockcroft, author and co-founder of Transparency International.[47] Aruna Roy, one of the founders of the Right-to-Information movement in India, characterizes corruption as: "the external manifestation of the denial of a right, an entitlement, a wage, a medicine..."[48] Thus, it constitutes a form of oppression and a loss of freedom that people can directly experience.

Adding People Power and Civil Resistance to the Anti-Corruption Equation

People power refers to the social, economic, political and psychological pressure that is exerted by significant numbers of individuals organized together around shared grievances and goals, conducting nonviolent tactics, such as civil disobedience, non-cooperation, strikes, boycotts, monitoring, petition drives, low-risk mass actions, power-holder engagement, community skills-building, and demonstrations. Gene Sharp, a seminal nonviolent resistance scholar, recorded over 198 types of tactics, and new ones are constantly generated by movements and campaigns, including those targeting corruption.[49] People power is a positive force that constructively confronts and seeks to change injustice and oppression.

Civil resistance—also called nonviolent resistance, nonviolent conflict and nonviolent action—is the civilian-based method to fight oppression and injustice through which people power is wielded. While active and strategic, it does not employ the threat or use of violence against human beings.

---

46. This systemic definition was developed by the author, who wishes to credit for inspiration, points made by Maria Gonzalez de Asis, World Bank, in an unpublished, working paper.

47. Laurence Cockcroft, *Global Corruption: Money, Power, and Ethics in the Modern World* (Philadelphia: University of Pennsylvania Press, 2012), 3.

48. Aruna Roy, "Survival and Right to Information," Gulam Rasool Third Memorial Lecture. MKSS website, http://www.mkssindia.org/node/42.

49. Gene Sharp, *Waging Nonviolent Struggle* (Boston: Porter Sargent, 2005).

People power and civil resistance impact corruption and produce change through three dynamics. First, they disrupt systems of graft and unaccountability, thereby making "business as usual" difficult or impossible. Second, they engage with powerholders and the public, in order to pull people towards their side, as well as to shift positions and loyalties within systems of corruption. Third, they apply (nonviolent) pressure through the power of numbers, that is, people collectively raising their voices over shared grievances and demands.

This framework is essential for developing new approaches to impacting corruption, gaining accountability, and building democracy. Traditional efforts to curb corruption have been top-down and elite-driven, with a focus on institutional development and reform, rules and integrity practices, such as public finance management. They are based on a flawed assumption that once anti-corruption frameworks are put in place, illicit practices will cease. But how can institutional mechanisms bring forth change, when they must be implemented by the very institutions that are corrupt? Those who are benefitting from graft are often expected to be the ones to curb it. Consequently, even when political will exists, it can be obstructed, because too many people have a stake in the dishonest status quo.

People power and civil resistance add a strategic advantage to curbing corruption. They can bring extra-institutional pressure to push for change and disrupt malfeasant systems when state and non-state powerholders are: indifferent to civic demands, beholden to special interests, corrupt and/or unaccountable, and institutional channels are blocked or ineffective.

What does this look like in reality?

Bosnia and Herzegovina: *Dosta!* (Enough!), a nonviolent, youth movement, promotes accountability and government responsibility to citizens, and seeks to foster civic participation across religious and ethnic groups in the country. In 2009 it launched a digital and on-the ground campaign that led to the resignation of Prime Minister Nedžad Branković over his acquisition of an upscale, state-owned apartment for approximately 500 euros through a series of administrative maneuvers. He left office a year and a half before his term was over.

Italy: *Addiopizzo* (Good-bye Protection Money) is a youth anti-mafia movement in Palermo that empowers businesses to publicly refuse to pay pizzo, educates schoolchildren about integrity, and mobilizes citizens to resist the Cosa Nostra crime group through simple, everyday acts, such as patronizing pizzo-free stores and businesses (reverse boycott). By 2012, 1,000 businesses joined the pizzo-free network, a new civic group, Libero Futuro (Future with Freedom), was formed by the older generation of anti-mafia advocates to complement the youth movement. The latter encourages and helps businesses go through denuncia, the process of testifying to the police and courts about mafia extortion.

Russia: The Movement to Defend Khimki Forest targeted corruption and impunity, and used both nonviolent action and legal efforts to prevent the bisection of an old-growth, state-protected woodland outside Moscow for a large highway and illegal development involving the French firm, Vinci. The European Bank for Reconstruction and Development and the European Investment Bank pulled out of the project. In 2010, then President Dmitry Medvedev temporarily suspended the project. In June 2013, Sherpa, the French human rights lawyers' group, along with other European NGOs, filed a formal complaint of corruption against Vinci with the Paris Prosecutor. In October 2013, the magistrate announced the opening of a preliminary enquiry into financial crimes. Nonetheless, construction began and the motorway is now open through the forest. While the movement did not succeed in changing the route or stopping the project, it valiantly delayed construction for years. Activists report that traffic is as bad as before, and there may yet be repercussions depending on the French court's verdict, which had not been announced as of October 2015.

Turkey: In 1997, the six-week "One Minute of Darkness for Constant Light" campaign pressured powerholders to tackle the crime syndicate, which refers to a nation-wide network of politicians, parts of the police, paramilitary groups linked to state security institutions, mafia and private sector. Through low-risk mass actions based on turning off lights for one minute every evening at 9:00 p.m., approximately 30 million people mobilized around the country over six weeks. As a result, it broke the taboo of exposing the country's crime syndicate, and led to judicial investigations, trials and verdicts.

These examples come from an international research project I conducted to document, analyze and distill general lessons from organized, sustained campaigns, movements and civic initiatives to impact corruption and impunity.[50] Sixteen cases were documented in total. In addition

---

50. The research culminated in a book: Shaazka Beyerle, *Curtailing Corruption: People Power for Accountability and Justice* (Boulder: Lynne Rienner 2014), and self-study curriculum, Freedom from Corruption. Information can be found here: www.curtailing corruption.org.

to the above four, grass-roots efforts were also studied in Afghanistan, Bangladesh, Brazil, Egypt, Guatemala, India, Indonesia, Kenya, Mexico, Philippines, South Korea, and Uganda.

Five Takeaways for Curbing Corruption and Reinforcing Democracy

At a minimum, there are five takeaways relevant to Europe and neighboring countries.

1. Organized, well-planned, strategic civic campaigns/movements power targeting corruption very often emerge in societies enduring poor governance, poverty, low levels of literacy, and severe repression, the latter perpetrated by the state, paramilitary groups, or organized crime. In spite of these tough contexts, or perhaps because of them, citizens are mobilizing, engaging in civil resistance, wielding people power to curb corruption and injustice, and building democracy from the bottom up.

2. Citizens-organized in grass-roots movements, campaigns and community initiatives-are protagonists and have achieved outcomes, for example:

    • *Afghanistan*: Community monitoring initiatives of reconstruction and development projects achieved an 82 percent success rate (460 out of 560), whereby problems were uncovered and rectified as a result of community pressure, or those responsible for the projects (contractors and the State) cooperated during the process, or no problems were found in an otherwise highly corrupt setting.

    • *Brazil*: Winning passage of the grass-roots Ficha Limpa (Clean Slate/Record) legislation, which prohibits candidates from taking office if they have been convicted of specific crimes by more than one judge (misuse of public funds, drug trafficking, rape, murder or racism).

    • *India:* Empowering regular people to refuse bribe demands by submitting Right to Information petitions and using the "Zero-Rupee" currency, and promoting values of integrity among university students, many of whom will become the next generation of officials, educators, business people and politicians.

    • *Indonesia:* Defending the Corruption Eradication Commission (KPK) from an organized plot led by senior officials in the police, judiciary and

Attorney General's office to neutralize it, and securing the release of two falsely imprisoned deputy commissioners.

- *South Korea:* 69 percent of candidates deemed "unfit to run for office" (59 out of 86) lost the 2000 National Assembly elections after a national blacklisting campaign.

- *Uganda:* SMS community monitoring of police intimidation and extortion together with locally-developed officer integrity training improved police behavior, and led to their requesting help from citizens and a civic group to overcome problems they faced within the institution.

3. Top-down and bottom-up approaches are complementary and synergistic. Bottom-up nonviolent campaigns, movements and local civic initiatives can:

- Empower and protect honest powerholders and integrity champions actively pursuing accountability, reform and change from within the system.

- Empower and protect honest state officials who simply don't want to engage in corrupt practices, that is, noncooperation with corruption.

- Disrupt vertical and horizontal forms of corruption, for example, through monitoring officials, parliamentarians, institutions, budgets, spending, public services, schools, hospitals, and development/anti-poverty programs.

- Create political will to enact policies, laws and administrative mechanisms to curb illicit financial flows and/or to implement them.

- Contribute to changing behaviors, practices and general norms regarding corruption.

4. Civic initiatives targeting corruption are incubators of democracy. They build democracy through action, such as informal elections, citizen-led surveys, monitoring elections and documenting fraud, and even voting for anti-corruption heroes. They are "exercises in participatory democracy that challenge the traditional 'rules of the game' in governance."[51] In my research, I observed that anti-corruption movements and campaigns were sometimes precursors to nonviolent democracy movements, or successors of them in new democracies. In the latter cases, veterans went on to lead bottom-up efforts against corruption and impunity.

---

51. Manuela Garza, "Social Audits as a Budget Monitoring Tool," International Budget Partnership Learning from Each Other Series, October 2012, 6.

5. Civil society, including regular people, can be the eyes and ears of anti-corruption efforts, from reform of the police to delivery of public services to development and reconstruction efforts. They often bring valuable input to the design of these efforts, as pointed out by the deputy editor of *Ukrainian Week*.

> *It is equally important for Ukraine's partners to interact with these [civil] initiatives and initiators on a regular basis to understand all the nuances of local political processes. These activists are knowledgeable enough to perceive these nuances, and most of them are not linked to the old system or its business interests. Ukraine's Western partners can make the Ukrainian government hear the voices of these activists much better than it does now.[52]*

—Anna Korbut

In conclusion, when political parties become entrenched, self-serving and corrupt, when voters face venal choices, when kleptocrats plunder their countries, when leaders veer to authoritarianism, democracy becomes a hollow shell. Organized civic initiatives, challenging the malfeasant status quo and engaging constructively with leaders and reformers, are upholding democracy from the bottom up. Their actions point to a new conceptualization of democracy that extends beyond representational political processes. Genuine democracy is a practice involving an active citizenry, government and state accountability, and the synergies between them.

---

52. Anna Korbut, "Reforms in Ukraine: No Room for Pessimism," *Judy Dempsey's Strategic Europe*, Carnegie Europe, August 6, 2015.

Part IV

How Effective Is the
EU's Democracy Promotion?

Chapter Nine

Constructing the EU as a Global Actor: A Critical Analysis of European Democracy Promotion[1]

Münevver Cebeci

The debate over the EU's actorness—especially its global actorness—has dominated European Foreign Policy Research (EFPR) for years. While some scholars underlined the EU's "international presence"[2] (rather than referring to it as an actor), some others have preferred to name it as "a global actor."[3] The first draft of the European Security Strategy, presented at the Thessaloniki European Council (June 20, 2003) by Javier Solana, reads as follows: "the European Union is, like it or not, a *global actor*; it should be ready to share in the responsibility for global security."[4] The main text of European Security Strategy, finally adopted on December 12, 2003 stated, instead: "the European Union is inevitably a *global player* [...] it should be ready to share in the responsibility for global security and in building a better world."[5] This difference in the wording of the two texts, by itself, is quite telling about the contested nature of the European Union (EU). It also shows the importance of language in the creation of a European identity and gives a hint as to how certain knowledge about the Union is produced and reproduced.

1. This chapter is a revised and updated version of the author's paper entitled "Constructing the EU as a Global Actor: European Foreign Policy Research Meets Global Challenges" presented at BISA-ISA Joint Conference 2012, Edinburgh, 20-22 June 2012. The research for this paper was supported by the Project Office (BAPKO) of Marmara University, Istanbul, with the project number SOS-D-090512-0186.
2. David Allen and Michael Smith, "Western Europe's Presence in the Contemporary International Arena", *Review of International Studies*, vol. 16, no.1 (1990), pp. 19-37.
3. Charlotte Bretherton and John Vogler, *The European Union as a Global Actor*, (London and New York: Routledge, 2006).
4. Council of the European Union, "A Secure Europe in a Better World." 10881/03 COSEC 3, Brussels, 25 June 2003, http://register.consilium.europa.cu/pdf/en/03/st10/st10881.en03.pdf (10 Nov. 2009).
5. Council of the European Union, "A Secure Europe in a Better World—European Security Strategy," Brussels, 12 December 2003, http://ue.eu.int/uedocs/cmsUpload/78367.pdf (12 Apr. 2009).

This chapter is based on the argument that the knowledge produced about the EU's global actorness is a positive one. In other words, the EU is constructed as "a *positive force* in world politics"[6]—i.e. "an ideal power."[7] This construction is mainly made through underlining the EU's *difference* as an actor in the world, which is post-modern and post-sovereign, which constitutes a model in terms of successful regional integration and promotion of democracy, human rights and the rule of law, and which acts as a normative power.

The EU's democracy promotion, on the other hand, constitutes an important part of its global actorness. Through its various tools, such as enlargement and trade conditionality, political dialogue, etc., it pursues its efforts at democratization in the world. Surely, the EU's image as a post-sovereign, post-modern entity, a model of peaceful integration and democracy, and a normative power, nurtures and legitimizes its democracy promotion efforts. In turn, these efforts add to and reproduce its representations that make it an "ideal power."

This chapter attempts to look into how the EU's identity in global politics is constructed in a specific way—both as a global actor and an ideal power; how such construction legitimizes its democracy promotion activities; and how the latter feed into such construction in turn. Its major argument is that despite the diversity in their approaches, both EFP analysts and practitioners help the construction of the EU as an ideal power, which legitimizes the Union's actions in global politics in general and its democracy promotion efforts in the world, in particular.

This study offers an analysis of European foreign policy through a discussion based on the "'ideal power Europe' meta-narrative" argument developed by the author in a former article.[8] The "ideal power Europe" meta-narrative is a concept used by the author to underline the power-knowledge relations behind the construction of the EU's identity as ideal. This conceptual framework is employed to reveal how the EFP researchers and practitioners convey the EU's story in a positive way and how such a positive depiction of the Union legitimizes its acts in global

---

6. Thomas Diez, "Constructing the Self and Changing Others: Reconsidering 'Normative Power Europe'," *Millennium: Journal of International Studies*, vol. 33, no.3 (2005), p. 613. Emphasis added.

7. Münevver Cebeci, "European Foreign Policy Research Reconsidered: Constructing an 'Ideal Power Europe' Through Theory?," *Millennium—Journal of International Studies*, vol. 40, no. 3 (2012), pp. 563-583.

8. Ibid.

politics. In such an endeavour, three major epistemological practices used by the EFP researchers and practitioners to convey a positive image of the EU are scrutinized: the discourse on post-sovereign/postmodern EU, the EU-as-a-model discourse and the normative power EU discourse. This chapter also makes a second reading of these three representations of the EU in such a way to reveal how the EU's actorness in global politics in general and its democracy promotion in particular are constructed. It attempts to elaborate on such construction critically and through a poststructuralist interpretation. The chapter starts with a definition of the conceptual framework adopted in this study. Then it looks into the three epistemological practices through which the EU's global actorness is conveyed in world politics as listed above. Finally, it provides an analysis of the EU's global actorness and its democracy promotion.

Actorness, Foreign Policy and Identity

Poststructuralist analyses of foreign policy claim that there is an open link between "foreign policy" and "identity" as the former is the major practice of creating an inside and an outside.[9] Foreign policy refers to the set of discourses and practices (institutions, procedures and processes) that constitute an actor's relations with its 'others'. In (re)turn, it is an actor's identity that legitimizes its foreign policy. Hansen argues that "identities and policies are constitutively or performatively linked."[10] This means that identity and foreign policy "are ontologically bound to each other."[11]

Similarly, "actorness," which is seen as "the ability to function actively and deliberately in relations to other actors in the international system,"[12] is closely related with identity construction. This is because actorness cannot be solely defined by technical criteria relating to the self (autonomy, capabilities, purposeful action, etc.) but it also finds meaning within the self's relations with the others, i.e., through communication, interaction, and recognition.

---

9. David Campbell, Writing Security—United States Foreign Policy and the Politics of Identity, (Revised Edition), (Minneapolis: University of Minnesota Press, 1998).

10. Lene Hansen, *Security as Practice—Discourse Analysis and the Bosnian War*, (London and New York: Routledge, 2006), pp. 10-11.

11. Cebeci, *op. cit.*, p. 565.

12. Gunnar Sjöstedt, *The External Role of the European Community*, (Farnborough: Saxon House, 1977), p. 15.

On the other hand, foreign policy researchers act as agents who convey certain knowledge about identities and policies of international actors. "Through articulating foreign policies and identities in a specific way," they serve "to legitimize foreign policies and [reinforce] their reproduction."[13] This is exactly the point, which shows their agency in creating the specific identities of international actors against their others. There is also a link between the knowledge provided by foreign policy researchers and by policy-makers (practitioners) as the latter use the knowledge produced by the former to legitimize their acts and in (re)turn the practitioners' discourse and acts feed into foreign policy research. This chapter looks into how an 'ideal' European identity is constructed by both EFP researchers and practitioners. The European discourse and practice on democracy promotion also adds to the construction of such an identity.

Marking the EU's Difference:
The EU as a Postmodern/Post-Sovereign Actor Discourse

The definition of the EU as "distinctive actor"[14] marks its identity in global politics. The Union is regarded as a "unique"[15] actor and a "hybrid polity."[16] The claim that the EU is unique is the most important way of referring to its *difference* from all other actors. Because the EU "is not directly analogous to any one of" the international actors, it "may therefore be considered a unique type"[17] which is "more than an intergovernmental organization, less than a state"[18]. One of the major discourses that marks the EU's *difference* from other actors revolves around its postmodern/post-sovereign/post-Westphalian nature.[19]

---

13. Cebeci, *op. cit.*, 565.

14. Karen E. Smith, "The European Union: A Distinctive Actor in International Relations," *The Brown Journal of World Affairs*, vol. 9, no. 2 (Winter/ Spring 2003), pp. 103-113.

15. See for example, Brian White, *Understanding European Foreign Policy*, (Hampshire and New York: Palgrave, 2001), p. 24.

16. See for example, Ian Manners, "Normative Power Europe: A Contradiction in Terms?," *Journal of Common Market Studies*, vol. 40, no. 2 (2002), p. 241. Also see: Bretherton and Vogler, *The European Union as a Global Actor*, 21 and 58-59.

17. White, *op. cit.*, p. 23.

18. Bretherton and Vogler, *op. cit.*, 21-22.

19. The EU is regarded by EFP researchers and policy-makers as postmodern and post-sovereign because it has supranational characteristics and its member states have thus transferred some part of sovereignty to the Union level. See, for example, James A Caporaso, "The European Union and Forms of State: Westphalian, Regulatory or Post-Modern?," *Journal of*

Manners and Whitman even claim that the international identity of the EU is "one which exists in contrast to the Westphalian norms of sovereignty and territoriality."[20] It is this underlined *difference* of the EU, which mostly legitimizes its acts in world politics. Manners argues that the EU "exists as being different to pre-existing political forms and that this particular difference pre-disposes it to act in a normative way." This statement also manifests how the knowledge produced and reproduced about the EU's *difference* as an actor gives it enhanced legitimacy to promote democracy in the world.

The EU's representation as a post-modern entity has become a theme of wide resonance in European studies, expanding upon a European practitioner's, Robert Cooper's[21], definition, which referred to the European state as post-modern and as "more pluralist, more complex, less centralised than the bureaucratic modern state but not at all chaotic, unlike the pre-modern."[22] Building on his arguments, many European studies scholars compared and contrasted the EU with its modern/pre-modern others such as the U.S., Russia and the Middle East;[23] underlining the "political incompatibility"[24] between them; establishing the EU's difference against its pre-modern, modern, and conflictual others; portraying it as "ideal" and legitimizing its intervention (implicit or explicit) in its others' domestic and international affairs.[25]

Common Market Studies, vol. 34, no. 1, (March 1996), pp. 45-48; William Wallace, "Europe after the Cold War: interstate order or post-sovereign regional system?," *Review of International Studies*, vol. 25, (1999), p. 222.

20. Ian Manners and Richard G. Whitman, "The 'difference engine': constructing and representing the international identity of the European Union," *Journal of European Public Policy*, vol. 10, no. 3 (2003), p. 382.

21. Cooper has worked for the EU at several different positions.

22. Robert Cooper, *The Post-Modern State and the World Order*, (London: Demos, 1996). p. 31.

23. See for example, Nicolai Wenzer, "Postmodernism and Its Discontents: Whither Constitutionalism After God and Reason?," *New Perspectives on Political Economy*, vol. 4, no. 2 (2008): 173-174 http://pcpe.libinst.cz/nppe/4_2/nppe4_2_4.pdf (3 February 2012); Martin Ortega (2003). "The Achilles Heel of Transatlantic Relations," in *Shift or Rift—Assessing US-EU Relations after Iraq*, ed. Gustav Lindstrom, Paris: European Union Institute for Security Studies, p. 162; and Ivan Krastev, "Russia as the "Other Europe'," *Russia in Global Affairs* 4, October-December 2007, http://eng.globalaffairs.ru/number/n_9779 (3 February 2012).

24. Krastev, *op. cit.*

25. Cf. Diez, *op. cit.*, p. 629. Surely this is not the case with the US. However, in the case of the US, the EU is compared and contrasted with it in terms of the latter's multilateralist and soft approach to democratization and crisis management and the former's unilateralist and military approach. See, e.g., Thomas Diez and Ian Manners, "Reflecting on Normative Power Europe", in Felix Berenskoetter and M.J. Williams, eds., *Power in World Politics*, (London and New York: Routledge, 2007), p. 180–3.

On the other hand, a second reading suggests that the EU's post-sovereign/postmodern nature does not represent a total break with the modern state, although Manners and Whitman claim that the international identity of the EU is "one which exists in contrast to the Westphalian norms of sovereignty and territoriality."[26] For example, Waever sees the post-sovereign EU as an entity, which exists besides the sovereign state—without "contesting state sovereignty."[27] This becomes all the more important for the EU's democracy promotion in the world. Haine argues: "The foundation of a 'post-modern' Europe is a competent and controlling State rather than a vigorous civil society. After all, the integration process was an elite-driven mechanism in which people had few if no say."[28] This statement explains the EU's technocratic approach to democracy promotion, and reveals how the European model of democracy, which is presented as 'ideal', cannot be successfully applied everywhere.

All in all, it can be argued that naming the EU as postmodern and post-sovereign goes beyond the practice of understanding the "nature of the beast."[29] It underlines and enhances the EU's difference from its "Others"; representing the European self as democratic, civilised, and peaceful (if not superior) and its others as undemocratic, conflictual, and uncivilised (if not inferior). Furthermore, it legitimizes the EU's actions in global politics in general, and its democracy promotion efforts in particular. The EU's actions in this regard are mostly based on an asymmetrical relationship, where the EU sets the standards of democracy, decides on the conditions to be applied on the target countries/societies, and expects them to follow suit. This can be regarded as "the dominative dimension of European foreign policy that arises from the EU's exercise of post-sovereign normative power."[30]

---

26. Manners and Whitman, *op. cit*, p. 382.

27. Ole Waever, "Identity, Integration and Security—Solving the Sovereignty Puzzle in E.U. Studies," *Journal of International Affairs*, vol. 48, no.2 (1995), pp. 389-481.

28. Jean Yves Haine, "The European Crisis of Liberal Internationalism", paper presented at the 7th Biennial Conference of the European Community Studies Association—Canada, "The Maturing European Union", Edmonton, AB, 25-27 September 2008, 12. http://www.ecsa-c.ca/biennial2008/Conference%20Program_files/Haine.pdf (14.10.2015)

29. Bretherton and Vogler, *op. cit.*, pp. 37-61.

30. Michael Merlingen, "Everything is dangerous: A Critique of 'Normative Power Europe'," *Security Dialogue* vol. 38, no. 4, (2007), p. 438.

Projecting the European Model:
The Discourse of Leading by Virtuous Example

Many EFP analysts and practitioners argue that the EU leads by *virtuous* example.[31] It is not only seen as a model of peaceful regional integration but it is also regarded as a model in promoting democracy, human rights and the rule of law. Solana, for example, lists the characteristics of the European model as: "compassion with those who suffer; peace and reconciliation through integration; a strong attachment to human rights, democracy and the rule of law; a spirit of compromise, plus a commitment to promote, in a pragmatic way, an international system based on rules."[32] There are also analysts who name the EU as a model in terms of having the best practices with regard to socio-economic and environmental policies.[33]

The EU-as-a-model discourse does not only help European practitioners legitimize their policies, but it also empowers the Union. In a critical article on NPE, Forsberg argues that viewing the Union as a *virtuous* example "points to the idea that the EU has power when it simply stands as a model for others to follow."[34] On the other hand, regarding the Union as a model also brings about the idea that the others are expected to imitate this model[35] and copy the EU's *best practices*.[36] It is through such discourse that the Union and its model are again portrayed as the ideal/ peaceful/ democratic/ civilized against its imperfect/ conflictual/ undemocratic/ uncivilized others.

Representation of the EU as a model can be read in various ways. Such a representation surely adds to the Union's international presence

---

31. See, e.g., Manners, *op. cit.*, p. 244.

32. Javier Solana, 'Identity and Foreign Policy', ESDP Newsletter, no. 3 (2007), p. 9.

33. See, e.g., Dominique Strauss-Kahn, "Building a Political Europe: 50 proposals for tomorrow's Europe", Rapporteur, Olivier Ferrand, April 2004, http://ec.europa.eu/dgs/policy_advisers/archives/experts_groups/docs/rapport_europe_strauss_kahn_en.pdf; and, Maria Joao Rodrigues, "The Influence of the European Socio-economic Model in the Global Economy," in Mario Telo, ed., *The European Union and Global Governance*, (London and New York: Routledge, 2009), pp. 104–27.

34. Tuomas Forsberg, "Normative Power Europe, Once Again: A Conceptual Analysis of an Ideal Type," *Journal of Common Market Studies*, vol.49, no. 6 (2011), p. 1197.

35. This is what Börzel and Risse refer to as "emulation". Tanja Börzel and Thomas Risse, "Diffusing (Inter-) Regionalism—The EU as a Model of Regional Integration," *KFG The Transformative Power of Europe Working Paper* 7, (Berlin: Freie Universitat, 2009). Note that Forsberg also cites Börzel and Risse: Forsberg, *op. cit.*, 1198.

36. Forsberg, *op. cit.*, p. 1198.

and visibility, empowering it against others. This surely contributes to the Union's relevance in the world.[37] Furthermore, it gives the legitimacy to the EU to apply conditionality on those countries that seek closer relations with the Union in order to get a share from its welfare and peace. In other words, it legitimizes the EU's asymmetrical approach in its enlargement, neighbourhood and trade policies, where the EU determines the content and the conditions of the relationship and the target countries are expected to accept such relationship, only with a symbolic say regarding the its pace rather than its content.

The EU usually asks the countries in other regions to adopt a one-size-fits-all model, especially in its democracy promotion efforts. The Euro-Mediterranean Partnership is the most important example of such a one-size-fits-all approach that does not take into account particular social, cultural, political and economic characteristics of target societies.[38] Despite the recent change in the rhetoric of a 'one-size-fits-all model' after the Arab uprisings—that "[t]he EU does not seek to impose a model or a ready-made recipe for political reform"—the Union still attempts to promote its own notion of "deep democracy" in its revised ENP.[39]

The EU-as-a-virtuous-example discourse brings about and nurtures the Union's claim that it represents the *best practices*. The EU's self-declared best practices also provide it with the power to set the rules of democratization. This legitimizes its asymmetrical approach towards third countries and regions. The problem with the imposition of the Union's best practices is that while doing so, the EU overlooks the specific characteristics of the target countries/societies and falls short of addressing grassroots needs. This encourages mimicry on the part of the target societies, inevitably reproducing the colonial practice.[40]

---

37. Roy Ginsberg, *Demystifying the European Union—The Enduring Logic of Regional Integration*, (Lanham: Rowman and Littlefield, 2007), p. 2.

38. See: Rafaella A. Del Sarto and Tobias Schumacher, 'From EMP to ENP: What's at Stake with the European Neighbourhood Policy towards the Southern Mediterranean?', *European Foreign Affairs Review*, vol.10, (2005), p. 17-38.

39. European Commission and High Representative of the European Union for Foreign Affairs and Security Policy, "A New Response to a Changing Neighbourhood—A Review of European Neighbourhood Policy", COM(2011) 303 final, Brussels, 25 May 2011. For more on the EU's rhetorical change in the revised ENP and its reflections in practice, see: Münevver Cebeci, "Deconstructing the 'Ideal Power Europe' Meta-Narrative in the European Neighbourhood Policy", in *The Revised European Neighbourhood Policy*, eds Tobias Schumacher and Dimitris Bouris, (Hampshire and New York: Palgrave, pp. n/a.

40. Cebeci, "European Foreign Policy Research Reconsidered", p. 572.

The EU as a Specific Type of Actor:
The Normative Power Europe Discourse and Its Discontents

Niemann and Bretherton contend that "approaches such as those on civilian and normative power Europe (NPE) are built on the assumption that the EU possesses sufficient actorness."[41] Manners also argues that one of the meanings of normative power is "as a characterization of a type of actor and its international identity."[42] The NPE discourse is based on the EU's "normative difference"[43] which is marked by its post-sovereign/postmodern presence, its virtuous example, and its promotion of democracy, human rights and the rule of law not only in Europe but also in the world. It is this difference which enables the EU to define what is 'normal' for other countries.[44]

Defining what is normal for others is problematic as it refers to a disciplinary and asymmetrical relationship. The "normative power Europe" discourse legitimizes the Union's imposition of a "silent disciplining power"[45] on other countries. This does not only reflect the "dominative dimension of European foreign policy"[46] and how EFP researchers contribute to it, but it also puts the EU in a superior position vis-a-vis those countries that are expected to fulfill EU conditionality if they want to have closer relations with the Union. Those countries are inevitably portrayed as the imperfect/undemocratic others (as those which can improve their situation only with the Union's help) whereas the EU's ideal characteristics are produced and reproduced through such discourse and practice.

Another problem with the NPE discourse is about the dichotomy between norms and interests. Claiming that the norms-interests

---

41. Arne Niemann and Charlotte Bretherton, "EU external policy at the crossroads: The challenge of actorness and effectiveness," *International Relations*, vol. 27, no. 3 (2013),p. 262.
42. Ian Manners, "The European Union's Normative Power: Critical Perspectives and Perspectives on the Critical," in *Normative Power Europe: Empirical and Theoretical Perspectives*, ed. Richard G. Whitman, (Hampshire and New York: Palgrave Macmillan, 2011), pp. 231-232.
43. See, for example, Manners, "Normative Power Europe: A Contradiction in Terms?," and Manners and Whitman, "The 'Difference Engine'."
44. Manners, "Normative Power Europe: A Contradiction in Terms?," p. 253.
45. Ole Waever, "The EU as a security actor—Reflections from a pessimistic constructivist on post-sovereign security orders," in *International Relations Theory and the Politics of European Integration—Power, Security and Community*, eds. Morten Kelstrup and Michael Williams (London: Routledge, 2000), p. 261.
46. Merlingen, "Everything is dangerous", 438.

dichotomy is a "false" one, Manners underlines that "the separation of norms and interests, both in terms of policy-making and policy analysis, is impossible."[47] Nevertheless, the author of this article still finds such an argument problematic because when interests of an entity (and of its members, as in the case of the EU) override its norms, insisting on naming that entity as a 'normative power' pertains to a power-knowledge relationship, where the dominative dimension of European foreign policy goes hand in hand with privileged EFP research scripts.

As a matter of fact, some of conditions that the EU expects the third countries to fulfil are normatively determined by the EU, as Manners argues[48] (as in the case of the abandonment of the death penalty). But more often, those conditions better serve the interests of the Union and its member states rather than solely being applied for normative purposes. The fact that the EU supported authoritarian regimes of North African countries for years for the sake of stability and security in the region, before the Arab uprisings, is a crucial example in this respect that can hardly be explained through the normative power Europe discourse. On the other hand, such practices on the part of the EU surely raise doubts about its democracy promotion efforts.

The EU's democracy promotion activities are shaped by the discourse of normative power, especially by the Union's claim to the universality of the norms that it represents. Nevertheless, the claim to be representing universal norms and values is also problematic as it also reproduces certain knowledge about the EU, legitimizing its acts in global politics. The discourse on the EU as representing universal norms inevitably constructs the Union's several others as either violating them, or having difficulties in complying with them. Thus, the EU's actorness in global politics is marked by its normative difference, which gives it the 'power' to legitimize its civilizing acts against others.

---

47. Ian Manners , "Sociology of Knowledge and Production of Normative Power in the European Union's External Actions", *Journal of European Integration*, vol. 37, no. 2, (2015), pp, 299-318, 300-301.
48. Manners, "Normative Power Europe: A Contradiction in Terms?".

The EU as a Global Actor and its Democracy Promotion in the World: Displacing the "Ideal Power Europe" Meta-narrative

There is a general understanding in EFPR that the EU is not a homogenous/monolithic[49] and full-fledged global actor. Even Bretherton and Vogler who argued for its global actorness in 1999 and the early 2000s have revised their approach and started to consider the Union as "a global actor past its peak"[50]. In their view, "[w]hile the EU will remain an important global actor, its ability to exert influence externally, which was at its peak in the post-Cold War period, has declined since the mid-2000s;" mainly because of "the disastrous impact of" the economic crisis in Europe and "the difficult renegotiation of UK membership."[51]

It should be noted at this point that although many analysts find problems with the EU's global actorness and its "normative" nature; they tend to focus on the *aspirations* of the EU and regard its future on positive terms. In a sense, the EU's 'ideal power' image is constructed more on the premise that it *aspires* to act in ideal ways, rather than on the basis that it acts in ideal ways. This is important because, in practice, it is usually very hard to distinguish between norms and interests, and the EU fails to act in some cases due to its non-unitary nature and associated problems with coherence.[52] Diez defines "three epistemological standings in" Manners' NPE approach: "as an ontological category for classification"—the EU example; "as an explanation of EU foreign policy"—especially EU conditionality; and "as a normative aim and critique of the present."[53] The third epistemological standing of NPE that he refers to also captures the point that this chapter seeks to make with regard to aspirations. Having a normative aim for the future means basing the NPE on a "future to be brought about."[54]

---

49. Note the exception of Bretherton and Vogler who take the EU as a singular unit in their analysis. Bretherton and Vogler, *The European Union as a Global Actor*.

50. Charlotte Bretherton and John Vogler, "Past Its Peak: The European Union as a Global Actor 10 Years after," in *The EU as a Foreign and Security Policy Actor*, ed. Finn Laursen (Dordrecht: Republic of Letters Publishing, 2009), 23–44; and Charlotte Bretherton and John Vogler, "A global actor past its peak?," *International Relations*, vol. 27, no. 3 (2013), pp. 375–390.

51. Bretherton and Vogler, "A global actor past its peak?," p. 387.

52. Cebeci, "European Foreign Policy Research Reconsidered," pp. 576-578.

53. Thomas Diez, "Normative power as hegemony," *Cooperation and Conflict*, vol. 48, no. 2 (2013), p. 204.

54. Jean-François Lyotard, "Memorandum on Legitimation," in *The Political*, ed. David Ingram, (Massachusetts and Oxford: Blackwell Publishers Ltd., 2002), p. 234.

Manners also acknowledges this aspirational dimension when he attaches the Union a "normative quality" on the basis of its aspirations; underlining "that the EU *should* act to extend its norms into the international system."[55] In his view, the EU can do this via ensuring consistency and coherence in its acts[56] in order to show "that the EU is not hypocritical in promoting norms which it does itself not comply with," and, "that the EU is not simply promoting its own norms, but that the normative principles that constitute it and its external actions are part of a more universalizable and holistic strategy for world peace." Manners concludes: "The creative efforts and *longer term vision* of EU normative power towards the achievement of a more just, cosmopolitical world which empowers people in the actual conditions of their lives should and must be based on more universally accepted values and principles that can be explained to both Europeans and non-European[s] alike."[57]

Through such logic, the EU's 'ideal' traits are established in any case. Even if it fails to act in "ideal ways" it suffices for the Union to "aspire" to act in ideal ways.[58] This is exactly the point which produces and reproduces the EU's actorness in global politics in the form of an "ideal power." The EU's identity is constructed positively against all other actors through its unique postmodern/post-sovereign nature, its virtuous example and its normative difference; not only with reference to what it is and what it does but also with reference to what it aspires to.

Neither the EU's global actorness nor its democracy promotion is without problems. EU practice usually does not match the 'ideal power Europe' discourse in many instances. This is also the case in the Union's democracy promotion activities. Without infringing the poststructuralist nature of this chapter, it would be helpful to have a look at the EU's practices in this regard, to see how the 'ideal power Europe discourse' employed by EFP researchers legitimizes them. This would also testify to Hansen's poststructuralist claim that foreign policy researchers act as agents that help "the construction of a link between policy and identity that makes the two appear consistent with each other."[59] EU practice usually displaces the 'ideal power Europe' meta-narrative that is con-

---

55. Manners, "Normative Power Europe: A Contradiction in Terms?," p. 252.

56. Ian Manners, "The Normative Ethics of the European Union," *International Affairs*, vol. 84, no. 1 (2006), p. 76.

57. *Ibid.*, 80. Emphasis added.

58. Cebeci, "European Foreign Policy Research Reconsidered," p.578.

59. Hansen, *Security as Practice*, p. 25.

veyed by EFP researchers in this regard, shattering the link between the Union's policy and identity.

For example, European foreign policy (especially EU conditionality) is pursued with the logic that the EU's model of democracy, human rights and the rule of law can fit all cases and can be successful in other parts of the world as well. However, this is not always the case in practice. An important problem in this regard is the EU's technocratic approach to democracy promotion.[60] Such a technocratic approach especially reveals itself in the EU's emphasis on governance aspects of democratization, which falls short of considering the specific political and cultural dynamics of the target societies. Such a technocratic approach inevitably brings about the creation of a "shallow"[61] form of democracy in the target countries. "Shallow democracy" in this sense refers to the minimum requirement of free elections; a parliamentary system based on majority rule; and a few selective political reforms. Referring to the case of Morocco, Kausch contends: "[H]opeful European talk of a regional model of democratisation is misplaced. Political reforms, instead of being steps in a consistent, overarching process towards democracy, have been ad hoc, selective and often superficial."[62]

Another problem in EU democracy promotion is that the EU, as an international organization, has to work, inevitably and mainly, with the governments of target countries.[63] Although this might seem as natural, corresponding mostly with the governments might be counter-productive for democratization because in most cases it is the governments of target countries that tend to limit democracy and fundamental rights and freedoms. This has been the case in North Africa for years, especially before the Arab uprisings. Echagüe refers to this as the EU's

---

60. See, e.g., Milja Kurki, 'Democracy through technocracy? Reflections on technocratic assumptions in EU democracy promotion discourse', *Journal of Intervention and Statebuilding* 5, no. 2 (2011): 211-234; and Piotr Maciej Kaczynski and Piotr Kazmierkiewicz, 'European Neighbourhood Policy: Differentiation and Political Benchmarks', EuroMeSCo Paper 44, September 2005, http://www.euromesco.net/euromesco/media/euromesco_paper_44.pdf (30 September 2013).

61. Vicky Reynaert, 'Preoccupied with the Market: The EU as a Promoter of "Shallow" Democracy in the Mediterranean', *European Foreign Affairs Review*, vol. 16, no. 5, (2011), pp. 623-637.

62. Kristina Kausch, "Morocco" *in Is the European Union Supporting Democracy in its Neighbourhood?*, Richard Youngs, ed., (Spain: FRIDE, 2008), p. 10 (9-31)

63. For a similar argument, see: Stefanie Kappler, 'Divergent Transformation and Centrifugal Peacebuilding: The EU in Bosnia and Herzegovina', *International Peacekeeping*, vol. 19, no. 5, (2012), p. 616.

"indulgence or, some would say, connivance with a non-democratic regime"[64] and "its receptiveness to government priorities,"[65] in the case of Jordan. On the other hand, it should not also be forgotten that EU conditionality also helps the governments of third countries legitimize their acts in domestic politics through the rhetoric of "EU induced reforms" where those acts might be met with harsh criticism and opposition without the EU tag.[66] This example also shows that the EU's normative power image conveyed by EFP researchers on the one hand and its practices oriented towards preserving security and stability—even preserving and pursuing its member states' interests—on the other, do not match.

An important ingredient of democracy promotion, support for civil society is also problematic in the case of the EU. Although the Union has an ambitious agenda for supporting civil society in its enlargement and neighbourhood policies, its practice on the ground suffers from certain discrepancies. The first one is that the EU tends to support professionalized civil society organizations, which seek their own interests (rather than the everyday needs of the locals), and in many cases grassroots actors cannot have their voice heard in the EU circles. In many cases, the EU has also been criticized for not incorporating civil society organizations in its negotiations with the governments of target countries (for example, in accession negotiations in the case of Turkey,[67] and, in negotiations of the Action Plans with ENP Partners, as in the case of Jordan[68]).

The EU also pursues a selective agenda in its conditionality, mainly based on its Member States' and its own interests. For example, despite grave human rights problems in Morocco and Jordan, these problems have not stopped the EU from "granting advanced status" to these countries in the ENP.[69] Although "norms and interests cannot so easily be separated and both are infused by each other,"[70] still this example

---

64. Ana Echagüe, "Jordan", in *Is the European Union Supporting Democracy in its Neighbourhood?*, ed Richard Youngs, (Spain: FRIDE, 2008), p. 33. (33-53)

65. Ibid., 44.

66. For a similar argument, see: Kappler, 'Divergent Transformation', 616.

67. Atila Eralp, 'The role of temporality and interaction in the Turkey-EU relationship', *New Perspectives on Turkey*, vol. 40, no. 1, (2009), p. 162.

68. Echagüe, "Jordan", 42.

69. Tobias Schumacher, "The EU and the Arab Spring: Between Spectatorship and Actorness", *Insight Turkey*, vol. 13, no. 3, (2011), pp. (107-119) 113.

alone suffices to show that the EU is not the "normative power" some analysts believe it to be. On the other hand, it is also widely observed that the EU also acts selectively in promoting democratization, prioritizing issues that are more popular among the European public, rather than addressing the needs of the locals. In the case of Turkey, for example, the EU has paid more attention to the Kurdish issue, civil-military relations, and the status of the Greek Orthodox theological/clergy school in Halki/Heybeliada for years, mostly overlooking the general human rights problems in the country until the Gezi Protests.[71]

The EU's promotion of its own model is also problematic in the sense that it does not take into account the specific political, social, economic and cultural characteristics of the target societies and rather imposes its own best practices in a one-size-fits-all fashion. The EU's discourse and insistence on its own model and best practices automatically put the Union in a dominant and dictating position in its relationship with the others where the EU sets the conditions and the others have to fulfill them. Haine summarizes the EU's problems with regard to democracy promotion as follows:

> The [EU] does not pay sufficient attention or give sufficient support to civil society, civic organizations, opposition parties, or NGOs. Moreover, when there is a democracy agenda, it relies on existing regimes, some robustly authoritarian, to implement liberal reforms, and for those, there are no real incentives to comply with democratic and human rights rules. Overall, the union's approach privileges order over reforms, stability over democracy, and the status quo over change.[72]

All in all, it can be claimed that the EU as an actor has a general problem about democracy promotion in other countries and its practices mainly lead to or nurture the creation of a superficial understanding of democracy pursued for instrumentalist reasons (for establishing closer relations with the Union). On the other hand, the EU's portrayal as an 'ideal power' in any case—even when it does not act ideally— surely legitimizes its governmentality, empowering it in the face of the

---

70. Diez, 'Normative Power as Hegemony', p. 201.

71. See several Progress Reports on Turkey by the European Commission for the EU's priorities in promoting democracy.

72. Jean Yves Haine, "The European crisis of liberal internationalism", *International Journal*, vol. 64, no. 2 (2009), pp. (453-479) 460.

others. Such construction leaves its others as *the defective*, which have problems that can only be solved through compliance with EU standards and which are "incapable"[73] of adopting necessary reforms without "assistance"[74] from the Europeans. The EU's asymmetrical approach towards those countries that seek membership in the EU or that would like to have access to European markets is justified through the employment of such an "ideal power Europe" narrative. This also brings about the imposition of the EU's best practices on others in a fashion that does not take into account the economic, cultural, political and social specificities of the countries concerned. The result is insensitivity towards the everyday needs of the peoples in the geographies that the EU intervenes—economically, politically or militarily.

Conclusion

This chapter has argued that the construction of the EU as a specific type of actor in global politics inevitably creates a positive European identity against its others, legitimizing the Union's application of some form of governmentality to various countries and regions. It has analysed thoroughly how the EU's identity in global politics is constructed in a specific way—as "a positive force"[75]—by European Foreign Policy (EFP) researchers and policy-makers/practitioners. It looked into three major epistemological practices that define the EU as a specific type of actor: the EU as a unique, postmodern/post-sovereign actor discourse, the discourse on the EU as an actor which leads by virtuous example, and the EU as a normative power discourse.

It has shown that a crucial part of the EU's actorness is based on its unique nature. For those who construct it as such, the Union's uniqueness reveals itself in its structural and functional traits as its member states have transferred parts of their sovereignty to the Union level and the EU thus enjoys pooled sovereignty. These traits refer mainly to the Union's supranational characteristics. This is exactly the point that leads to the construction of the EU's identity as postmodern/post-sovereign, transcending the modern/sovereign state. On the other hand, this study

---

73. Senem Aydin-Düzgit, *Constructions of European Identity—Debates and Discourses on Turkey and the EU*, (Hampshire and New York: Palgrave Macmillan, 2012), pp. 67, 96, 145, 152.
74. *Ibid.*, 45,67,77-98.
75. Diez, "Constructing the Self and Changing Others."

has revealed that a different interpretation is also possible: that the EU's construction as such refers to the legitimization of the EU's governmentality in world politics.

This chapter has further put forward that the representation of the EU as a virtuous example for others also legitimizes the EU's imposition of its own model and best practices on others. This surely nurtures the Union's actorness in global politics as it provides relevance to its role and actions. Such a self-claimed role makes the EU apply a one-size-fits-all approach in its relations with other regions that falls short of addressing the specific economic, cultural, social and political needs of the target societies.

The discourse on the EU's normative power has also been scrutinized in detail in this chapter. It has shown how the Union's representation as a normative power has given it the justification to define what is normal for others. It has also argued that the EU's normativity is highly contested due to the norms/interests dichotomy and it is very hard to distinguish whether the EU acts on its own interests or seeks to pursue normative claims in some cases. On the other hand, the quest for being a normative power and representing universal values endows the EU with the legitimacy to impose its own civilizational standards on others—an action which is very much criticized by some (although very few) EFP researchers, because they see it as a neo-colonial attempt.

Lastly, this chapter has attempted to displace 'the ideal power Europe' meta-narrative especially through looking into how its normative aspirations for the future legitimize its governmentality today and how the EU's practice on the ground shatters the 'ideal power Europe' image that is conveyed by EFP researchers to make the Union's identity and policies seem consistent with each other. It has shown, through scrutinizing the EU's democracy promotion activities in the world, that the EU practice does not usually match the NPE identity attached to it. It has also revealed that the EU's democracy promotion efforts do not go beyond the portrayal of the EU as an ideal entity which promotes universal values and norms and of its others (the target societies) as imperfect—as societies which need the EU's help in order to become democratic, etc.

All in all, it can be concluded that the EU's global actorness and its ideal traits are represented as characteristics that can be maintained under any circumstances. Even the Union's own internal problems such as financial crises (e.g., the Euro crisis) or political crises (e.g., the rene-gotiation of the UK's membership) cannot seriously damage its ideal image constructed by EFP researchers and policy-makers.[76] It can only be regarded as "a global actor past its peak,"[77] but still as an "impor-tant"[78] one—and definitely not as a failing one. This shows how the image of an 'ideal power' is maintained (produced and reproduced) even when the EU is experiencing hardships—if not failing. Any future work on the EU's actorness should thus take into account how the EU's iden-tity as an 'ideal power' is constructed against its imperfect others and how this legitimizes its role and actions in global politics.

---

76. Cf. Bretherton and Vogler, "A global actor past its peak?," p. 387.

77. *Ibid.*

78. *Ibid.*

Chapter Ten

Human Rights and Democracy Promotion: EU Blows on an Uncertain Trumpet

Geoffrey Harris[1]

For if the trumpet give an uncertain sound, who shall prepare himself to the battle?

I Corinthians 14:8

In the decades since 1973 and the first enlargement of the European Community, as it was then called, and up until the financial crisis of 2008, Europeans approached neighbors, potential new members and others around the world with something to offer: the lessons of a successful, attractive, and often inspiring project. A project that seemed to achieve a triumphal advance at the beginning of the 21st century with the peaceful reunification a continent hitherto divided by war and ideological conflict. This had been achieved on the basis of common values: democracy, human rights and the rule of law.

The concept of democracy promotion as such was not, initially, the basis of a conscious policy. As the European project became more ambitious such policies have been put in place, European institutions have developed their own terminology reflecting a view that they should be assisting the development and stabilization of democracy.

Twenty years after the apparent triumphs of the EU, the establishment of a single currency and the enlargement of the Union, these basic values face unexpectedly strong challenges from both inside the Union and in its neighborhood.

In the second decade of the 21st century the European idea is facing a crisis of confidence. The institutions of the EU do not seem to inspire even their own citizens. Whatever internal challenges the EU now faces in terms of populist challenges to EU membership, immigration, terrorism and the economy, these challenges can only be confronted and

---

1. The views expressed in this paper are strictly personal and do not necessarily reflect those of the European Parliament.

resolved through democracy. Elections and referenda will decide how the EU goes forward. It does, however, already seem clear that the profound nature of the current crisis risks undermining the power of attraction of the EU as well as its ability to influence its region and build on the huge achievements of the last 70 years.

1973–1989: Steady Progress Based on Common Values

On October 17th, 1989, Commission President Jacques Delors addressed the students of the College of Europe in the following terms:

> The European Community, and the peoples and nations that it encompasses, will exist truly only if it has the means to defend its values and to apply them for the benefit of all, in short, to be generous. Let us be powerful enough to command respect and to promote our values of freedom and solidarity. In a world such as ours, there can be no other way.[2]

The promotion of these values had already been a growing element in the emerging structure of European foreign policy cooperation even in the 1970s. Indeed, perhaps the most convincing argument for Europe to show greater confidence in these values is provided by a measured and objective re-examination of the historical consequences of the Helsinki process of the 1970s. This was a triumph of 'soft power' achieved almost by accident in a Europe divided and, with many countries, dominated by outside powers. The USA and the USSR both in their own ways were committed to an extremely 'realistic view' of how to achieve stability in Europe. At the time, Europe (the Community then had only nine member states) was, just as now, deeply affected by an international economic crisis and the Community was at the time tinkering with its own very weak diplomatic machinery for 'European Political Cooperation.'

In spite of this very low profile, compared, say, with NATO, it emerged that

> Human rights became part of the trans-European agenda only through the initiative of the European Community, which intro-

---

2. http://www.cvce.eu/obj/address_given_by_jacques_delors_bruges_17_october_1989-en-5bbb1452-92c7-474ba7cf-a2d281898295.html.

duced its first as a topic for substantive East-West cooperation, and later as a principle of relations among European States.[3]

If it was possible for the EC to achieve so much in the decades after 1975, there is no reason to be quite so pessimistic as to the potential of the modern EU to build on its achievements and in doing so to play its full part in enhancing respect for universal human rights.

A normative agenda was, therefore, part of a specific European contribution to East-West relations advanced at a time when the U.S. administration (Nixon and Kissinger) had little faith at all in multilateral diplomacy and showed little sign of any commitment to interpreting the advancement of human rights in their foreign policy. The EC was not only interested, at a minimum, in improving contacts among Europeans, but was also looking for a distinct identity as a basis for developing its international role.

In the 1980s the accession of Greece, Spain and Portugal followed inevitably from their overthrowing of fascist dictatorships. This marked another historic achievement for Europeans and European values.

The structures and the situation today may be relatively new, but Europe's presumption as an international actor are, therefore, not quite so new. Since the original creation of 'European Political Cooperation' in the 1970s, it has, however, been 40 years—quite a long time to realize something fairly obvious: that a European foreign policy without a structure to implement it had little chance of success. With the establishment in 2009 of the European External Action Service, the establishment of such a structure made a major step forward.

1990–2008: From Hubris to Uncertainty

By the beginning of the 1990s, the EC had not only recognized the need for deeper political integration but had digested a re-united Germany and initiated a process which would eventually lead to a fuller 'big bang' enlargement of the Union in 2004. In 1995, Sweden, Austria and Finland had joined the EU, having understood that following the end of the Cold War European integration it could no longer be dismissed as a

---

3. Daniel C. Thomas, *The Helsinki Effect - International Norms, Human Rights and the Demise of Communism*, (New Jersey: Princeton University Press, 2001), pp 54-54.

divisive process, but was in fact the basis for a wider, stable union of democratic countries.

At the beginning of the 1990s, the EU established a set of criteria on which future applicants for membership would be judged. The Copenhagen criteria laid down that even before beginning accession negotiations, applicants for membership would have to established democracy and the rule of law, with full multi-party elections and freedom of expression. Earlier enlargements had, more or less, taken this for granted, but in Copenhagen the basic principle was codified clearly.

The European flag was brandished in the cities of East Germany in the revolutionary atmosphere after 1989 just as it would be brandished in Kiev in the second decade of the 21st century. The European idea had become quite literally an alternative, sometimes revolutionary and always inspiring motive for those in Europe seeing their countries as part of a family of peoples united by a set of basic values. From the Balkans to the Caucasus, the idea continues to attract and inspire movements and leaders seeking stability, peace and prosperity in their countries and regions.

The current situation is, therefore, quite different from that in pre-1989 Central and Eastern Europe, whose communist rulers regularly faced verbal and political attacks for failing to accept the universal values to which they had signed up in 1948 and again in 1975 in the Helsinki process. As an ECFR paper (Dennison and Dworkin) in 2011 put it:

> The world that the EU confronts at the beginning of the 21st century is, in many ways, a more realist one than could have been anticipated 20 years ago. The shift of political and economic power away from the West has curtailed the scope for international action to alter the internal arrangements of individual countries.

Even so, whilst sophistication and flexibility are undoubtedly necessary, the EU should not, as the authors put it, "lose faith in the universal appeal of such fundamental values as the right of all individuals to be free from oppression and to live under a regime that governs through their consent."[4]

---

4. Towards an EU Human Rights Strategy for a Post-Western World, ECFR/42, September 2010, p. 12.

The value of the European integration project and the potential of the EU as a normative or soft or ethical power is already the subject of vast academic literature, which will no doubt be extended to analyse the impact of the new structures established in the last few years.

New Challenges: Economic Crisis and Upheaval in the Neighbourhood

It should, however, not be overlooked that the structures now put in place and the context since the financial crisis of 2008 and the beginning of the Arab revolutions in 2011 are quite new.

Dworkin and Dennison, again, have neatly summarised the new situation:

> European leaders who had become used to seeing stability and political reform in the Arab world as opposing principles have been forced to re-think their approach ... to be effective the EU must develop a strategy that takes full account of the inherent complications of supporting universal values in a region where Europe cannot act as an unchallenged standard bearer.[5]

Richard Youngs of FRIDE has looked at the impact of the economic crisis on Europe's emerging foreign policy.[6] He looks at the potential consequences for Europe's political strength of an inevitable but relative economic decline and the institutionalization of a two-speed Europe as the Eurozone countries deepen their own integration (or at least the marginalization of Britain and some other countries). The EU's ability to provide external messages could, he argues, be compromised if the euro crisis and its management seem to undermine the idea of economic liberalization and good governance being somehow interlinked.

Resurgent Russia

Events in Georgia in 2008 and Ukraine after 2013 confirmed the failure of the EU to establish a peaceful neighborhood. The president of

---

5. Europe and the Arab Revolutions. A New Vision for Democracy and Human Rights, ECFR/42, November 2011, p. 1.

6. European Foreign Policy and the Economic Crisis: What Impact and How to Respond? FRIDE working paper no. 111, November 2011.

Russia seized on an unexpected opportunity to undermine a Union whose values he perceived as a threat to his regime and his regional predominance. The fact that European integration now faces strong domestic challenges even from extreme right movements should not lead authoritarian regimes around the world to feel secure in their rejection of these basic values.

After Kelety: Mass Influx of Refugees into the EU

In the summer and autumn of 2015 it seemed as if a new historical phase was opening as the EU and its member states responded in a disjointed manner to the arrival of hundreds of thousands of refugees and migrants escaping war and oppression in the Middle East and North Africa. Images of refugees camped in a Budapest railway station and of dead bodies washing up on the beaches of southern Europe had as much impact on public opinion and politics as the events in Eastern Europe in 1989. On August 31, Chancellor Merkel, attempting to get a grip on an unravelling crisis, said that the refugee crisis facing Europe was testing the core ideals of universal rights at the heart of the European Union. It is far too soon to assess the impact of these dramatic events, but they do also confirm the domestic impact of failed European attempts to contribute to the peaceful evolution of North African and Middle Eastern countries.

Evolving Structures, Developing Policies

The European Union remains committed, as stated in Article 21 of the Lisbon Treaty of 2007, to take the "principles which have inspired its own creation" as the guide for its "action on the international scene." To live up to such an approach will, however, require much more than the creation of a new diplomatic machine, the development of the ability really to speak and act as a genuine Union in international organisations and in specific third countries, the adoption of new policy documents, guidelines and action programmes. It will, however, like the political and economic integration process itself, be precisely that: a process. Just as the EU developed as a sui generis political structure so a new type of international actor is taking shape. It will take time to develop and such a process so will inevitably face internal and external challenges.

The Union in 2003 had already adopted a European Security Strategy[7] calling for a more "capable" and "responsible" EU ready to take on new tasks including support for human rights as part of a wider conception of Europe's mission in the world. Lisbeth Aggestam[8] has explained how the concept of Europe as a civilian power developed after the end of the Cold War into a more idealistic conception of 'normative power Europe'.

Similarly a specific European Human Rights Policy is not exactly a new idea. In 2001 the Commission published a first communication on "The European Union's role in promoting human rights and democratization in third countries." At the end of 2011 an apparently similar document emerged with a significantly different title: "Human Rights and Democracy at the heart of EU external action—towards a more effective approach."[9]

The 2011 communication began with an extraordinarily innocuous reference to the cataclysmic historical developments taking place while this contribution to policy development was being slowly drafted. It states: "The events of 2011 in the Middle East and North Africa show the central importance of human rights and democracy."[10] Such a low-key reference to "events" almost echoes the efforts of the Chinese Communist Party to define what happened in Tiananmen Square in 1989 as an "incident."

Whilst the dictators of North Africa and the Middle East were not unaware of the occasional criticisms they received from European countries or institutions (more often the Parliament than the Council or Commission) they had no reason to be troubled by them. With the exception of Syria, all the other countries of the region had stable institutionalized political and economic relations with the EU, including a low level 'dialogue' on human rights and, sometimes, limited opportunities for EU financing of democracy assistance projects or civil society activities. In the case of Tunisia, as well as Israel, human rights issues did not prevent the EU from actively considering even upgrading their bilateral relations. Some of the regimes like Algeria and Morocco were partially democratic; all were, to varying degrees, repressive. The dis-

---

7. European Council, Brussels, 12 December 2003.
8. Lisbeth Aggestam: Ethical Power Europe? *International Affairs*, Vol. 84, no, 1, 2008, p. 2.
9. COM (20211) 886 final, 12.12.2012.
10. COM (20211) 886 final, 12.12.2012, p. 5.

creet approach to human rights taken by Europe in what is now, in effect, an earlier historical epoch ending with the revolution in Tunisia, makes it all the more difficult for the EU now to advance democracy in the context of reversal of the Arab spring. Regimes have been overthrown and their successors seem in no mood to accept the kind of conditionality implicit in EU aid offers based on the principle of 'more for more' and 'less for less'. In fact the EU had simply been too defensive about its own values and now it risks paying the price.

A reactive unambitious approach would contradict the ambitions of the Lisbon Treaty and fail to inspire confidence inside and outside of the EU. The ongoing Eurozone crisis had already undermined the EU's external image when the refugee crisis added an even more daunting threat to unity with governments at odds with one another and public opinion deeply divided. Devising an outward looking, forward-thinking regional could certainly help renew the EU's sense of purpose but earlier failures of vision, leadership and anticipation are having a potentially destructive effect.

After the Lisbon Treaty entered into force in 2009, the European Parliament led calls for a review of human rights policy generally calling for new structures and a coherent set of goals and policies. At the beginning of 2011, Parliament decided to launch its own examination of EU policies and actions to promote democracy. Parliament's rapporteur Veronique de Keyser MEP reflected the optimism of the moment:

> Nobody imagined how much this topic would be pushed into the limelight by the events in Tunisia and Egypt, toppling two entrenched despots and making many more of their counterparts fear the power of the 'Arab street' and its rallying cry for 'dignity, bread and freedom.' Then, when speaking about democracy support in external relations in February, everything seemed to be set for a 'paradigm shift'...Too evidently had the EU's approach to the southern neighbourhood and other parts of the world been dominated by diplomatic Realpolitik, economic self-interest or the fear of instability....,
>
> the Arab spring should be encouragement to really integrate democracy support into our external relations policies and development programming, to truly enable our EU delegations around the world to support democratic governance and human rights - which requires financial means and human resources and sometimes exerting pressure as to enhance the rule of law, foster independent

media and democratic institutions that can 'deliver' and keep each other in check. It should also mean that aid conditionality becomes practice rather than theory. (...)we must keep previous commitments and the political will to make our external policies overall more democracy-friendly. ...Building democracies in the Arab world and elsewhere will take many years but, if we make a long term commitment and keep it, chances of success have never been better.[11]

The context in which this commitment is to be met has become much more problematic. Certainly Europe should learn the lessons of failed attempts at accommodation with dictators on its southern borders and in living up to the objectives set for the EU in its basic treaties ensure its relevance as a political project for its citizens and its international partners in the years ahead.

Experience suggests that the development and rethinking of how best to use whatever 'normative' power the EU retains has to avoid two extremes. On the one hand the extreme of excessive self-importance or even hubris of the kind that was evident in the immediate period after the collapse of communism in the USSR. Avoiding this does not, however, mean adopting an excessively modest view of Europe´s achievements and potential in a way that avoids careful examination of how the EU goes about its business, as if there is no need to bother too much with the mechanisms since the potential outcome is, by definition, limited. That is the other extreme that should be avoided. Similarly, recognition of the genuine problem of 'double standards' should not involve a further debilitating excess of European self-criticism.

Leading by Example?

In 1998 a number of academics presented a report on the potential of the EU to enhance its leadership on human rights by linking its external projection with its internal policies.

> The irony is that the Union has, by virtue of its emphasis upon human rights in its relations with other states and its ringing endorsements of the universality and indivisibility of human rights highlighted the incongruity and indefensibility of combining an

---

11. European Parliament: Office for the Promotion of Parliamentary Democracy, Newsletter, 2 June 2011.

active external policy stance with what in some areas comes close
to an abdication of internal responsibility.[12]

Their basic insight that internal and external policies are 'two sides of
the same coin' was recognised by Baroness Ashton in her own metaphor
of '360 degree coherence.' The difficulty the EU has had in handling
the massive influx of refugees reflects on the one hand a consequence of
failing to encourage peaceful democratic reform in its neighbourhood,
as well as an inability to take a rights-based approach to immigration
and asylum. The consequences have been among the elements contributing to anti-EU and anti-immigrant populism.

Achieving such coherence between external and internal policies will
be an ongoing challenge. Meanwhile those who, in effect, oppose European values adopt attack as the best means of defense of their reactionary repressive policies at home. In December 2011 Russia published
a report on the *Human Rights Situation in a Number of the World's States.*
This document even quotes prestigious international and American
NGOs, which the Russian authorities normally ignore when their own
actions are exposed.[13] Actions taken by the EU and its member states in
such areas as asylum policy or counter-terrorism are often profoundly
problematic, but to dismiss Europeans' right to seek to extend the
recognition of human rights around the world is merely self-serving
rhetoric by regimes who maintain their power precisely by repression
and elimination of opposition. Even those governments which do so
have themselves signed up to the UDHR of 1948 and other texts that
they do not respect in letter or in spirit. By 2015 the challengers to
human rights and democracy seemed to be in the process of seizing the
initiative in a more explicit fashion.

Downgrading the Importance of EU Human Rights Policy?

After the 2014 European elections, Baroness Ashton was replaced by
Federica Mogherini as the EU High Representative and Vice President
of the Commission for foreign and security policy, and in July 2015, the
EU revisited its human rights strategy and explicitly reaffirmed its

---

12. 'Leading by Example: A Human Rights Agenda for the European Union for the Year
2000'. http://www.lue.lt/AEL/.
13. Russia spoofs the Human Rights Report by Tyler Roylance, Freedom House Blog, and
January 3rd 2012.

intention to keep human rights at the heart of the EU agenda.[14] Recognizing the context of widespread human rights violations the EU Council considered that "this Action Plan should enable the EU to meet the challenges through more focused action, systematic and coordinated use of instruments at its disposal...). The Action Plan adopted on the basis of this review contained 34 precise objectives under five headings:

- Boosting ownership of local actors such as parliaments, election management bodies, civil society
- Addressing human rights challenges including freedom of expression, promoting religious freedom, the rights of women and children, indigenous peoples, but also economic and social rights
- Ensuring a comprehensive human rights to conflicts and crises using the new EU Conflict Early Warning System
- Fostering better coherence and consistency addressing issues like migration, human trafficking, as well as the human rights aspects of trade and investment policies whilst pursuing a right based approach to development cooperation
- A more effective EU human rights and democracy support policy with local human rights country strategies based on consultation of civil society as well as public diplomacy

In spite of this apparently positive development, critics were quick to notice that the most recent document adopted and the structures put in place to implement it did not appear very convincing. As Richard Youngs put it,

> While this action plan includes many admirable elements, it is strikingly low key compared with the more traditional security and defence reviews underway. Tellingly, many working on these new foreign policy strategies know nothing of the democracy and human rights strategy. This shows that the EU's promise of cross-fertilization between different areas of external relation remains unfulfilled.
>
> If the new action plan is to correct a widespread suspicion that democracy and human rights are decreasing in priority, the EU and its Member States will need to demonstrate stronger political will and define better tactics of democracy support.[15]

---

14. Council of the European Union 20 July 2015.
15. Carnegie Europe, July 2015.

The point being made here is that while the European Union is reviewing its neighborhood policy, its approach to common defence and security, as well as dealing with major issues in relation to migration, trade and energy, it should constantly include reflection on the human rights aspect in these policies.

The growth of terrorism in the European Union with fears of the real threats coming from returning jihadist fighters has been noted in both the U.S. and Europe. Congressional discussions have taken place on the opportunities provided within a borderless space such as the Schengen area for EU citizens who happen also to be terrorists. The refugee crisis of 2015 is a potential threat to Schengen by itself. Europe and America face the common problem of maintaining balance between civil liberties and counter-terrorism measures. European political life does not as yet reflect the deep fear of major terrorist attacks that is apparent in the U.S. It is, however, all too likely that the kind of political polarization seen in America will extend to Europe.

European institutions have hitherto been committed to at least attempt to set some basic conditions to trade and aid agreements with third countries. Such conditionality has even been applied to agreements with the U.S. A most dramatic example of this came in the spring of 2010 when Parliament blocked a draft agreement concerning the tracking of terrorist finances via the SWIFT banking transfer system. This led many in Washington to wake up to Parliament's new powers under the Lisbon Treaty. This is the "assent procedure" whereby no agreement between the EU and a so-called third country can come into effect without a positive vote of over half of all MEPs, i.e. 'all' MEPs, not just those in the room at the time of a particular vote. Within weeks of the vote Vice President Biden was addressing the Parliament as a sign of renewed respect for its role. It also became clear after the negotiations for a Transatlantic Trade and Investment Partnership that such an agreement might fail to be ratified unless European concerns about US intelligence gathering in Europe were addressed.

In fact the U.S. and EU could try to do more together to ensure human rights conditionality. Egypt would be an excellent example for study as to how the West not only failed to engage effectively to promote democracy in Egypt but has now been obliged to recognize its impotence as a new military regime abuses human rights on a massive scale. The fact that Russia is ready to deepen cooperation with this regime only sharpens the dilemma.

The issues of enforcing labor rights and countering human trafficking regularly arise in discussions of trade agreements being negotiated by the US and the EU and common approaches could be developed. Certainly in relation to Europe's neighborhood the absence of effective common strategies is obvious. The current situation in relation to the Assad regime in Syria comes years after failed attempts to bring the country into some kind of relationship with the EU. Regrettably the EU developed a whole strategy for a Euro-Mediterranean Partnership without learning the lessons of the Helsinki process and insisting on a substantial human rights part of the package.

EEAS Structure—Potential for Trans-Atlantic Cooperation

In 2010 when the EU agreed to the legislation establishing the EEAS it achieved an agreement that obliged Baroness Ashton to formally and explicitly commit herself to

> Give high priority to the promotion of Human Rights and good governance around the globe and promote its mainstreaming into external policies, throughout the EEAS. There will be human rights and democracy structure at headquarters level as well as focal points in all relevant Union delegations with the task of monitoring the human rights situation and promoting an effective realisation of EU human rights policy goals.[16]

The European Parliament had insisted "that the decision on where to place human rights in the structure of the EEAS is of great importance" and requested "the setting up of a Human Rights and Democracy Directorate with the tasks of developing a robust EU human rights and democracy strategy." The expectation was expressed that "this approach prevents human rights from being isolated and is the only way to ensure full compliance with the provisions of the Lisbon Treaty."[17]

In 2011 such a Directorate was established; the fact that it was abolished in 2015 was much regretted by the European Parliament and NGOs. It remains to be seen whether this will really result in a downgrading of human rights in EU external relations.

---

16. Statement by the HRVP to the European Parliament, July 7 2010.

17. EP resolution on Human Rights in the World 2009 and EU policy on the matter (paragraph 4), adopted on December 16th, 2010.

In July 2012 the High Representative appointed a special EU Special Representative on Human Rights.[18] A former Greek Foreign Minister and MEP, the mandate of Stavros Lambinidis, includes enhancing the Union's effectiveness, presence and visibility in protecting and promoting human rights in the world, notably by deepening Union cooperation and political dialogue with third countries, relevant partners, business, civil society, international and regional organisations; and through action in relevant international fora. Mr. Lambinidis regularly visits the U.S.

Within each EU delegation there is a dedicated official to monitor human rights and cooperation with U.S. embassies also takes place.

Like the U.S., the EU carries out human rights dialogues with governments around the world. Whilst it can be argued that any dialogue is better than no dialogue, the real impact of this instrument has often been challenged. With allies, most notably the U.S., dialogue is a framework in which arrangements can be discussed in relation to work together on common objectives. Issues where differences persist, e.g. the death penalty and Guantanamo, can also be addressed. Talking can, however, be a trap and engaging in a human rights dialogue with such countries as China, Russia and Iran has never seemed likely to produce significant reform as both EU and the U.S. seek to resist the authoritarian backlash in Europe's neighborhood they should always attempt common messaging towards the regimes they are dealing with and learn the lessons when they fail. European institutions, sometimes in cooperation with U.S. legislators and foundations, regularly observe elections in the OSCE area and take the opportunity to encourage countries to live up to their commitments flowing from the Helsinki process.

Looking at the failure of both to contribute to an irreversible establishment of democracy in Central Asia, one expert has written:

> With each regional election, Western monitors are disappointed by lack of genuine choice and policy debate, while leaders claim dizzying numbers in the polls.... The ideas, values, and practices promoted by the U.S. and EU in Central Asia have been culturally insensitive, inconsistent, unimportant, and, therefore, lacking credibility for Central Asian governments and people. Western policymakers and academics have developed a sophisticated understanding

---

18. http://eur-lex.europa.eu/legal-content/EN/TXT/HTML/?uri=CELEX:32014D0385 &from=EN.

of what democracy is about and this understanding emphasizes political pluralism, elections, and civic engagement, among other things. Yet, these ideas are largely divorced from how democracy and democratization are understood in Central Asia. The regional elites downgrade democracy to a lower priority than economic prosperity and security. Central Asian citizens perceive democracy as an empty ideological framework or a recipe for mayhem. These attitudes toward democracy have been bolstered by the fatigue and resentment of the Central Asian populations to the externally driven ideologies that have been a constant reality for the Central Asian societies subjected to Russian colonialism, Sovietization, and post-Soviet democratization.[19]

Democracy Promotion: A Distinctive European approach.

The fact of different priorities perhaps reflecting different historical experiences may be illustrated by the initiative taken by Poland during its presidency for a European Endowment for Democracy. It was the European Parliament which in the 1990s insisted on a major "democracy" element in the assistance programmes originally just for Poland and Hungary (PHARE) which were put in place after the 1989 revolutions. Attempts over the years to abolish or hide away the EIDHR within other external assistance programmes have been regularly resisted by Parliament and those member states which insist that the EU should not be shy about its global ambitions in relation to democracy and human rights.

The timing and origin of the EED's proposal also illustrates the fact that the post-Lisbon institutional structure of the EU is designed to strengthen the EU's collective capacity whilst leaving much space for member states to advance their own ideas and interests. In the second part of 2011, Poland held the rotating Presidency of the EU and as a country whose own peaceful revolution in the 1980s had been profoundly influenced by outsiders responded with understandable emotion to the events of the Arab Spring which unfolded in the months leading up to the beginning of its Presidency. Even if the historical analogy may well turn out to be overstated, the reaction and thus the Polish initiative was logical and understandable. Poland's underground "Soli-

---

19. http://www.demdigest.net/democracy-promoters-fault-central-asia/.

darnosc" movement had benefitted from under-the-radar 'democracy promotion' assistance in particular from the U.S foundations. It is by no means clear that the transposition of the U.S. National Endowment for Democracy model to Europe will be feasible but the idea is indeed an inspiring one that cannot be dismissed. As explained in a European Parliament report,

> The intention is to set up a semi-autonomous entity which could support democracy activists and democratic developments around the world in an un-bureaucratic way and which would not be directly associated with EU diplomacy on the European Commission.[20]

Two years later the 2014 Annual Report of the European Endowment for Democracy described its objectives, not in terms of promoting democracy as such but explained that:

> In the face of closing spaces for democracy and freedom, the democracy support agenda has been brought back into the geopolitical game. EED focuses on local and grassroots needs, on the young fledgling and unsupported, who struggle to fight for democracy and reopen these free spaces.

The Polish initiative, the Ashton review, the regular demands by the European Parliament for a more coherent and courageous approach, the very active campaigning by NGOs in the Human Rights and Democracy Network in Brussels[21] all showed that in spite of the widely reported crisis of confidence in the European integration process there has always been pressure for Europe to enhance its profile in this field.

Two years after the EED was established, Richard Youngs took a positive view of its achievements.[22] He explains that with a budget of less than $10 million it has achieved both a good profile and organizational flexibility and independence. The decision of its board to extend EED activities beyond the EU neighborhood reflects a conscious response to Russian soft power efforts to bolster support or minimize opposition to its hard power adventurism.

---

20. Report by Alexander Graf Lambsdorff, EP Document A7-0061/2012.
21. www.hrdn.eu.
22. http://carnegieeurope.eu/strategiceurope/?fa=61190.

Others see a lack of substance in EU human rights and democracy promotion leading to a crisis in the whole exercise. Sonja Grimm analyses the strategy and highlights the strength of the challenge now to be faced by the authoritarian backlash. She writes that

> Authoritarian incumbents have started to 'push back' liberalisation efforts, and to crackdown on domestic oppositional non-governmental organisation and popular uprisings, as well as international democracy promotion. Thereby, they spoil European democracy promotion efforts. Autocrats have learned techniques either to challenge the opposition and to undermine their legitimacy or to co-opt (and thereby muzzle) oppositional forces. Strategies of repression have successfully ridden out popular uprisings in a majority of countries affected by the Arab spring and the colour revolutions. Autocrats have started to include domestic elections in their policy mix. Although it seems to be a risky strategy that could potentially throw them out of office, many have succeeded in creating stability and even legitimacy for their authoritarian rule.[23]

The challenge of the EU in the years ahead will be to keep up the courage of the convictions that have carried European countries so far in the last 40 years. As mentioned at the beginning of this chapter, European leaders and institutions have never been completely at ease with the concept of 'democracy promotion'. The many achievements referred to above have been the result of dialogue, assistance and the force of attraction rather than the outcome of a conscious proactive policy to promote and advance democracy as such. Even attempts to establish a 'European consensus on democracy' have not come to fruition. In this sense, it is fair to argue that what the EU aims to support is unclear.[24]

Various official documents mention a range of objectives: political reform, free elections, building of institutions, fighting corruption, supporting independence of the judiciary, sustaining civil society, as well as gender equality and free market economies. Europeans have particularly, since the 2003 Iraq invasion and its catastrophic consequences, been less willing to adopt the hubristic language of democracy promotion. This may be defined as the effort by governments, foundations and

---

23. http://www.demdigest.net/eu-democracy-promotion-crisis/.
24. For more on this see *The Substance of EU Democracy Promotion* edited by Wetzel and Orbie Palgrave 2015.

NGOs to spread democracy as a political system. Europeans seem to prefer the concept of democracy assistance or support, namely, direct, positive measures to aid or advice on the establishment and strengthening of democratic systems. This can involve applying a principle of conditionality, not only towards countries seeking EU membership but also in relationships based on trade and financial assistance. Programs of support for civil society or the development of the capacity of parliaments to function effectively have been for Europeans key elements of this overall effort. In this sense, the term democracy promotion seems more ambitious, or perhaps intrusive; on the other hand, democracy assistance cannot or should not be seen as a half-hearted version of democracy promotion. It does, however, reflect, from a European perspective, a more realistic assessment of what can be achieved without military action or covert operations.

Challenges Ahead: Common Transatlantic Responses?

In both America and Europe there are those who dismiss the others' contribution as reflecting double standards, special interests and differing views of the relationship between soft and hard power. The simplistic 'Mars vs. Venus' description of these differences is extremely unhelpful. A competitive approach in unhelpful, even if it is clear that different views on the justification for the U.S.-led military intervention in Iraq are always the air. Often the U.S. is impatient with Europe's preference for multilateral over bilateral approaches. In the Cold War era the U.S. was more comfortable with under-the-radar operations but with the advent of the EED this difference has also been diminished, at least in Europe's neighborhood. Contrary to some caricatures, the EU and its many of its member states in Albania, Bosnia and Macedonia as well as outside Europe in the Democratic Republic of Congo, Sierra Leone and Coté d'Ivoire. In relation to its European Neighborhood Policy Instrument the EU is somewhat more intrusive than similar U.S. actions.

Since 2003 the EU has been involved in over 20 missions within the framework of its European Security and Defense Policy. Such missions in Ukraine, the Caucasus and Palestine confirm that the EU can and does have a hard power contribution to offer. In all such missions officials are obliged to take into account human rights aspects and there is an element of coercion in EU actions in post-conflict situations.[25]

Engagement with unpleasant regimes is unavoidable for both Europe and America and no amount of academic study can produce a formula to avoid apparent double standards. Both Europe and America engage with rivals and ideological competitors. On each side of the Atlantic policies towards Arab dictators have not really been so different even if in relation to Iraq or Libya arguments over military action have raged. Indeed they rage within Europe and within the U.S. The U.S. tends to be more rhetorically outspoken than most European leaders who tend to shy away from explicit talk of democracy promotion.

Failure of Cooperative Engagement

Since 2011 this failure has been all too apparent and even after such events as the beginning of a civil war in Syria both Europe and the U.S. have appeared unable to define any meaningful effective response. The rise of ISIS did not have the same mobilizing effect on public opinion as did the arrival in southern and Eastern Europe of hundreds of thousands of refugees. 'Mars' is not very strong in Washington or Brussels, in fact, leaving millions in the Arab countries feeling abandoned in the face of increasingly brutal oppression.

Differences between European and American approaches based on different emphases in relation to the concept of democracy promotion should therefore not be exaggerated. Both can be accused of double standards and both are prepared to use military force and sanctions to advance their goals. Often Europe is prepared for engagement as well as criticism of regimes violating human rights (Iran and Cuba). Relations with Egypt under the Al-Sisi presidency face both with the same dilemma. Both face the explicit challenge to universal values from China and Russia.

---

25. For more on this see "Venus approaching Mars? by Tanja Börzel and Thomas Risse in Amichai Magen, Thomas Risse and Michael A. McFaul, eds., *Promoting Democracy and the Rule of Law: American and European Strategies* (Hounsmills: Palgrave Macmillan, 2009).

Many critics point to the failure of Europe and America to foresee the events of the Arab Spring and advance the movements for change in the region, as if, somehow, external intervention to enforce change was a serious option. European efforts to engage Arab regimes before 2011 were ongoing, but the idea that the Euro-Mediterranean partnerships would be a modern version of the Helsinki process lacked a solid foundation. Europe can and does support those seeking political change, and can and does assist in the establishment of democratic institutions. But the initiation of the process depends on the peoples of the countries concerned. European institutions can and do criticize regimes which violate human rights, but the EU is in no position to enforce or initiate revolutionary change. Indeed, this is not what happened in Europe in the 1980s, and to imagine otherwise is to develop policies based on an illusion of power, which, if carried out, could prove counterproductive.

In short, without 'people power' on the spot, outside promotion or assistance for the development democracy is unlikely to achieve very much. In his second inaugural address in January 2005, President George W. Bush spoke of "the policy of the U,S, to seek and support the growth of democratic movements and institutions in every nation and culture, with the ultimate goal of ending tyranny in our world." His successor abandoned this approach and it is unlikely that any EU or European national leader would make such a bold expression of intent. Indeed, the head of policy planning in the State Department in the early years of the George W. Bush presidency, Richard Haass, considered that it is neither desirable nor practical to make democracy promotion a foreign policy doctrine."[26]

Whilst the instruments and agencies of American human rights and democracy promotion can provide models for European institutions, it is clear that the EU is not in any position even to imagine an approach based as Guilhot has put it on "the structural subordination of the field of human rights to the field of state power." In Brussels there is certainly interaction between officials, parliamentarians, institutions, civil societies and organizations, but Europe has a more pluralistic environment than the U.S., and it is hard to imagine the development of what Guilhot describes as one in which "no real distinction is made between activists, movements for democracy and human rights, and Washington policy consultants."[27] One

---

26. *The Economist*, 21.106, p. 26.
27. Nicolas Guilhot, *The Democracy Makers*, (New York: Columbia University Press, 2005), p. 182.

can, however, observe in Europe a similar process of professionalization of democracy support; but for the foreseeable future, it seems likely that the high hopes of the early 1990s and the initial optimism after the Arab Spring began are unlikely to return. On the other hand, Europe is unlikely to fall victim to the wishful thinking that the movement towards democracy around the world is some kind of irreversible process. It may be that at a time of economic and political crisis, support for democracy has moved down Europe's external relations agenda.

An acceptance of the limits of Europe's power may still prove is a wiser basis for the development of a coherent policy than hubris based on a misreading of what really happened in Europe at the end of the Cold War. As John K. Glenn of the German Marshall Fund pointed out, at the beginning of the Obama presidency:

> The experience of post-Communism compels advocates of democracy promotion to be modest, recognizing that democracy is never exported but always driven from within and, frequently fragile, subject to backsliding." International efforts to support democracy are best advanced through promotion of resources and expertise as new democracies build and sustain reform.[28]

As Europe struggles with the consequences of events in its neighborhood, the U.S. is choosing new leadership. Both face domestic divisions and confident rival powers with an alternative set of values. Modesty in the cause of democracy promotion should not, however, lead to the abandonment of a cause that inspires so many to look towards Europe and America as models of a better way of life.

Europe does sometimes blow a more uncertain trumpet than America but both face the same difficulty in getting heard in a world where others have their own melodies to offer.

---

28. GMF Policy Brief: The Myth of Exporting Democracy: Lessons from Eastern Europe after 1989, 21.04.09.

The Center for Transatlantic Relations at the Johns Hopkins University Paul H. Nitze School of Advanced International Studies cordially invites you to

Challenges of Democracy in the Center and the Periphery: The European Union and Its Neighbors

March 30, 2015 • Johns Hopkins University
SAIS • 1717 Massachusetts Avenue NW •
Room 500 • Washington, DC

The decline of political democracy due to the material limits of financing the welfare state has led to arguments that "democracy is spreading at the peripheries of the world, but exhausted in the center." Developments in the European Union's neighborhood test this argument, since the negative trends in the periphery also clearly pose a major challenge to one of the main and shared values of the EU and the U.S. in forming foreign policy—democracy promotion, through coercion, conditioning and attraction.

The aim of this conference is to evaluate the state of democracies and find answers to some burning questions: Will this de-democratization trend, which challenges a normativized image of Western democracy as a universal model to which non-Western societies aspire, evolve into different models of "quasi-democracy" for each state or authoritarian regime, or will Western-style democracy as a model recover?

Agenda

10:00-10:15   Welcoming Remarks

András Simonyi, Managing Director, Center for Transatlantic Relations, Johns Hopkins University SAIS & Former Hungarian Ambassador to the U.S.

10:15-11:45   Challenges of Democracy in the EU: Is There a Role for the U.S.?

Moderator: Esther Brimmer, Professor, the George Washington University

- Thomas O. Melia, Executive Director, Democracy International and former Deputy Assistant Secretary, Bureau of Democracy,Human Rights and Labor

- Jocelyne Cesari, Senior Fellow, Berkley Center for Religion, Peace and World Affairs and Professor in the Department of Government, Georgetown University

- Andrew Srulevitch, Director of European Affairs, Anti-Defamation League

11:45-13:00   Challenges of Democracy in the Aspirant Countries of the EU

Moderator: Debra Cagan, Senior State Department Fellow, Center for Transatlantic relations, Johns Hopkins University SAIS

- Aylin Ünver Noi, Visiting Scholar, Center for Transatlantic Relations Johns Hopkins University SAIS & Professor, International Relations, Istanbul Gedik University

- Federiga Bindi, Senior Fellow, Center for Transatlantic Relations, Johns Hopkins University SAIS & Professor, Political Science, University of Rome Tor Vergata

- Renata Stuebner, Senior Program Specialist Balkans, Governance, Society and Law, USIP

- Dajana Dzindo, Visiting Scholar, Center for Transatlantic Relations, Johns Hopkins University SAIS

13:00-14:00   Lunch

14:00-15:15   Challenges of Democracy in the Eastern Neighborhood of the EU

Moderator: Donald N. Jensen, Resident Fellow, Center for Transatlantic Relations, Johns Hopkins University SAIS

- Michael Leigh, Senior Advisor, The German Marshall Fund of the United States

- Alex Sokolowski, Head of Democracy Unit, USAID Bureau of Europe and Eurasia
- Shaazka Beyerle, Visiting Scholar, Center for Transatlantic Relations, Johns Hopkins University SAIS

15:15-16:30 How Effective is Western Democracy Promotion?

Moderator: Antonio Álvarez-Couceiro, Fellow, Center for Transatlantic Relations, Johns Hopkins University SAIS, and Founding Secretary-General, Club de Madrid and Founding Trustee and Vice President/Executive Director of the Conference on Democratic Transition, FRIDE

- Amy Hawthorne, Senior Fellow, Rafik Hariri Center for the Middle East, Atlantic Council
- Bastian Hermisson, Executive Director, Heinrich Böll Foundation North America
- David Kramer, Senior Director for Human Rights and Human Freedoms, the McCain Institute & Former U.S. Assistant Secretary of State for Democracy, Human Rights and Labor; Former President, Freedom House

16:30 Closing Remarks

András Simonyi, Managing Director, Center for Transatlantic Relations, Johns Hopkins University SAIS & Former Hungarian Ambassador to the U.S.

About The Authors

Shaazka Beyerle is a Nonresident Fellow, Center for Transatlantic Relations (CTR), School of Advanced International Studies (SAIS), Johns Hopkins University; Senior Advisor, International Center on Nonviolent Conflict, and author, *Curtailing Corruption: People Power for Accountability and Justice* (Lynne Rienner 2014), and *Freedom from Corruption: A Curriculum for People Power Movements, Campaigns and Civic Initiatives* (2015). She has contributed chapters in: *Is Authoritarianism Staging a Comeback?* (Atlantic Council 2015); *Conflict Transformation: Essays on Methods of Nonviolence* (McFarland 2013); and *Civilian Jihad: Nonviolent Struggle, Democratization and Governance in the Middle East* (Palgrave 2010). She regularly publishes articles, most recently on corruption and extremism (*Foreign Policy*) and global financial corruption (*Diogène*). Ms. Beyerle teaches and speaks about citizen empowerment and strategic nonviolent action. She testified at a US Congress Committee on Security and Cooperation in Europe hearing, and most recently presented at: the 16th International Anti-Corruption Conference; Columbia Law School Center for Public Integrity; Fletcher School for Law and Diplomacy; Georgetown University, Harvard University; and US Institute of Peace. She's a Friend of the International State Crime Initiative (Queen Mary University-London, Harvard, University of Hull), Editorial Board member, *State Crime*, and an elected Coordinating Committee member, UN Convention Against Corruption Civil Society Coalition.

Münevver Cebeci is an Associate Professor at the European Union Institute (a Jean Monnet Centre of Excellence), Marmara University in Istanbul. She has taught several courses, including "European Foreign Policy", "Security Studies" and "International Relations Theories" since 2001. Her course "International Politics of the EU" was awarded as a "Jean Monnet Permanent Course" by the European Commission in 2002–2007. She gave lectures (as a guest) at various universities; including the College of Europe-Natolin and Canterbury Christ Church University. She is a former visiting fellow of WEU (now the EU) Institute for Security Studies. She holds a PhD in EU Politics and International Relations from the European Union Institute, Marmara University, and MSc in International Relations from London School of Economics (as a

Jean Monnet scholar) and an MA in International Relations from the Social Sciences Institute, Marmara University. Her research interests include European Foreign Policy and Security Studies. She has published two books and numerous scholarly articles in journals and edited books. Her latest book *Issues in EU and US Foreign Policy* (an edited volume) was published by Lexington Books in 2011. Cebeci is also the author of "European Foreign Policy Research Reconsidered: Constructing an 'Ideal Power Europe' through Theory?" published in *Millenium-Journal of International Studies* in 2012.

Leila Hadj-Abdou is a Research Fellow at the Department of Politics, University of Sheffield (UK). She specializes in international migration politics and the governance of ethno-cultural diversity. Prior to coming to Sheffield Leila held positions at the Johns Hopkins University, School of Advanced International Studies (SAIS) in Washington D.C. and the University of Vienna. She was a visiting researcher at the University College Dublin, the CNRS in Paris, and the Institute for Higher Studies in Vienna. She holds a Ph.D. from the European University Institute.

Geoffrey Harris is currently the Deputy Head of the European Parliament Liaison Office with the US Congress. This office is charged with the development of relations between the European Parliament and the US Congress and works to raise the Parliament´s profile in the United States. He was until 2012 the Head of the Human Rights Unit within the Secretariat General of the European Parliament (Directorate General for external policies DGEXPO). This unit provides the back-up for the EP sub-committee, a parliamentary body working in the framework of the Foreign Affairs Committee of the European Parliament. The unit also provided back-up for all initiatives and aspects of the work of the institution concerning human rights (the President, the Development and External Trade committees and the Inter-parliamentary delegations, as well as the Annual Sakharov Prize Award). From 1976-1989 he was an official of the (then) largest Group in the EP, the Socialist Group and from 1989–1992 he was the diplomatic adviser to the President of Parliament. From 1992–2004 he was the EP official charged with the organization of inter-parliamentary relations with all the candidate countries (Joint Parliamentary Committees) and with other countries in Europe but outside the EU. This included Russia, the Western Balkans, South Caucasus as well as Ukraine, Moldova and Belarus. He is a regular lecturer and participant in academic conferences and is the author of one book, published by Columbia U.P. in 1993 *The Dark Side of Europe—the Extreme Right in Europe Today.*

Mak Kamenica is the Executive Director of the America-Bosnia Foundation, and Deputy Chief of Party of the USAID Energy Investment Activity (EIA) project in Bosnia and Herzegovina. Mr. Kamenica holds a M.Sc. in Electrical Power Engineering from the Faculty of Electrical Engineering, University of Sarajevo, and a certificate in Business Project Management from the New York University. Mr. Kamenica was a Fulbright Visiting Scholar at the New York Institute of Technology. His previous experience includes being the Deputy Chief of Party of the four-year USAID Enterprise Energy Efficiency (3E) Project, in Bosnia and Herzegovina, and an Advisor/Intern at the Mission of Bosnia and Herzegovina to the United Nations in New York on issues that concern energy efficiency, climate change, environment and sustainability.

Sir Michael Leigh is Senior Fellow at the German Marshall Fund (GMF) of the US in Washington DC and visiting scholar at the Paul H. Nitze School of Advanced International Studies (SAIS) of Johns Hopkins University in Washington. Since 2011 he has led GMF's project on Eastern Mediterranean energy, which focuses on the geopolitical implications of gas discoveries in the region. He has written and lectured extensively on the future of the EU and the Eurozone, enlargement and Eastern Partnership, particularly Ukraine, Turkey's relations with the EU and their common neighborhood, as well as Europe's response to political change in the Mediterranean and Middle East. He currently coordinates and moderates the European and Eurasian Studies Program Distinguished Lecture series at SAIS. Sir Michael became director-general for enlargement at the European Commission in 2006 after serving for three years as external relations deputy director-general with responsibility for European Neighbourhood Policy, relations with Eastern Europe, Southern Caucasus, Central Asia, Middle East and the Mediterranean countries. Earlier he was chief negotiator with the Czech Republic and other candidate countries. He contributed to the development of the single market and the common fisheries policy. He began his career as assistant professor of international relations at Johns Hopkins University, SAIS in Bologna, Italy and lecturer in international relations at the University of Sussex. He holds a Bachelor's degree in Philosophy, Politics and Economics from Oxford University and a PhD in Political Science from M.I.T.

Professor Daniel P. Serwer (Ph.D., Princeton) directs the Conflict Management Program at the Johns Hopkins School of Advanced International Studies (SAIS). He is also a Senior Fellow at its Center for Transatlantic Relations (CTR) and affiliated as a Scholar with the Middle East Institute. His current interests focus on the civilian instruments needed to protect U.S. national security as well as transition and statebuilding in the Middle East, North Africa and the Balkans. His *Righting the Balance: How You Can Help Protect America* was published in November 2013 by Potomac Books. Formerly vice president for centers of peacebuilding innovation at the United States Institute of Peace, he led teams there working on rule of law, religion, economics, media, technology, security sector governance and gender. He was also vice president for peace and stability operations at USIP, where he led its peacebuilding work in Iraq, Afghanistan, Sudan and the Balkans and served as Executive Director of the Hamilton/Baker Iraq Study Group. Serwer has worked on preventing interethnic and sectarian conflict in Iraq and has facilitated dialogue between Serbs and Albanians in the Balkans. Serwer blogs at www.peacefare.net and tweets @DanielSerwer

Alexander Sokolowski serves as the Democracy and Governance Division Chief in the Bureau for Europe and Eurasia at the United States Agency for International Development (USAID) in Washington where he focuses on strategy and cross-sectoral issues related to the promotion of democracy, human rights and good governance in the region. From 2003 to September 2009, he served as Senior Political Processes Advisor in USAID's Europe and Eurasia bureau. He was one of the main drafters of USAID's new Strategy on Democracy, Rights and Governance (2013). Prior to joining USAID in June 2003, he taught Comparative Politics at George Washington University. He received his Ph.D. in Politics from Princeton University in 2002, writing his dissertation on the structural and political determinants of fiscal and social policy failure in Yeltsin's Russia. He has served as a Foreign Policy Research Fellow at the Brookings Institution (2000-2001). He also holds master's degrees from Princeton (2000) and the Fletcher School of Law and Diplomacy (1994). Through the mid to late 1990s, he worked for the National Democratic Institute's Moscow office as a Political Party Program Officer and Political Analyst. Fluent in Russian, he has published articles on Russian politics and democratization in academic journals (*Europe-Asia Studies, Demokratizatsiya*) and opinion pieces (*The Moscow Times*). He has co-taught a course on democratization at Boston University's Washington Program.

Mario Telo is Jean Monnet Chair of International Relations in Brussels and Professor of EU institutions in Rome-LUISS University. Emeritus President of the Institute European Studies of the Universite libre de Bruxelles (ULB). He has been elected a Member of the Royal Academy of Sciences in 2007. He has been advisor to the European Commission, European Parliament and the Presidency of the European Council. Among his 35 books we mention the most recent ones: *The EU Foreign Policy* (2013), *The EU and New Regionalism* (2014), *The Politics of Transatlantic Trade Negotiations* (2014), and *Interregionalism and the EU* (2015).

Sasha Toperich is a Senior Fellow at the Center for Transatlantic Relations (CTR), at the Johns Hopkins University Paul H. Nitze School of Advanced International Studies (SAIS). He is also President of the America-Bosnia Foundation, President of the World Youth Leadership Network, and a world-renowned pianist. Dr. Toperich has also held several diplomatic positions for Bosnia-Herzegovina. In 2002-2003, he was advisor to the Ambassador of Bosnia-Herzegovina to the United Nations, from 2003-2007, he was a Special Envoy of the Presidency of Bosnia and Herzegovina to the United States; and in 2009 and 2010, he served as Counselor at the Permanent Mission of Bosnia and Herzegovina to the United Nations. He is a co-author of two papers in the book Unfinished Business: Western Balkans and the International Community (Brookings Institution/CTR, 2012) titled *The Regulatory Environment in the Financial System in Bosnia and Herzegovina and How to Improve It* and *A New Paradigm for the Mediterranean: U.S.-North Africa- Southeast Europe*. Dr. Toperich is the Director of the Mediterranean Basin Initiative and chairman of the Supervisory Board at the Mediterranean Development Initiative in Tunisia.

Aylin Ünver Noi is Nonresident Fellow at the Center for Transatlantic Relations (CTR), the Johns Hopkins Paul H. Nitze School of Advanced International Studies (SAIS). She is Director of European Union Application and Research Center and Assistant Professor at International Relations department, Istanbul Gedik University. She also teaches "International Politics of the European Union I-II" courses at European Union Institute (a Jean Monnet Centre of Excellence), Marmara University. She affiliated as Associate Researcher at European Institute for Research on Mediterranean and Euro-Arab Cooperation–MEDEA, Brussels. She holds a BA from the Department of International Relations, Bilkent University, Ankara and an MA and a PhD from the Department of European Union Politics and International Relations,

European Union Institute, Marmara University, Istanbul. She is the author of the books *The Euro-Mediterranean Partnership and the Broader Middle East and North Africa Initiative: Competing or Complementary Projects?* (2011) and *Avrupa'da Yükselen Milliyetcilik- The Rise of Nationalism in Europe* (2007) as well as several scholarly articles and chapters published in journals and edited books. She is also editor of the book *Islam and Democracy: Perspectives on the Arab Spring* (2013). Ünver Noi writes for Huffington Post at her blog.